LIFE IN CHRIST

LIFE IN CHRIST

Lessons from Our Lord's Miracles and Parables

The Miracles of Our Lord

Volume 12

Charles H. Spurgeon

We love hearing from our readers. Please contact us
at www.anekopress.com/questions-comments with
any questions, comments, or suggestions.

Life in Christ, Vol. 12
© 2023 by Aneko Press
All rights reserved. First edition 1891.
Revisions copyright 2023

Cover Design: Natalia Hawthorne
Cover Painting: Matt Philleo
Editors: Ruth Clark and J. Martin

Aneko Press

www.anekopress.com

Aneko Press, Life Sentence Publishing, and our logos are trademarks of
Life Sentence Publishing, Inc.
203 E. Birch Street
P.O. Box 652
Abbotsford, WI 54405

RELIGION / Christian Life / Spiritual Growth

Paperback ISBN: 979-8-88936-262-3
eBook ISBN: 979-8-88936-263-0

10   9   8   7   6   5   4   3   2   1

Available where books are sold

Contents

Chapter 1

Sheep Who Shall Never Perish

My sheep hear my voice, and I know them, and they follow me: and I give unto them eternal life; and they shall never perish, neither shall any man pluck them out of my hand. My Father, which gave them me, is greater than all; and no man is able to pluck them out of my Father's hand. I and my Father are one. (John 10:27-30)

Our Savior did not hesitate to preach the deeper doctrines of the gospel to the most miscellaneous assembly. When he began to preach where he was brought up, they all gathered around him with admiration, until he preached the doctrine of election; and then, immediately, they were so enraged that they would have destroyed him. They could not bear to hear of the widows of Israel being passed by, and the woman of Zarephath being chosen; nor of a heathen leper healed, while the many lepers of their own race were left to die. Election seems to heat the blood and fire the wrath of many. Not that they care to be chosen of God themselves, but, like the dog in the manger, they would keep other people out of the privilege. Not even to prevent these displays of bad temper did our Lord keep back the discriminating truths of the Word.

Here, when addressing the Jews, he did not hesitate to speak, even to a rude rabble, concerning that glorious doctrine. He says, *Ye believe not, because ye are not of my sheep, as I said unto you.* He does not lower

1

the standard of doctrine; but he holds his ground, and carries the war into the Enemy's camp.

The notion that certain truths are not fit to be preached to a general assembly, but are to be kept for the special gathering of the saints, is, I believe, horribly mischievous. Christ has not commanded us to keep a part of our teaching *sub-road* – reserved from the common folk, and set aside for the priests alone. He is for openly proclaiming all truth. *What I tell you in darkness, that speak ye in light: and what ye hear in the ear, that preach ye upon the housetops* (Matthew 10:27). There is no truth that we need to be ashamed of, and there is no truth that will do any harm.

We grant you that every truth can be twisted, but even this would be a lesser evil than the concealment of it. Whatever the doctrine may be, ungodly men can pervert it according to their own lusts; and if we have to stop preaching a doctrine because of the possibility of perverting it, we shall never preach anything at all, for every truth may be perverted, and made to be the mother of infinite mischief. Our Savior did not teach his disciples to keep certain things for the instructed few who were able to receive them; but he bade us to publish all the great truths, since they are necessary for conviction, for conversion, for edification, for sanctification, and for the perfecting of the people of God. Even to his brutal opponents he exhibited but little reserve. He flashed in the faces of his adversaries this grand, but humbling truth: *Ye believe not, because ye are not of my sheep.* Your unbelief is just an evidence that you were not chosen, that you have not been called by the Spirit of God, and that you are still in your sins.

The Jews had said to him, *If thou be the Christ, tell us plainly* (John 10:24). They professed that they wanted to know more certainly concerning him. This was a vain claim, for he had told them all they needed to know, and they had not believed him. Therefore, he answered them to a large degree by making them know more about themselves.

Sometimes the point in which a man is deficient is not as to the gospel, but as to his own need of it. He may know all of Christ that is needful for his salvation, but he may not know enough about himself and his own lost condition; therefore, he is not in the way in which Christ becomes precious to him, because he is ignorant of his deep and terrible need. So, the Savior began to talk to them, not so much about himself as about his people, and what they were to be. *My sheep hear my voice, and I know them, and they follow me.*

I pray God, the Holy Spirit, to bless the word to many, that they may learn more about the work of Christ in their hearts, and more about their need of it, and thus may be led to seek Jesus, and find him tonight as their Savior and their Shepherd.

There are two things in my text that will suffice for our meditation. First, here is *a description given* of the Lord's people. *My sheep hear my voice, and I know them, and they follow me.* And then, secondly, there is *a privilege secured* to them, namely, their everlasting, unquestionable safety. *I give unto them eternal life: and they shall never perish, neither shall any man pluck them out of my hand. My Father, which gave them me, is greater than all; and no man is able to pluck them out of my Father's hand. I and my Father are one.*

First, and all that I can say will be but little, considering the largeness of the subject, let us notice the description here given of the people of God.

They are first described by *a speciality of possession: **My** sheep* (emphasis added). All men are not sheep, for some are foxes, or ravening wolves, and others are compared to dogs and lions. All persons who might be called sheep are not Christ's sheep. All do not belong to his flock. All are not gathered into his fold. There is a speciality of possession. There may be many sheep, but the Savior speaks of *my sheep,* those whom he chose of old, those who were given him of the Father, those who have been bought with his blood, redeemed from among men, and in due time have been ransomed by his power, for he has bought them back from the hand of the Enemy, and therefore claims them to be his own. *The Lord's portion is his people.*

Other lords have their portion, and Christ takes his portion. His people are the lot of his inheritance. He speaks of *my sheep* as a peculiar heritage whom, as a shepherd, he claims for his own. Of these he is the sole Owner. He is not merely their Keeper, but also their Possessor. We read of the hireling shepherd, *whose own the sheep are not;* but in the case of our Good Shepherd, *he putteth forth his own sheep* (John 10:4).

There is *a speciality of character* about them. They are *my **sheep*** (emphasis added). They are dependent, timid, trembling, obedient, and teachable; they are made sheep by his own Spirit. They have received

3

a nature that is not that of the doggish world, nor that of the swinish multitude, nor that of the wolfish persecutor; but that of men indwelt by the Spirit of God, who are therefore clean, gentle, loving, and gracious. He calls them *my sheep,* for they have a special relationship to himself: they are like Jesus. Being his sheep, he has become their Guardian as well as their Proprietor, and they look up to him as such. They are sheep to him, and he is a shepherd to them.

We may judge ourselves by considering whether or not we are Christ's sheep. Do we acknowledge ourselves as belonging to him, spirit, soul, and body? Do we regard ourselves as being, in relation to him, no wiser, no stronger than sheep to a shepherd? I know some who are certainly no sheep of Christ's flock, for they will be led by nobody in heaven, or on earth, but must have their own way. They are critics of the Bible, not disciples of it. They might be very good dogs, but they are very strange sheep. They would make very respectable wolves, for they are great in destructive criticism; but they certainly are not sheep, and their temper and spirit are such that they would disdain the character, if they understood it. "What! To go where I am led? To lie down where I am bidden to lie down? Not to choose my own way? Just to see nothing, and know nothing; but to have my eyes in *his* head, and my wisdom in *his* mind? To be shepherded by another mind than my own? Is it so? Am I to be nothing but a sheep to the Lord Jesus?"

Yes, it is even so; therefore, the modern wise man is indignant, and proudly repudiates the character of a sheep. As for us, we accept all that the name implies. O brethren, we can play the man before other people, but when we come before our Lord, as the sheep is a mere animal in comparison with its shepherd, we feel ourselves to be less than that. How often have we cried with David, "*So foolish was I, and ignorant: I was as a beast before thee* (Psalm 73:22). O my Lord, in your presence I sink as low as low can be, and you become very high, yes, all in all to me, the Shepherd of my weak, vacillating, trembling spirit!" There is a speciality, then, about these people in the description. I have only time to hint at it.

*A chief mark of Christ's people is attention. My sheep **hear*** (emphasis added). They can hear, because they have had spiritual ears given to them. Once the Shepherd might have spoken all day long, and they would not have heard him; but it is not so now. Even from the cross our Lord's melancholy cries were all unheard by them; but now he has given them spiritual capacity and perception, and they can hear, and they do hear what his dying love would make them know and understand. Their Lord has spoken to them. They have heard his voice, and have known it to be his; they still hear it, and they distinguish between his voice and other voices. *A stranger will they not follow, . . . for they know not the voice of strangers.* They now so hear that voice as to hear it in a true way, and joyfully to acknowledge it by obeying it.

Do you not say, sometimes, to a child that is disobedient, "Did you not hear me speak, child?" So, Christ may say to many who hear with the outward ear, but who will not yield obedience, that they have not heard him; indeed, they have not listened with the inner ear. Their ear does not reach down to their heart, and thus, for spiritual purposes, it is no ear at all. It is an awful thing when the ear is a closed-up passage, shut against the voice of the Savior.

You can tell the sheep of Christ by their being marked in the ear. *My sheep hear my voice.* They may not hear a good deal that other people hear; they may even be glad to be deaf to it. There are many calls that are exceedingly musical to carnal ears, but which have no compelling attractiveness for them. They try to be deaf to some voices from which they could gather nothing but temptation; but they hear Christ's voice. They are all there when he speaks: their soul sits at the door to hear his softest whisper. They try to hear: they charge themselves to take heed that they lose no sound from heaven. They do hear, but they long to hear yet more completely, and to be more obedient to that voice that rings through the chambers of their soul. Oh, what a hearing we have sometimes given to Christ! I have heard him with my body, my soul, and my spirit, or at least I have thought so; but whether in the body, or out of the body, I could not tell. If in the body, every pore has been an ear for my Lord's sweet voice. As though my blood were tingling from the crown of my head to the sole of my foot, so has my spirit been wholly and entirely affected by the charming tones of the voice of the Well-beloved. Oh, that he would speak tonight! Can you not hear him? Beloved, is he not now calling us? Do you not rejoice to hear him?

No music's like his charming voice,
Nor half so sweet can be.

So you see, a noteworthy specialty of the elect ones lies in their attention to Jesus, their Shepherd. He calls in vain to others, but his sheep hear his voice.

Another mark of the Lord's people is intimacy. My sheep hear my voice, and **I know them** (emphasis added). *I know them.* Yes, *the Lord discerns them.* He singles them out, for *the Lord knoweth them that are his.* Sometimes *we* do not know them; but he says, *I know them.* In cloudy times they do not know themselves, but he says, *I know them.* When a child of God does not know whether he is a child of God or not, his Father knows his own children, and the Great Shepherd knows his own sheep. His is a discernment that never fails. The hypocrite cannot get into the true fold of Christ. He may get into the visible fold, but not into the real spiritual fold of Christ; for Christ does not know him, and he bids him to depart. This is the very seal upon the foundation – *The Lord knoweth them that are his.* His eyes discern between the righteous and the wicked, between him that fears God and him that fears him not; his is a knowledge of quick and certain discernment.

But this might make us tremble if we did not know that the expression *I know them* means *a knowledge of commendation. I know them,* says the Shepherd; "I take delight in them. I know their secret sighs and mournings. I hear their private prayers. I know their praises in the silence of their hearts. I know their consecration, and their aspirations for perfect service. I know their longings and their lovings. I know how they delight in me. I know how they trust my promise. I know how they look to my atoning blood. I know how in their inmost souls they rejoice in my name. I know them, and approve their secret thoughts." O sweet word, understood in that sense! And this is one part of the character of the Lord's people – that he did foreknow them in his sovereign grace; and now he personally knows them by taking delight in them.

This divine complacency leads to a very *intense observation* of them. *He knoweth the way that I take* (Job 23:10). *The Lord knoweth the way of the righteous* (Psalm 1:6). He has an eye upon them, and he marks their paths. His ears are open to their cry, and he hears their petitions.

Though there be all the world for his omniscience to consider, yet he looks upon each one of his saints as much as if there were only that one person in the universe. Oh, to think of this! *I know them* sounds like music in this sense. He that knows the stars, and knows the infinite multitude of living creatures in the universe, has a special and unique knowledge of his own chosen ones. *I know them,* says he; and he intends by that to mean an intense observation.

Now, beloved, just try a little here, to see whether you come into this number – *I know them.* Does the Lord know you as his own? Has he had personal interaction with you, and you with him? Or will he have to say to you at the end, *I never knew you?* Why, some of you have made him know you! You have gone to him in such trials, and in such troubles, and you have cried to him in such bitterness and anguish, that, if he asks your name, you can say,

> Once a sinner near despair
>> Sought thy mercy seat by prayer;
> Mercy heard, and set him free;
>> Lord, that mercy came to *me!*

"When you did help me in great need, when you did pass by my great sin, then did you know me, O my Lord! Do you ask me who I am? Ah, my Lord! you know my name." Just as some men know right well the beggar who is often at their door, so does the Lord for certain know some of you, for you go every day begging at his gate, and you receive a constant charity from his hand. Besides that, you go every day thanking him for the mercies you receive. He knows your name: the name of one who is drowned in debt to his infinite bounty. He can never forget your groans and cries, and day by day your praises are a memorial to him. By his love, and pity, and compassion, he is sure to remember you. Sooner *can a woman forget her sucking child* (Isaiah 49:15) than your God can forget you.

Well, here are things well worth noting – specialty, attention, and intimacy. Are these yours?

But here is one more: *actual obedience.* How does he put it? *I know them, and **they follow me*** (emphasis added). All the Lord's sheep are marked in the foot as well as in the ear. The foot and ear marks must be in every sheep of the Lord's flock. *They follow me.* That is to say, they openly acknowledge him as their Shepherd. Other shepherds come, and other sheep go after them; but these sheep know the Lord Jesus, and they follow him. He alone is their Leader. They are not ashamed to acknowledge it. They take up the cross, and follow the Cross-bearer, and they bear his name.

More than that, they practically carry out their open acknowledgment, and they follow him in daily life, copying his example. They not only say, "He is my Leader," but they also follow him. Christ's sheep try to follow in the track that the Shepherd marks for them. Christ's people are never so happy as when they can put down their feet where Christ put his feet down. The very marks that he has left by his bleeding footsteps we would desire to follow, all the day, and every day. Beloved, look carefully to this! Do what Jesus did, according to your measure and power. This is what the people of God try to do. If you do not endeavor to be like Christ, you are not his sheep; for of his sheep it is true: *I know them, and they follow me.*

And this is personally operative upon them. I could not tell you exactly in English words, but the Greek word here gives a kind of personality to the whole company. *My sheep hear my voice,* that is, the whole of the flock of God. *I know them,* that is, again, the whole flock of them, all together. But, *they follow me* is in the plural number. It is as though it said, "They, each one, follows me." We who are the Lord's chosen hear *en masse,* and the Lord knows the whole church, for, as a whole, it is redeemed by Christ; but we individually follow – each one for himself, through grace. We each one follow him. *They follow me.* I like that singular personal pronoun. It is not written, "They follow my commandments," though they do. It is not said, "They follow the route that I have mapped out for them," though they do that. But, *they follow me* (emphasis added) distinctly. In their individual personality they follow their Lord in his individual personality. They have recognized him above his words, above his ways, and even above his salvation. *They follow me,* says he. This is a grand mark of a Christian – not merely a life of morality, a life of integrity, and a life of holiness, but a life of all these in connection with Christ. They follow *him,* not holiness, nor morality, nor integrity apart from Christ, but they follow *their Lord.*

A good life is good in any man. We cannot speak evil of virtue, even when we find it in the ordinary moralist; but this is not the complete mark of Christ's sheep. The virtues of Christ's sheep are *in connection with himself.* The Christian is holy, and all that, but that is because he follows his perfect Master, and keeps close to him. This is one of the peculiar and unfailing marks of the child of God.

I have run through, very briefly, the description, and I now leave you to meditate upon it when you are alone. This description of the sheep of Christ is worthy of reading, marking, and inwardly digesting.

But my main object tonight is to show you the great privilege here conferred on the people of God. Christ has secured to them the priceless blessing of eternal security in him. No sheep of Christ shall ever be lost. None that he has purchased with his blood, and made to be his own, shall ever wander away so as to perish at last. This is the doctrine of the verses now before us. At any rate, if I wanted to express that doctrine, I could not find words in which I could set it forth more definitely or more completely than is done by the words before me.

The security of the people of God lies, first of all, in *the character of the life that they have received.* Listen to this: *And I give unto them eternal life.* All the spiritual life that all the sheep in the flock now possess has been given to them by their Shepherd. Never was there another flock of which this could be said. No shepherd but this one can give life to his sheep; but he gave them all the true life that they have. No, stop: he not only gave them life, but he also sustains that life by a constant gift. Observe, it is not written, "I *gave* to them eternal life," but *I give unto them eternal life* (emphasis added). They are always living by virtue of the life that he is always giving. They are constantly receiving life from him, according to that assurance: *Because I live, ye shall live also* (John 14:19). What he always gives they must always receive, and therefore it cannot cease.

Notice the nature of that life. *I give unto [my sheep] eternal life* (emphasis added). Now, you all know what *eternal* means; or I say, rather, none of you can form an idea of eternity that can grasp all its length of endurance. Only this: you know it has no end, and cannot therefore close. If anybody said that he had eternal life and lost it, he would be flatly contradicting himself. It could not be eternal, or else he would still have it. If it is eternal, it *is* eternal, and there is no end to it; and there is an end of further argument about it.

If the life that Christ gives us, when we are born again, can die, it is not *eternal* life, or else words have ceased to have any meaning at all. In its nature, as being the work of the Holy Spirit, and a releasing from God, the life bestowed in regeneration is an undying one. Has not the Holy Spirit described us as *being born again, not of corruptible seed, but of incorruptible, by the word of God, which liveth and abideth for ever* (1 Peter 1:23)? The life of God imparted by the Holy Spirit must live forever. As the gift is continuous, and it is always being given, and as it is in itself eternal life, it must always exist.

But, principally, I dwell upon *the glorious character of the Giver. I give unto [my sheep] eternal life.* The life that Christ gives is not that poor, inferior life that lasts for the convert for only about three weeks, and then dwindles down and dies out; or, say, for three months, and then the revival is over, and the convert is spun out and done for, and has to begin again. Such is the religious life that is pumped up by men; but it is not so with the life that comes from God. I said that the *false* convert begins again, though how he begins again I know not, because I read in Scripture of people being born again; but I have never read of their being born again, and again, and again, and again. I am told that some of our religionists have had their people converted and born again more times than they can count; and I heard that a woman had been born again twelve times down at a certain meeting, but he who stated the fact said shrewdly that he feared it was not done well the last time. No, I do not think it will ever be done well in that way. He that is born again, according to Scripture, has received eternal life, and this is the only life worth receiving. I would not preach my very soul away in order to proclaim such a twopenny, worthless, and temporary salvation as that, but to preach the Lord Jesus as giving *eternal* life is worth living for and dying for.

I tell you, sirs, it is this that brought me to Christ. While I was still young, and thinking over matters, I saw young lads who were brought up with me, excellent in character, who left their homes to be apprenticed, and after a while the temptations of the world overcame them, and they went astray, and had no religion at all. But when I read that

Christ gave his sheep eternal life, I looked at it as a kind of moral life insurance for my soul, and I came to Christ, and trusted him to keep me to the end. I shall suffer a grievous disappointment if I ever find out that the life of God in me is not eternal, and that the new birth does not assure final perseverance. I did not go up to the booking office and take a ticket for a quarter of the distance to heaven; but I took my ticket for all the way through. I trust, no, I know, that according to my faith, so will it be unto me. I am very glad to have my through-ticket with me, and I believe that unless the train of almighty grace smashes up – which it never will – I shall get through to the celestial terminal as surely as ever divine power can draw me there; for so it is written, *I give unto [my sheep] eternal life.*

Now, depend upon it, it is what you hold out to people that has much to do with how they behave themselves afterwards. Tell them that if they believe in Christ, they are going to get not eternal life, but life for a little while – life for as long as they take good care of it, and I fear it will prove to be so. It may do them good to get the poor little change you offer them; but as surely as they are converted to a temporary life, they will die out before long. You told them that they would. You did not propose any more to them. But when you propose to them this – "Here is everlasting life to be had by believing in Christ. It is not temporary, but eternal life" – why, then they grip it as such. They believe in Christ for that, and according to their faith it is unto them; and the Lord and Giver of life is glorified in giving to them this great and splendid gift, the gift of all gifts. *I give unto [my sheep] eternal life.*

I do not know in what other way to preach from this text than the one in which I am preaching from it. Somebody says, "Oh, that is Calvinism!" I do not care what it is. It is scriptural. I have this inspired Book before me, and I cannot see any meaning in the words before me if they do not mean that those who have received life from the Lord Jesus have an endless inheritance. I cannot make them mean anything else. *I give unto [my sheep] eternal life* must mean that believers are eternally secure. "It is dangerous doctrine," cries one. I have not found it dangerous, and I have tested it these many years. I conceive that it would be far more dangerous to tell people that they could be truly converted, and yet the work of grace would end in six months, and then they could come back again, and begin again, and do so as many times as they liked; whereas the Word of God tells them that *if they shall fall away,* it is impossible *to renew them again unto repentance* (Hebrews 6:6). Men may fall and be restored; but if they fall away utterly, there remains no other work that can be done for them.

If this everlasting life could die, the Holy Spirit would have done his best, and nothing more would remain to be done. If it were so that this salt that is good should lose its savor, by what means could it be salted? See what a gulf opens before you; and do not look for a work that will not endure every possible strain. Oh, that you may get this eternal life!

So, we take a step further. The children of God are safe, again, not only because of the life they receive, but also because of *the inner dangers that are averted.* Take the next sentence – *And they shall never perish.* They have a tendency toward spiritual sickness, but their Shepherd will doctor them so that they shall never perish. They are sheep, and have a tendency to wander; but their Shepherd shall keep them so that they shall never perish. Time tests them, and they grow old, and the novelty of religion wears off; but they shall never perish. Think what you will of them, *they shall never perish,* for so the promise stands.

The first statement, *I give unto them eternal life,* is as broad as it well can be, and this is broader still – *they shall never perish.* The rule has absolutely no exception. The whole of them shall be preserved. Let them live to be as old as Methuselah, they shall never perish, whatever temptation may attack them. They may be tested, and troubled, and broken down so that they may be hardly able to live; but *they shall never perish. Never* is a long day; but it is not longer than grace will last. Blessed be God, this grand promise stands fast – *They shall never perish.*

Now we must go a step further. We have no time to urge these arguments at any great length. They are safe, next, by *outer injuries being prevented. Neither shall any man pluck them out of my hand.* Many will pluck at them, but none shall pluck them away. The devil will give many a horrible pluck and pull, to get them away; but out of the Great Shepherd's hand he shall never take them. Their old companions, and the memory of their old sins will come and pluck at them very hard, and very cunningly; but the Savior says, "None shall pluck them out of my hand." So, first, here is their security: *they are in his hand,* that is, in his *possession* and he grasps them as a man holds a thing in his hand, and says, "It is mine." Neither shall any take them away from being under his *protection*. Never shall they be plucked away from Christ.

When he says this, he pledges his honor to preserve them, for if it could be that one were plucked out of his hand, then would the devils in hell rejoice, and say, "He could not keep them. He said that he would, but he could not. We have managed to pluck this one, or that one, out of the pierced hand of their Redeemer." But such a horrible exultation shall never be heard throughout the ages of eternity. *They shall never perish, neither shall any man pluck them out of my hand.*

Someone wickedly said, "They may get out of his hand themselves." But how can this be true, when the first sentence is: *They shall never perish*? Treat Scripture honestly and candidly, and you will admit that the promise, *they shall never perish,* shuts out the idea of perishing by going out of the Lord's hand by their own act and deed. *They shall never perish, neither shall any man pluck them out of my hand.* Who is to loosen the clasp of that hand that was pierced with the nail for me? My Lord Jesus bought me too dearly ever to let me go. He loves me so well that his whole omnipotence will work with that hand, and I cannot be plucked away from that dear, firmly held grip.

Now, to make quite sure about it, and to pile on the comfort, the Savior goes on to add *the care and power of God himself.* Our Lord says, *My Father, which gave them me.* The saints of God are safe because the Father gave them to his Son. He did not give him a transitory inheritance. He did not bestow on him something that he might, after all, lose. Will the Lord Christ lose what his Father gave him? You know how people say, "Oh, I hope that if a burglar takes anything from my house, he will not take that cup, which is an heirloom. My father gave it to me." If a man had to defend his property, he would be sure to take care of that which was a very special gift, given in his honor, as a memorial of a great work.

So it is with our Lord Jesus: he values that which his Father gave him. I delight in that thought. I picture my blessed Lord looking at each one of his believing people, and saying, "My Father gave you to me." That poor woman, that struggling young man, that decrepit old lady, that man who is half-starved, but who loves his Lord – Jesus says of each one, "My Father gave this soul to me." He cannot lose what his Father gave him. He would die again sooner than he would lose them. His death has made their salvation safe beyond all jeopardy. He laid down his life for the sheep. The lion came, and leaped into the fold; but the Shepherd met the lion; yes, he received him on his naked breast, and held him there. It was a terrible tug. The Shepherd sweat great drops of blood as he held the monster; but he tore him, and he hurled him to the earth, and said, "It is finished," *and it was finished.* He has so saved all his flock until now that we are sure that he will never lose one of those whom his Father committed to his trust. "My Father gave them to me."

Then he goes on to say that *his people are kept by the Father's power*; for he says, *My Father, which gave them me, is greater than all; and no man is able to pluck them out of my Father's hand.* Beloved, although God gave us to Christ, he did not cease to care for us himself! Our sweet text last Sunday night I must bring to your memory. I could not fully preach from it, but the text was enough without a sermon: *All mine are thine, and thine are mine; and I am glorified in them* (John 17:10). We tried to show you how we were nonetheless the Father's because we were the Son's, and nonetheless the Son's because we belonged to the Father. So here Jesus in effect says, "My Father gave you to me; yet he takes care of you nonetheless, but all the more. Because he is determined that what he gave to me shall be mine, the Lord will put forth his wisdom and power to preserve you."

Let me by a symbol illustrate the latter words of the text. There lie the children of God in the hand of Christ. Do you see that firmly closed hand? They are safe enough there. Jesus says, "No man shall be able to pluck them out of *my hand.*" But see the Father: he puts his hand over the hand of Jesus! There now; you are inside two hands, *And no man is able to pluck them out of **my Father's hand*** (emphasis added). Oh, the serene security of those who hear the voice of Christ, and whom he calls his sheep! A doublehanded force keeps them safe against all ill. Pluck away, Satan! You will never pluck them away from the hand of Jesus and the hand of his Father! *Quit separabit? Who shall separate us from the love of Christ?* (Romans 8:35). It is impossible to be done.

And then the Savior finishes all by saying that while he has spoken of the Father and himself as two – and two they are as persons – yet *in their divine essence they are but one.* He says, *I and my Father are one,* and especially one in love for his people. *The Father himself loveth you* (John 16:27), even as he loves his Son; and, while you read the love of Christ in his death, you must read the Father's love quite as much in that great sacrifice.

It is true of our Lord Jesus that *Christ also loved the church, and gave himself for it* (Ephesians 5:25); but it is equally true of the Father that *God so loved the world, that he gave his only begotten Son* (John 3:16). They are one in an infinite love to all those who, called according to the divine purpose, are following Christ, and hearing his voice. I fall back with great joy upon this blessed conviction – that he will not permit those to perish who have received eternal life at his hands. Of course, if you have only taken temporary life – if you only believe in that – you will get no more than you believe. Your gift will be measured by your faith.

But if you say, "I gave myself up to Christ that he might be Alpha and Omega to me; and I wholly trust myself to him without reserve, throughout all my life, to save me." then he will do it; *for I . . . am persuaded that he is able to keep that which I have committed unto him against that day* (2 Timothy 1:12). *He which hath begun a good work in you will perform it until the day of Jesus Christ* (Philippians 1:6). *The path of the just is as the shining light, that shineth more and more unto the perfect day* (Proverbs 4:18).

You are safe in Christ's hand. Know it, and feel the joy of it. "Oh," says one, "but if I thought so, I would run into sin!" I am sorry for you, that things act very strangely upon you. Nothing binds me to my Lord like a strong belief in his changeless love. "Oh, but it would be far safer to tell your hearers that they may be overcome by sin, and perish!" I will not tell them what I do not believe. I will not dishonor my Lord by a falsehood. Shall I come home to your house, and tell your children that if they do wrong, you will cut their heads off; or that if they disobey you, they will cease to be your children? If I were to propound that doctrine, your children would grow angry at such a slander upon their father. They would say, "No, we know better than that!" Far rather would I say to them, "My dear children, your father loves you; he will love you without end, therefore do not grieve him." Under such doctrine true children will say, "We love our ever-loving father. We will not disobey him. We will endeavor to walk in his ways."

15

'Tis love that makes our willing feet
    In swift obedience move.

Our loving Lord will not cast away those to whom he is bound by marriage bonds. "Well, but suppose we sin." He will chasten us and restore us. "If I believed that doctrine, I would live as I like," says one. Then you are not one of his sheep, for his sheep love holiness, and will not love iniquity. The change effected by the new birth is such that a man will not return to his old ways of sin and folly. This is the doctrine, and how can you make it to be an indulgence to sin? True saints never turn the grace of God into licentiousness, but the very mention of eternal love leads them to careful obedience.

One thing I must say at the end. Some ministers preach a gospel with a very wide door to it, but there is nothing to be had when you get within. I am sometimes told that I make my door a little too narrow. It is not true, for I preach the gospel to every creature under heaven, with all my might; but if the door be narrow, there is something worth having when you enter by it. Even if the way be narrow, if you once get in, then you *have gotten* in, and you have found eternal life, and you shall never perish, neither shall any pluck you out of Christ's hands. Sinner, come and have an eternal blessing! It is worth having. Come and have it! If you believe, you shall assuredly be saved. *He that believeth and is baptized shall be saved;* saved from sin so as never to go back and live in it again; so saved as to be made holy; so saved as to be preserved in holiness. Holiness shall be the set of the main current of your life until, made perfectly holy, you shall dwell with God above.

Into his hands let us commit our spirits , and we may rest assured that they shall be safe eternally. Amen.

Chapter 2

Eternal Life

*And I give unto them eternal life; and they
shall never perish, neither shall any man
pluck them out of my hand.* (John 10:28)

S ome will say that this is a mixed congregation, and that such a
doctrine as this should not be advanced in the presence of ungodly
men and women. This shows how little such objectors read their Bible,
for this very text was spoken by the Savior, not to his loving disciples,
but to his enemies. Read the thirty-first verse of the chapter, and you
will see the temper of the congregation to whom Jesus Christ preached
upon this subject – *Then the Jews took up stones again to stone him.* So
that an indignant multitude of bigots had this hurled into their face by
the Savior, that although they might reject him, and because of their
willful obstinacy might miss the blessings of grace, yet those blessings
were rich and rare.

He would have them to know that what they lost was inexpressibly
precious, and that his message was not to be despised without great
damage to their souls. Thus, if there be a mixed multitude here – and
I fear the allegation is true, that there are many here who cannot comprehend the preciousness of the things of God – yet, for the same reason
that prompted the Savior to preach of this doctrine to the wicked in his
day, we will do the same now, that they may know what it is they lose

by losing Christ, what those comfortable things are that they despise, and what are the inestimable treasures that those must miss who seek after the treasures of this world, and let their God, their Savior go.

We have no time to loiter, and let us therefore, as the bee sucks honey from the flower, seek after the sweet essence of the text, *I give unto them eternal life.* The connection tells us that the pronoun *them* refers to Christ's sheep, to certain persons whom he had chosen to be his sheep, and whom he had also called to be such. Lest we should be in the dark as to who they are, our Savior has kindly put us in possession of the marks by which his sheep may be discovered. We cannot read the secret roll of election, nor can we search the heart, but we can mark the outward conduct of men; and the verse before the text tells us by what signs we are to know God's people. *My sheep hear my voice, and I know them, and they follow me.*

The marks are the hearing of Christ, and then the following of Christ, first, by faith in him, and then by an active obedience to his precepts. *Faith which worketh by love* (Galatians 5:6) is the mark of Christ's sheep, and it is of true believers that he speaks when he says, *I give unto them eternal life; and they shall never perish, neither shall any man pluck them out of my hand.* Would to God that all of us wore the garb of the elect, namely, active, sanctifying faith! Oh, that we all listened to the Great Shepherd's voice, that we received the truth that he delivers, and then resolved by his grace to follow him to whatever place he goes, as the sheep follow the shepherd.

Having thus explained to whom the text belongs, we will now handle it in a threefold manner. The text implies, first, *somewhat concerning the past of these people;* the text plainly states, in the second place, *a great deal about the present state of these people;* and thirdly, the text not obscurely hints at *something about their future.*

In the first place, the studious reader will observe that the text implies somewhat concerning the past history of the people of God.

It is said, *I give unto them eternal life.* There is an implication, therefore, *that they had lost eternal life.* Every one of God's people fell in Adam, and all have fallen also by actual sin; consequently, we came under condemnation, and Christ Jesus has done for us what Her Majesty the Queen has sometimes done for a condemned criminal – he has brought us a free pardon. He has given us life. When our own desert was eternal destruction from the presence of the Lord, Jesus Christ stepped in, and he said, "You are forgiven; the sentence shall not take place upon you; your offense is blotted out; you are clear." No, I think the text implies that there was something more than condemnation; there was execution. We were not only condemned to die, but we were also already spiritually dead. Jesus did not merely spare the life that ought to have been taken, and in that sense gave it to us, but he also imparted to us a life that we had not before enjoyed.

It is implied in the text that we were spiritually dead; no, we are not left here to our own suppositions, nor even to our own experience, for the apostle Paul has said, *You hath he quickened, who were dead in trespasses and sins.* What, Paul, dead? Are you not mistaken? Perhaps they were only a little sick? No, we are ready to admit, O apostle, that they were sick and near to death, but surely they had a little vital energy, a little power to assist themselves! "No," says the apostle, "you were dead, *dead in trespasses and sins.*" The work of salvation is tantamount not only to the healing of the sick, but also to the actual resurrection of a dead man from his grave. All the saints who are now alive unto God were once as dead as others, quite as corrupt and offensive as others, and as much an ill smell in the nostrils of divine justice by reason of their sins as even the most corrupt of their fellows.

We had altogether gone out of the way; we had altogether become abominable, for *there is none that doeth good, no, not one* (Psalm 53:3). When we were all shut up under sin, then Jesus Christ came into the region of death, and brought life and immortality to us. Life was forfeited by all the saints; spiritual life they had none. Jesus the Invigorator has made them alive unto God.

Is it not also very clearly implied that, so far from having any life, *these people could not otherwise have obtained life except by its being given to them*? It is a rule well known to all biblical students that you never meet in God's Word with an unnecessary miracle, that a miracle is never worked where the ordinary course of nature would suffice. Now, my brethren, the greatest of all miracles is the salvation of a soul. If that soul could save itself, God would not save it, but would let it do what it could do; and if the spiritually dead could revive themselves, rest assured, from the analogy of all the divine transactions, that Jesus Christ would not have come to give them life.

I believe that it would be utterly impossible for any one of us to enter heaven, let us do what we might, unless Jesus Christ had come from heaven to show us the way, to remove the bolts and bars for us, and to enable us to tread in the path that leads to glory and immortality. Lost! lost! lost! The race of man was utterly lost, not partly lost, not thrown into a condition in which it might be ruined unless it worked hard to save itself; but so lost, that but for the intercession of a divine arm, but for the appearance of God in human flesh, but for the stupendous transaction upon Calvary, and the work of God the Holy Spirit in the heart, not one dead soul ever could come to life. Eternal life would not be the peculiar work of the Lord Jesus if man had a finger in it, but now man's power is excluded and grace reigns.

It is clearly to be seen in the text, by a little thought, *that eternal life was not the merit of any one of God's people, for it is said that it is given to us.* Now, a gift is the very opposite of a payment. What a man receives as a gift he certainly does not deserve. If it be given to us, then it is no more a debt; but if it be a debt, then it can be no more a gift. None of us merits eternal life, or ever can merit it. Mere mortal life is a gift of divine mercy: we do not deserve it; and as for the eternal life spoken of in the text, it is a blessing too high for the fingers of human merit to hope to reach it. If a man could work never so hard for it, nevertheless, upon the footing of the law it would be impossible for him to obtain it. Man merits nothing but death, and life must be the free gift of God. *The wages of sin is death;* that is to say, it is earned and procured as a matter of debt; *but the gift of God,* the free-grace gift of God, *is eternal life* (Romans 6:23).

Now, this is a very humiliating doctrine, I know; but it is true, and I want you all to feel it. Children of God, I know you do. Do you see the hole of the pit from where you were drawn? Do you see it? Or have you grown proud recently? Those fine feelings and prayings of yours, have you stuck them like feathers in your cap? I pray you recollect what you were! You are proud! Do not forget the dunghill where you once grew! Remember the filth out of which God took you, and instead of being scarlet with the garments of pride, your cheeks may well be scarlet with a blush! Oh! may God forbid, once and for all, that we should glory, for what have we to glory in? What do we have that we have not received?

It is clear, too, from the text, that *those who are now righteous would have perished but for Christ.* Christ says, *They shall never perish.* Promises are never given as luxuries. There is a necessity, therefore, for this promise. There was a danger, a solemn danger, that every one of those men who are now saved would have perished eternally. Sin made them heirs of wrath even as others, so Scripture tells us; and justice must have overwhelmed them with the rest, if distinguishing grace had not prevented it.

Even now it is solemnly true, that there is no reason why a truly righteous soul should not perish, except that Christ still prevents it. You are alive, but you would not be spiritually alive for an hour unless the Holy Spirit continued to pour his vital energy into your soul. You shall be preserved, but, mark you, it is stated as a promise, and therefore it is not at all a matter of natural necessity. Apart from grace, you are in fearful danger of apostasy, and probably you have fears about it even now, like the apostle, who feared lest after having preached to others, he himself should be a castaway. It is a very proper fear, a fear that will often come upon sincere souls who feel a holy jealousy of themselves.

But we need have no fear when we come to the promise of God, for if we are really in Christ we have a guarantee of security, since Christ's own word is: *They shall never perish.* The promise was certainly given because it was needed. There is a danger of perishing; there are ten thousand risks of perishing; only omnipotence itself keeps off the fiery darts of Satan. The blessed Physician gives the antidote, or else the poison would soon destroy us; he who swears to bring us safely home protects us from a thousand foes, who otherwise would work our ill. *They shall never perish.*

It is also implied, *that naturally the people of God have ten thousand enemies who would pluck them out of Christ's hand.* They were once in the hand of the Enemy; they were once willing bondslaves of Satan. All this they know, and all this they are willing to acknowledge. I would to God that some here would feel the truth of that which I have been saying. You self-righteous ones will say, "I am all right; I do my best, I go to a place of worship." Now, soul, that is right enough in itself, but if you boast of it, it is an evidence that you know neither God nor yourself. When I have heard of some who have boasted that they felt no inbred sin, I have wished that they would read the story of the Pharisee and the publican.

At the Fulton Street Prayer Meeting, a brother asked for the prayers of believers because he felt so much the corruption of his own heart, the temptations of Satan, and especially the natural vileness of his own nature. A brother stood up on the opposite side of the hall and said he thanked God that that was not his experience; he did not feel any corruption, and his heart was not depraved. The other one made no reply, but a friend present read these words:

> *Two men went up into the temple to pray; the one a*
> *Pharisee, and the other a publican. The Pharisee stood and*
> *prayed thus with himself, God, I thank thee, that I am not*
> *as other men are, extortioners, unjust, adulterers, or even*
> *as this publican. I fast twice in the week, I give tithes of all*
> *that I possess. And the publican, standing afar off, would not*
> *lift up so much as his eyes unto heaven, but smote upon his*
> *breast, saying, God be merciful to me a sinner. I tell you, this*
> *man went down to his house justified rather than the other:*
> *for every one that exalteth himself shall be abased; and he*
> *that humbleth himself shall be exalted.* (Luke 18:10-14)

A sense of sin is a blessed sign either of pardon received or of pardon to come. He that says he has no sin makes God a liar, and the truth is not in him. He who will not confess his sin shall never be acquitted; but he who with a broken and a trembling heart goes to the foot of the cross shall find forgiveness there. This much, then, upon the past estate of the heirs of heaven.

And now, to plunge at once into the subject. The text sheds a flood of light upon the present state of every believer.

We shall have to give you hints rather than a long exposition; so kindly take the first sentence, which speaks of *a gift received. I give unto them eternal life.* This gift is, first of all, *life.* You will make strange confusion of God's Word if you confound life with existence, for they are very different things. All men will exist forever, but many will dwell in everlasting death; they will know nothing whatever of life. Life is a distinct thing altogether from existence, and implies in God's Word something of activity and of happiness.

In the text before us it includes many things. Note the difference between the stone and the plant. The plant has vegetable life. You know the difference between the animal and the plant. While the plant has vegetable life, yet it is altogether dead in the sense in which we speak of living creatures. It has not the sensations that belong to animal life. Then again, if we turn to another and higher grade, namely, mental life, an animal is dead so far as that is concerned. It cannot enter at all into the mysterious calculations of the mathematician, nor revel in the sublime glories of poetry. The animal has nothing to do with the life of the intellectual mind; as to mental life, it is dead.

Now, there is a grade of life that is higher than the mental life – a higher life quite unknown to the philosopher, not put down in Plato, nor spoken of by Aristotle, but understood by the very lowliest of the children of God. It is a phase of life called "spiritual life," a new form of life altogether, which does not belong to man naturally, but is given to him by Jesus Christ. The first man, Adam, was made a living soul, and all his descendants are made like unto him. The second Adam is made an invigorating spirit, and until we are made like the second Adam, we know nothing of spiritual life. This body of ours is by nature adapted for a soulish life. The apostle tells us, in that wonderful chapter in Corinthians, that the body is sown – what? *A natural body.* The Greek is "a soulish body" – but *it is raised* – what? *A spiritual body* (1 Corinthians 15:44). There is a soulish body, and there is a spiritual body. There is a body adapted to the lower life that belongs to all men, a mere mental existence; and there is to be a body that will belong to all those who have received spiritual life, who shall dwell in that body as the house of their perfected spirit in heaven.

The life that Jesus Christ gives his people is spiritual life; therefore it is *mysterious. Thou hearest the sound thereof, but canst not tell whence it cometh, and whither it goeth: so is every one that is born of the Spirit* (John 3:8). You who have mental life cannot explain to the horse or the dog what it is; neither can we who have spiritual life explain to those who do not have it what it is. You can tell them what it does and what its effects are, but what the "spark of heavenly flame" may be, you yourselves do not know, though you are conscious that it is there.

It is spiritual life that Jesus Christ gives his people, but it is also more:

23

it is *divine life*. This life is like the life of God, and therefore it is *elevating.* "We are made," says the apostle, *"partakers of the divine nature"* (2 Peter 1:4). *Being born again,* says the apostle, *not of corruptible seed, but of incorruptible* (1 Peter 1:23).

We do not become divine, but we receive a nature that enables us to sympathize with Deity, to delight in the topics that engage the Eternal Mind, and to live upon the same principles as the most Holy God. We love, for God is love. We begin to be holy, for God is three times holy. We pant after perfection, for he is perfect. We delight in doing good, for God is good. We get into a new atmosphere. We pass out of the old range of the mere mental faculties; our spiritual faculties make us akin to God. *Let us,* said he, *make man in our image, after our likeness* (Genesis 1:26). That image Adam lost; that image Christ restores, and gives to us that life that Adam lost in the day when he sinned, when God said to him, *In the day that thou eatest thereof thou shalt surely die* (Genesis 2:17). In that sense he *did* die; the sentence was not postponed. He died spiritually immediately after he touched the fruit, and this long-lost life Jesus Christ restores to every soul who believes in him.

This life, you will gather from my remarks, is *heavenly life*. It is the same life that expands and develops itself in heaven. The Christian does not die. What does the Savior say? *Whosoever liveth and believeth in me shall never die* (John 11:26). Does not the mental life die? Yes. Does not the mere bodily life die? Alas, but not the spiritual life. It is the same life here that it will be there, only now it is undeveloped and corruption impedes its action.

Brethren, nothing of us shall go to heaven as flesh and blood, but only as it is subdued, elevated, changed, and perfected by the influence of the spirit life. Do you not know *that flesh and blood cannot inherit the kingdom of God; neither doth corruption inherit incorruption* (1 Corinthians 15:50)? Then what is the "I," the "myself," that shall enter heaven? Why, if you be in Christ a new creature, then that new creature and nothing but that new creature, the very life that you have lived here in this tabernacle, the very life that has budded and blossomed in the garden of communion with God, the life that has led you to visit the sick and clothe the naked and feed the hungry, the life that has made tears of repentance stream down your cheeks, the life that has caused you to believe in Jesus – this is the life that will go to heaven; and if you do not have this, then you do not possess the life of heaven, and dead souls cannot enter there. Only living men can enter into the land of the living. *As we have borne the image of the earthy, we shall also bear the image of the heavenly* (1 Corinthians 15:49). Even now the heavenly life heaves and throbs within us.

I think it may also be inferred from all this that the life that Christ gives his people is *an energetic life*. If the spiritual life is poured into a man, it raises him above his former state, and lifts him out of the range of merely carnal comprehension. He himself is discerned by no man. *For ye are dead, and your life is hid with Christ in God* (Colossians 3:3). You cannot expect the world to understand this new life. It is a hidden thing. It will be a mystery to yourselves, a wonder to your own hearts. But oh! how active it will be! It will fight with your sins, and will not be satisfied until it has slain them. If you tell me you never have a conflict within, I tell you I cannot understand how you can have the divine life, for it is sure to come into conflict at once with the old nature, and there will be perpetual strife.

The man becomes a new man at home; his wife and family observe it; he is a different man in business; he is a changed man altogether, whether you view him in connection with his fellow man or with his God. He is a new creature. He feels that the new and wondrous life that has been planted in him has made him of a different race from the common herd, and he walks among the sons of men feeling that he is an alien and a stranger. *Beloved, now are we the sons of God, and it doth not yet appear what we shall be: but we know that, when he shall appear, we shall be like him; for we shall see him as he is.*

I wish there were more time to describe the inward life, but this must suffice to indicate the blessing that Jesus gives to the believer by the work of the Holy Spirit.

There is a word in the text that qualifies it: *I give unto them **eternal life*** (emphasis added). *Eternal* means "without end." If Christ puts the life of God into a man, that life cannot be taken away. It cannot die; that would be impossible. When I have heard one say that you may be a child of God today but that next week may find you a child of the devil, I have supposed that the word *eternal* according to him could only have meant five or six days; but according to the dictionary I use, according to the mind of the Spirit, *eternal* means "without end." If, then, a man says, "I had spiritual life once, but I do not possess it now," it is clear that either he is mistaken altogether or he never had it at all. If Jesus had said, "I give unto them life that shall last for seven years, but that may perhaps be quenched and put out under temptation," I could understand a man saying that he had fallen from grace; but if it be *eternal life*, then it must be *eternal*; there is no end to it, it must go on.

The mere existence of the soul we believe will be never-ending, but it will be no help to the ungodly that it will be so. It is not for Christ to give us mere immortality of existence, for that will be a fearful curse to some men. Lost souls would be glad enough if they could be rid of their immortal existence, but Christ gives an eternal life, a holy life, a happy *life*, which is infinitely more than existence. Existence may be a curse, but life is a blessing. This life begins here: *I give unto them.* Not "I shall give," but *I give.* Not "I will give it to them when they die," but "I give it to them here, *I give unto them eternal life.*"

Now, my friend, you have either got eternal life, or you are still in death. If you have not received it, you are *dead in trespasses and sins,* and your doom will be a terrible one; but if God has given you eternal life, fear not the surrounding hosts of hell nor the temptations of the world, for the eternal God is your refuge, and underneath you are the everlasting arms.

This life *is given as a free gift* to every one of the Lord's people, and is bestowed by the Lord and by no one else.

Let us turn now to the second part of the blessing. Here is *preservation secured. They shall never perish.* Certain gentlemen who cannot endure the doctrine of final perseverance manage to slip away from the next sentence: *Neither shall any man pluck them out of my hand,* and suggest, "but they may get out themselves." No, no, no, because the text says, *They shall never perish.* Our present sentence that we have now in hand puts aside all suppositions of every kind about the destruction of one of Christ's sheep. *They shall never perish.* Take each word. **They shall never perish** (emphasis added). Some of their notions may perish, some of their comforts may perish, some of their experiences may perish, but they never shall. That which is the essence of the man, his true soul, his inward renewed nature, shall never be destroyed.

See then, Christian, you may be deprived of a thousand things without any violation of the promise. The promise is not that the ship shall not go to the bottom, but that the passengers shall get to the shore. The promise is not that the house shall not be burned; the pledge is that you who are in the house shall escape. *They shall never perish.* Take another word: *They shall never **perish*** (emphasis added). They shall go very near it perhaps. They shall lose their joys and their comforts, but *they shall never **perish**.* The life in them shall never be starved out, nor beaten out, nor driven out. If you once get leaven into a piece of bread you cannot get it out; you may boil it, you may fry it, you may bake it, you may do what you like with it, but the leaven is in it, and you cannot get it out. Get the soul saturated with the grace of God, and you can never eradicate it. The man himself shall never perish. He may think he shall, the devil may tell him he shall, his comforts may be withdrawn, he may go to his deathbed full of doubts and fears about himself, but he *shall never perish.*

Now, this is either true or it is not. You who think it is not true tell the Lord so; but I believe that it is a most sure and infallible fact, for Jehovah says it. I do not know how it is that they do not perish, it is a wondrous thing; but then it is all a marvel throughout from first to last. Now take the word *never*. We have shown how long the preservation endures: *They shall **never** perish* (emphasis added). "Well, but what if they should live to be very aged, and should then fall into sin?" *They shall **never** perish.* "Oh! but perhaps they may be assaulted in quarters where they least expect it, or they may be beleaguered by temptation." *They shall **never** perish.* "Well, but a man may be a child of God and yet go to hell." How so, if he can *never* perish? Why, that word *never* includes time and eternity, it includes living and dying, it includes the mountain and the valley, the tempest and the calm. *They shall **never** perish.*

> In every state secure,
> Kept by the eternal Hand.

Beneath the wings of the almighty God, night with its pestilence cannot strike them, and day with its cares cannot destroy them; youth with its passions shall be safely passed; middle age with all its whirl of business shall be navigated in safety; old age with its infirmities shall become the land of Beulah; death's gloomy vale shall be lit up with the coming splendor; the actual moment of departure, the last and solemn article, shall be the passing over of a river dry-shod. *When thou passest through the waters, I will be with thee; and through the rivers, they shall not overflow thee: when thou walkest through the fire, thou shalt not be burned; neither shall the flame kindle upon thee,* says the Lord (Isaiah 43:2). *They shall **never** perish.*

There is a way of explaining away everything, I suppose, but I really do not know how the opponents of the perseverance of God's saints will get over this text. They may do with it as they will, but I shall still believe what I find here, that I shall never perish if I am one of Christ's people. If I perish, then Christ will not have kept his promise; but I know he must abide faithfully to his Word. *[He] is not a man, that he should lie; neither the son of man, that he should repent* (Numbers 23:19). Every soul that rests on the atoning sacrifice is safe, and safe forever; *they shall **never** perish.*

Then comes the third sentence, in which we have *a position guaranteed* – in Christ's hand. We have not time to expound it. It is to be in a place of honor; we are the ring he wears on his finger. It is a place of love: *I have graven thee upon the palms of my hands; thy walls are continually before me* (Isaiah 49:16). It is a place of power: his right hand encloses all his people. It is a place of property: Christ holds his people; *all his saints are in thy hand* (Deuteronomy 33:3). It is a place of discretion: we are yielded up to Christ, and Christ wields a discretionary government over us. It is a place of guidance, a place of protection: as sheep are said to be in the hand of the shepherd, so are we in the hand of Christ.

As arrows in the hand of a mighty man to be used by him, as jewels in the hands of the bride to be her ornament, so are we in the hand of Christ. Now, what says the text? It reminds us that there are some who want to pluck us from that place. There are those who, with false doctrine, would deceive, if it were possible, the very elect. There are roaring persecutors who would frighten God's saints, and so make them turn back in the day of battle. There are scheming tempters – the panderers to hell, the jackals of the lion of the pit, who would rather drag us to destruction. Then there are our own hearts that would pluck us from that place.

You know in the text before us we need not read the word *man*, for it is not in the original. The translators have put the word *man* in italics to show that it is not in the Greek, and so we may read it – "Neither shall *any* pluck them out of my hand." Not only any *man*, but also any *devil*. Nothing that is present shall do it, and nothing to come – no principality, no power, nothing whatsoever that is conceivable. "None shall pluck them out of my hand." It does not merely include men, who are sometimes our worst foes, for the worst that we have are those of our own household; but it also includes fallen spirits. None shall be able to pluck us out of his hand. By no possibility shall any be able, by any of their schemes, to remove us from being his favorites, his property, his dear sons, his protected children. Oh, what a blessed promise!

Now, do you know, while I have been preaching to you about this, I have been thinking a little about my own history before I knew the Lord? One of the things that made me want to be a Christian was this. I had seen some young lads that I was at school with; they were excellent lads, and some of them had been held up as patterns of imitation to me and to others. I saw them, though only a very few years older than myself, turn out as foolish and ungodly as well could be, and yet I knew them to have been excellently well disposed as boys, no, to have been very patterns; and this kind of thought used to cross my young brain: "Is there not some means of being preserved from making a shipwreck of my life?"

When I came to read the Bible, it seemed to me to be full of this doctrine: "If you trust Christ, he will save you from all evil; he will keep you in a life of integrity and holiness while here, and he will bring you safely to heaven at the end." I felt that I could not trust man, for I had seen some of the very best wandering far from truth. If I trusted Christ, it was not a chance as to whether I should get to heaven, but a certainty; and I learned that if I rested all my weight upon him he would keep me, for I found it written, *The righteous also shall hold on his way, and he that hath clean hands shall be stronger and stronger* (Job 17:9). I found the apostle saying, *Being confident of this very thing, that he which hath begun a good work in you will perform it* (Philippians 1:6), and similar expressions.

"Why," I reasoned, "I have found an insurance office, and a good one too; I will insure my life in it; I will go to Jesus as I am, for he bids me; I will trust myself with him." If I had listened to the Arminian theory I would never have been converted, for it never had any charms for me. A Savior who casts away his people, a God who leaves his children to perish, is not worthy of my worship, and a salvation that does not save outright is neither worth preaching nor listening to. When I stand here and say to this assembled mass, "Trust my Master, believe him, and it is no matter of question as to whether you shall be saved, for he has said that *he that believeth and is baptized shall be saved*," I feel that I have something to say that is worth listening to.

My dear friend, with a new heart and a right spirit you will be a new man. As you now are, if you were to be pardoned tonight you would be condemned tomorrow, for the tendencies of your nature would lead you astray. But if God shall put a new nature into you, your old nature shall not be able to control it. The new immortal principle shall get the mastery; you shall be kept from sinning; you shall be preserved in holiness, and though you will have to mourn over your imperfection, yet you will feel that you have God's own life in you. Though you will realize that you are not perfect, yet you will wish you were, and this wishing to be so will be a sign of grace in your soul, and these wishes and desires will go on growing stronger and stronger, until, having mastered sin by the power of the Spirit, the day shall come when this body shall be dropped off, and the new life, unburdened with the vile rags that it was compelled to wear while it was here, shall leap in its disembodied existence into perfection. And then it shall wait for the trumpet's sound, and the body itself, purified and made fit for the new and higher life, shall be again inhabited, and so both the body and the soul, delivered from all sin, shall be an everlasting testimony to the promise of Christ; for those who rest in him shall have eternal life, *and they shall never perish, neither shall any man pluck them out of [his] hand.*

I have anticipated the last point, as to the outlook of my text into the future.

If God has given you eternal life, that fulfills all the future. Your spiritual existence will flourish when empires and kingdoms decay. Your life will live on when the heart of this great world shall grow cold, when the pulse of the great sea shall cease to beat, and when the eye of the bright sun shall grow dim with age. You possess *eternal* life.

When, like a moment's foam that melts into the wave that bears it, the whole universe shall have gone, and left not a wreck behind, it shall be well with you, for you have *eternal life*. Yon have an existence that will run parallel with the existence of the Deity. *Eternal life*! Oh! what an avenue of glory is opened by those words: *eternal life*! *Because I live*, says Christ, *ye shall live also*.

As long as there is a Christ there shall be a happy soul, and yonder shall be that happy soul. As long as there is a God there shall be a beatified existence, and you shall enjoy existence, for Jesus gives you eternal life. Spin on, old world, until your axle is worn-out. Fly on, old Father Time, until your hourglass is broken, and you shall cease to be! Come, mighty angel! Plant your foot upon the sea and upon the land, and swear by him that lives that time shall be no more, for even then every Christian shall still live, because Christ gives unto them eternal life.

Does not the next sentence also look into the future? – *They shall never perish*. They shall never cease to exist in perpetual blessedness! Never cease to be like God in their natures – never. Consider that you have been in heaven a thousand years – Can you realize it? A thousand years' blessed communion with the Lord Jesus! A thousand years in his bosom! A thousand years with the sight of him to ravish your spirit! Well, but you will have just as long to be there as if you had never begun, for you shall never, never perish.

When the millennium shall come, or when the judgment shall sit, and when all the great transactions of prophecy shall be fulfilled, these need not distress you, for if you trust Christ you shall never – oh! turn that word over in your heart – you shall never, never, never, never, never perish! What an eternity of glory, what unspeakable delight is wrapped up in this promise – *They shall never perish*!

Then, surely, this is another glance into the future – *Neither shall any man pluck them out of my hand*. We shall be in his hand forever, we shall be in his heart forever, we shall be in his very self forever – one with him, and none shall pluck us from that place. Happy, happy is the man who can lay claim to such a promise as this!

Oh! there are some of you to whom I wish this promise belonged! It is very rich, and very full of comfort; I wish it belonged to you. Do you say, "I wish it belonged to me"? Oh friend, I am glad to hear you say that! Do you know, soul, that there is but one key to open this precious treasure, and that is the key of the cross of the Lord Jesus? What do you say? Can you trust him?

When one told me the other day that she could not trust Christ, I looked her in the face and said, "What has he done that you should not trust him? Can you trust me?" "Yes," she said, "I can trust my fellow creatures, but I cannot trust God." Oh! I thought, what terrible blasphemy! It was honestly spoken, and it was spoken by one who did not perceive the greatness of the offense in it, but I do not know that there is any worse thing that can be said than that – "I cannot trust God." Well, sir, you have made him a liar then! That is the practical result of it; for if you believe a man to be honest you can always trust him. Can I trust my fellow man, and not trust God? Oh! the horror of that thought! There is such an amount of blasphemy in it that I must not quote it again! Not trust Christ! "Well," says one, "but may we not have a merely natural trust and so be deceived?"

I do not know of any trust in Christ except a spiritual one, nor do I believe in any other. If you trust Christ you have not done that of yourself. There was never a soul that did trust Christ unless he was enabled to do it by God the Holy Spirit, and if you wholly and simply trust Christ, you need not ask any questions about natural trusting or spiritual trusting. If you trust the Lord Jesus wholly, you are right. Rest on him then; rest on him only, wholly, and solely, and if you perish, then I do not understand the gospel, and I cannot comprehend what the Bible means. I will tell you one thing, and then close. If you trust Christ and you perish, then I must perish most certainly, and so must all my brethren and sisters here who have believed in Jesus. It is all over with us if it is all over with you.

When there is a storm, one passenger cannot very well go to the bottom, if he is in the ship, unless the whole of the ship's company goes too. We must go together. We have gotten into the lifeboat, and if the lifeboat goes down with you, it must go down with all the saints, and all the apostles, and all the martyrs too. They went to heaven resting upon Christ, and if you rest on Christ you will get there also.

Oh sinner, may you be led today to rest on Jesus and on Jesus only, and then take the text. Do not be afraid of it – *I give unto [my sheep] eternal life; and they shall never perish, neither shall any man pluck them out of my hand.*

Chapter 3

A Sharp Knife for the Vine Branches

Every branch in me that beareth not fruit he taketh away: and every branch that beareth fruit, he purgeth it, that it may bring forth more fruit. (John 15:2)

These are *the words of Jesus.* Unto you that believe he is precious – and every word that he speaks is precious for his sake – you will be sure, then, to give every syllable its weight, and to let each word fall upon your soul as coming directly from his lips. These are the words of our *Lord Jesus* just before his departure *from the world.* We reckon the words of dying men to be worth storing, and especially of such a matchless man as our Lord and Master. It may be said of him, *Thou hast kept the good wine until now* (John 2:10); for, in this chapter, and in that which follows, we have some of the choicest, deepest, and richest words that the Master ever uttered.

You will endeavor, then, to hear him speaking as upon the verge of Gethsemane; you will listen to these sentences as coming to you associated with the groans and bloody sweat of his agony. *These are words, moreover, about us,* and, therefore, are to be received by us with profound attention. The most of us who are here are in Christ, some one way or another; the majority of us profess to be Christians; so the text, then, is directed to us. When Jesus speaks about anything, it is weighty, and it demands our ear; but when he speaks about ourselves to ourselves, we must give him the heart as well as the ear, and give most earnest heed to the things that he speaks to us, lest by any means we let them slip by.

We may have to regret one day that we did not listen to his voice in love, for we may have to hear it when we *must* listen to it, when the tones have become those of judgment, and Jesus the judge shall say unto us, *I know you not* (Luke 13:25), even though we shall venture to plead that we ate and drank in his presence, and that he taught in our streets.

Having, then, your solemn attention, we will read the text again: *Every branch in me that beareth not fruit he taketh away: and every branch that beareth fruit, he purgeth it, that it may bring forth more fruit.*

The text *suggests self-examination, conveys instruction,* and *invites meditation.*

In the first place, it suggests self-examination.

I hear in these solemn words the tones of his voice of whom Malachi said, *Who may abide the day of his coming? and who shall stand when he appeareth? for he is like a refiner's fire, and like fullers' soap* (Malachi 3:2). I discern in these two heart-searching sentences the voice of him of whom John said, *Whose fan is in his hand, and he will thoroughly purge his floor, and gather his wheat into the garner; but he will burn up the chaff with unquenchable fire* (Matthew 3:12). Truly the Lord's *fire is in Zion, and his furnace in Jerusalem* (Isaiah 31:9). Happy shall that man be who can bear to be thrust into the flame, and to be covered with the hot coals of the burning truths here taught; but he shall be found rejected who cannot bear the trial.

Observe that our text mentions *two characters who are in some respects exceedingly alike;* they are both branches, they are both branches in the vine: *Every branch in **me*** (emphasis added). How much alike persons may be apparently, who in God's sight stand at opposite poles of character! Both the persons described in the text were in Christ: in Christ in different senses it is plain, because the first persons were not so in Christ as to bring forth fruit. Consequently, as fruit is that by which we are to judge a man, they were not in Christ effectively, graciously, influentially, or so as to receive the fruit-creating sap. If they had brought forth fruit, their fruitfulness would have been a sign that they were in Christ savingly.

Who will venture to say that a man who yields no fruit of righteousness can really be a Christian? Yet they were in Christ in some sense or other; that is to say, the two characters were equally esteemed to be Christians. Their names were enrolled in the same church register; in the common judgment of men they were equally Christian; according to their own profession, they were so; in many other respects that we need not now catalog, they were both in Christ as his professed disciples, as soldiers professedly fighting under his banner, as servants wearing his garb.

These two persons were probably equally sound in their doctrinal views; they held the same precious truth. If they heard falsehood, they were equally earnest to denounce it. When they listened to the gospel, they received it with joy, and so received it as to be willing to assist in the spread of it, and even to make sacrifices for its extension. These persons were equally attentive to ordinances. How often has it happened that two persons of widely different state before the Lord have been baptized at the same hour, in the same water, into the same name of the Father, and of the Son, and of the Holy Spirit, and have then broken bread together with equal apparent fervency, and with equal professions of enjoyment and devotion! These people have been equally fair in their profession; their moral conduct has in the judgment of all onlookers been much the same; they have avoided everything of ill repute; and they have in their measure sought after that which was comely and lovely in the estimation of men. Ah! there will often be found two who publicly pray alike, have an equal gift in prayer – and what is worse, preach with equal earnestness and zeal, to all appearance, who have family prayer maintained with the same consistency – and yet for all this, the end of the one shall be to be cast away as a branch to be burned, while the end of the other shall be to bring forth fruit unto perfection, with everlasting life as the reward.

Ah! friends, man can counterfeit cleverly, but when the devil helps him, he becomes master of the art. You will see pieces of coinage that it is almost impossible for you to discover to be mere counterfeits by their appearance, or even by their ring; in the scales they almost deceive you, but you put them into the fire, and then the discovery is made. Doubtless there are thousands in all Christian churches who have the stamp and the imprint of the King upon them, and look like the genuine shekels of the sanctuary, but who, after all, are only fit to be like bad money, fastened down on the footstool of the judgment seat, with a nail driven through them, to their everlasting rejection and disgrace.

How can we tell a bold man from a coward? Two soldiers wear the same military clothing; they will talk equally loudly of what they will do when the enemy shall come. It is the battle that tests and proves them; some peculiar phase of the conflict will bring out the difference. But until the battle comes, how easy it is for the coward to play the hero, while perhaps the bravest man may modestly shrink into the rear! Our text, then, brings before us two characters apparently alike.

Then, in the second place, *it shows us the distinction between them* – the great and solemn difference. The first branch brought forth no fruit; the second branch bore some fruit. *By their fruits ye shall know them* (Matthew 7:20). We have no right to judge our neighbors' motives and thoughts, except so far as they may be clearly discoverable by their actions and words. The interior we must leave with God, but the exterior we may judge, and must judge. There is a sense in which we are not to judge men; but there is another sense in which he would be an extreme fool who did not constantly exercise his judgment upon men. *By their fruits ye shall know them* is our Lord's own doctrine of sacred criticism. If you would judge men and judge yourselves, this is the one test – *by their fruits.*

Now then, what say you professing Christians who are present here today, you who are so regular in your attendance upon the means of grace? Will you now search yourselves to see whether you have any fruit? So that you may be helped in such an investigation, let me remind you that the apostle Paul has given us a list of these fruits in his fifth chapter of the epistle to the Galatians. He says in the twenty-second and twenty-third verses, *The fruit of the Spirit is love, joy, peace, long-suffering, gentleness, goodness, faith, meekness, temperance.* Nine kinds of fruit: all these should be in us and should abound. Let us question ourselves whether we have any of them.

Say, professing Christian, have you brought forth the fruit of *love*? Searching question, this is! I do not ask you, Can you talk of love? but do you feel it? I do not say, Is love upon your tongue? but does love rule your heart? Do you love God as a child loves his father? Do you love the Savior from a sense of gratitude to him who bought you with his blood? Do you feel the love of the gracious Comforter who dwells in you, if you are indeed a child of God? What do you know about love for the brethren? Do you love the saints as saints, whether they belong to your church or not; whether they please you or serve your special purpose or not? Say, do you love God's poor? Do you love God's persecuted and despised ones?

Answer, I pray you. What about love for the kingdom of the Lord's dear Son, and for the souls of men? Can you sit still and be satisfied with being saved yourself, while your neighbors are being damned by the thousands? Are your eyes never wet with tears for unrepentant souls? Do the terrors of the Lord never get hold upon you, when you think of men plunging themselves into hell? *He that loveth not his brother whom he hath seen, how can he love God whom he hath not seen?* (1 John 4:20). Have you this fruit, then? For if not, *every branch in me that beareth not fruit he taketh away.*

Next comes *joy*. Does your religion ever give you joy? Is it a mere matter of duty, a heavy chain for you to drag around like a convict, or is your religion a harp for you to dance to the tune of? Do you ever rejoice in Jesus Christ? Do you know what the "joy of the Lord" means? Does it ever give you joy to think that he is the same even when the fig tree does not blossom, and the herd is cut off from the stall? Do you feel a joy in reading the promises of God's Word?

Have you a joy in secret prayer; that joy that the world never gave you, and cannot take away from you? Have you a secret joy, like a spring shut up, a fountain sealed, that is only open to you and your Lord, because your fellowship is with him, and not with the sons of sin? He that never mourned because of sin has never repented; but he who has never rejoiced because of forgiveness cannot have seen the cross. Come, then, have you produced this fruit of joy? The Lord give it more and more to you! If you have never had it, then hear the sentence – *Every branch in me that beareth not fruit he taketh away.*

Next follows *peace*. Oh, blessed fruit! An autumn fruit, mellow and sweet, and fit for an angel's tooth. It is the fruit that the blessed ones feed upon in heaven – peace with God, peace of conscience, peace with one's fellow man, *the peace of God, which passeth all understanding, [and which] shall keep your hearts and minds through Christ Jesus*

(Philippians 4:7). *Great peace have they which love thy law: and nothing shall offend them* (Psalm 119:165). *Therefore being justified by faith, we have peace with God through our Lord Jesus Christ* (Romans 5:1).

Ah! my friends, some of you make a great deal of noise perhaps about religion, and yet never have peace of conscience. This is what ceremonialists never can obtain. *We have an altar, whereof they have no right to eat which serve the tabernacle* (Hebrews 13:10) of outward ordinances, and carnal, vain, and lofty ceremonies. Of our altar, where the finished sacrifice is eaten as a peace offering, they cannot eat. They find no peace after all their masses, and holy offices, and processions, and sacred hours, and priestcraft, and I know not what else. Poor slaves, they go down to their graves as much in bondage as ever, with the dreary prospect of a purgatorial fire before them; with no delightful prospect of waking up in the likeness of Christ; and with no sense of the truth of that glorious passage: *And ye are complete in him* (Colossians 2:10). He that has Christ has this one of his fruits, namely, peace. He who knows no peace with God, has good need to tremble.

Mention is next made of *longsuffering.* I fear there are many professing Christians who have very little of this, a quality that may be viewed in many aspects. There is patience, which bears God's chastising hand, and does not turn against him, but says, *The Lord gave, and the Lord hath taken away; blessed be the name of the Lord* (Job 1:21). There is long-suffering towards God, suffering long. Then there is long-suffering towards man, bearing persecution without apostasy, bearing slander and reproach without revenge, bearing the errors and mistakes of mankind with tender compassion. The believer should have much of this.

Some of us, perhaps, may be naturally quick-tempered; grace must overcome angry passions. It is not for you to say, "I cannot help it"; the fruit of the Spirit is long-suffering – you must help it. If there is no change in your temper, then there is no change in you at all; you have need to be converted. If the grace of God does not help you in a measure to keep under that temper that will be there, but which you must restrain, you have need to go to God and ask him to make sound work in you, for there is no work of grace there yet. We must have long-suffering, or we may be found fruitless, and then woe unto us.

Next in order is *gentleness,* by which I understand kindness. The

Christian is a man of kindness. He recognizes his kindness with his fellow man, he wishes to treat them as his kin. He has compassion for those who are suffering; he endeavors to make his manners kind and courteous. He knows that there is a natural offense in the cross to carnal men, so he does not wish therefore to make any offense of his own. He desires in his own life not to be sullen, suspicious, harsh, proud, and domineering, but he seeks to imitate his Master, who said of himself, *Take my yoke upon you, and learn of me; for I am meek and lowly in heart* (Matthew 11:29).

The believer in Christ should be gentle towards all men with whom he comes in contact. This is one of the fruits of the Spirit, and, I may add, a fruit of the Spirit in which many professing Christians are terribly deficient. Do not think that I judge you. I judge you not – there is one that judges you, it is this word of God that we speak. Gentleness is the fruit of the Spirit, and if you do not have it, then you do not have this fruit of the Spirit; and what says the text? *Every branch in me that beareth not fruit he taketh away.*

We are next reminded of *goodness,* by which is undoubtedly meant charity, benevolence, generosity, not merely kindliness of manner, but also bounty of heart. Oh, what a fine thing it is when our Christianity gives us a noble spirit! We cannot all be nobles in pocket, but every child of God should be a noble in his heart. "Come in," said a poor Scotch woman to some of the Lord's people. "I have room for ten of you in my house, but I have room for ten thousand of you in my heart." So should the believer say, "Come in, you that are in need; I have not the power to help many of you, but I have the will to help all of you if I could." The Christian should be like his Lord and Master, easily pleaded with, ready to communicate, making it his delight and his business to distribute, like a cloud that is full of rain, and empties itself upon the earth; like the bright and sparkling sun scattering his beams abroad, and not hiding or hoarding his light. If you have not this fruit of the Spirit in some measure, I implore you to remember the solemn words of the text: *Every branch in me that beareth not fruit he taketh away.*

Then comes *faith,* by which is probably not meant the grace of faith that is rather a root than a fruit, yet that is included. The fruit of the Spirit is indeed faith in God; without this, there is not even the commencement of anything like security in the soul. Do you believe on the Son of God? Do you have faith? If you have faith but as a grain of mustard seed, it is a sign of life within you. If you have little of it, pray, *Lord, Increase our faith* (Luke 17:5). But the faith here, I think, means faithfulness – faithfulness towards God, faithfulness towards conscience.

How little some Christians make of that nowadays! Why, they swallow their consciences. There are ministers who subscribe to words that they know to be deceiving the people, and help to buttress a church that is doing its utmost to lead this nation into downright Roman Catholicism. The good and gracious ministers in the Establishment are the prop and pillar of it, and by their influence they maintain a system that enables traitors to pollute this land with Roman Catholicism. O that our friends had a little more tenderness of conscience, and would come out from their unhallowed alliance with the Roman Catholic ritualists. How earnestly do I pray that none of us have the remotest connection with anything that would take us back to that antichrist that God hates, which he so hates that he has bidden his servant John to call the apostate church by a dreadful name, a brand of infamy, a name that God never uses until he has cast off and utterly abhorred a thing.

My brethren, may your consciences be faithful, and may you be faithful to your consciences. Men who trifle with doctrines, it seems to me, little know what sins they commit. I say to you who trifle with doctrines that you are as bad as thieves; you are worse, for the thief only robs men, but you rob God and your own souls. By helping to foster error, you are heaping together the elements of a pestilence that, unless grace prevents it, will utterly destroy this land. We must have faithfulness also in our dealings with our fellow man in business. Saints are men of honor still. The Christian man *sweareth to his own hurt, and changeth not* (Psalm 15:4). He does not take an oath, but his word is his bond. O that we may have this fruit of the Spirit: faithfulness, directness, straightforwardness, doing the right thing, loving the truth, and walking uprightly before the Lord our God!

The next fruit is *meekness*. May we possess much of this, for there is a peculiar benediction promised to the meek: *Blessed are the meek: for they shall inherit the earth* (Matthew 5:5). The Christian is to be as harmless as a dove. In his Master's battles, he is to be as bold as a lion, but for himself and for his own cause, he is to be tender, gentle, shunning debate, loving quietness, ready to take a rebuke rather than to administer one, and feeling himself to be weak and frail. Moses was the meekest of men, often provoked, but only once speaking unadvisedly with his lips. It is marvelous how he bore with the people; they were the most provoking people in the world, except ourselves – but yet, like a nurse is tender with a sick child, even so was he with a foolish people. How often did they provoke him and grieve his spirit! He grew indignant, and dashed the two tablets of stone upon the ground when he saw the idolatry of the people. Moses, the meekest of men, could not bear that; and God's meekest servants grow wrathful when they think of the idolatry into which this land is sliding so rapidly. But meek we must be towards all men; and if we have not this fruit, the Master says, *Every branch in me that beareth not fruit he taketh away.*

Do not forget *temperance* (or moderation), which is now generally used in respect to meats and drinks, but which has a far wider significance, though it includes that. The man who indulges the appetites of the flesh, and cannot control himself as to eating and drinking, need not pretend to be a Christian. He has first to prove that he is equal to a beast before he may pretend to be a child of God; he has first to show that he is a man before he may claim to be a Christian. Those who indulge in drunkenness shall drink of the wine of God's wrath before long, and then how bitter will their sweet wines be to them! How will that which has been sweet to the throat be as poison in the bowels forever and ever! If we do not have that kind of temperance, then evidently we can know nothing about true religion. But there must be an equal temperance in all other things: a temperance in your dress, in your expenditure, in your temper, and indeed in every act. There is a moderation to be observed, a narrow road to be followed, which the tutored eye of the spiritual man can see, and which it is a fruit of the Spirit for the spiritual foot to tread. God grant that we may have these fruits.

Beloved in the Lord, I am persuaded that no truth needs to be pressed more upon my own soul and yours than this: that positive fruit is the only test of our being in Christ. It is so easy for us to wrap ourselves up in the idea that attention to religious ceremonies is the test, but it is not so, for *except your righteousness shall exceed the righteousness of the scribes and Pharisees,* who were the most religious people of their day, *ye shall in no case enter into the kingdom of heaven* (Matthew 5:20). I know it is easy to think, "Well, I do not indulge in drunkenness; I am no rogue; I do not do this or that." This is little to the matter. Remember that the judgment will not be about those things that you do not do, but about positive things.

How does Jesus Christ put that judgment matter? *I was an hungred, and ye gave me no meat: I was thirsty, and ye gave me no drink: I was a stranger, and ye took me not in: naked, and ye clothed me not: sick, and in prison, and ye visited me not* (Matthew 25:42-43). The absence of positive fruit was that which condemned the lost. *Every tree,* says John the Baptist, *which bringeth not forth good fruit is hewn down, and cast into the fire* (Matthew 3:10). He does not say, "Every tree that bears bitter fruit, or sour grapes," but *Every tree which bringeth not forth good fruit.* Fruitless professing Christians, tremble! I may not speak so as to make this truth penetrate as I wish it would into your inmost souls, but I pray the eternal Spirit to make it like fire in the bones of every deceived man and woman. If my Lord shall come to you, my friend, day after day, as he once came to the fig tree, and should find leaves upon you and no fruit, I tell you he will say, *Let no fruit grow on thee henceforward for ever* (Matthew 21:19), and you shall wither away. That is his own parable! The master of the vineyard said to the husbandman, *Behold, these three years I come seeking fruit on this fig tree, and find none: cut it down; why cumbereth it the ground?* (Luke 13:7). And when the husbandman interceded, you will remember his intercession went only so far: *If it bear fruit, well: and if not, then after that thou shalt cut it down* (Luke 13:9). Jesus the Intercessor agrees with his Father the Husbandman; Mercy agrees with Justice; if there be no fruit, the tree must come down.

May I implore you to lay these things to heart. You must bear fruit unto God by the power of the Spirit, or it is down with you. God fingers his axe this morning; it is sharp, and if he does but lift it, woe to you, barren fig tree! Woe, indeed, to me also, if I be found barren in the day of the Lord's appearing.

In closing this weighty business of self-examination, I must remind you that our Lord tells us that although these persons were in some points alike, *the solemn difference between them led to a solemn result. Every branch in me that beareth not fruit he taketh away.* There are many ways in which the Lord takes away barren branches. Sometimes he allows the professing Christian to apostatize. He gets rich, and then he will not go to the place of worship that he used to frequent when he was a poorer man and was humble enough to hear the gospel; he must go to some fashionable place where he can listen to anything but the truth; and thus by his own pride he is taken away. Or else he is allowed to fall into open sin.

We always should regret the falls of professing Christians, but sometimes it is possible that discovered sins may be a blessing, for they take away from the church men who never ought to have been there, and who were an injury to it. Many bright professing Christians have stood well for a long time, but at last they have been snuffed out by the church by reason of their outward sins. God has taken them away. Some have been taken away in a more terrible sense by death; God has removed them. They have lived in the church and died in the church, but have been taken away in solemn judgment, and cast into the fire. Then there is a taking away that is the worst of all, when the Master shall say, *Depart from me, ye cursed.*

Now, do observe it: these were respectable people; these were people like you, decent, good people, who attended a place of worship, and contributed, and were very moral, but still they did not have grace in their souls. They had nominal Christianity, but not the fruit of the Spirit; and what was done with them? "Lord, cannot some mild means be used? How sad to see these branches cut off!"

"No," says he, "if they bring not forth fruit, they must be taken away."

"But Lord, they never reeled in and out of the gin palace! Lord, they were much too good and much too amiable to be around among the debased and the debauched!"

"Take them away; they brought no fruit, and they must be taken away."

"But Master, they were so diligent in the use of ordinances; they were so constant and regular in the form of prayer!"

"They brought forth no fruit," says he, "so take them away. There is only this one thing for them: if they had through saving faith been made to bear the fruit of the Spirit, they would have been saved; but as there was no fruit, take them away."

What is done with that which is taken away? If I could take you just outside the garden wall, I would let you see a heap of weeds and slips that are taken from the vine, and there they are heaped together with a little straw, and the gardener burns them. The other branches with their purple clusters are in honor, but these dishonored things are burned outside the gate. I cannot picture to you that day of doom, that tremendous fate that shall come upon fruitless branches of the spiritual vine – outside the gate, with a great gulf fixed between them and heaven, where the smoke of their torment goes up forever and ever, *where their worm dieth not, and the fire is not quenched*. If such people are cast away, what will become of some of you? If these good people who were in Christ, in a way, still perish because they brought forth no fruit, O you who are like hemlock in the furrows of the field, you who produce the grapes of Gomorrah and the apples of Sodom, what shall be your doom in the day of account when the Master shall come forth in robes of judgment to execute righteousness among the sons of men?

I'll touch briefly on the second point. The text conveys instruction.

Looking at it carefully, we observe that *the fruit-bearing branches are not perfect*. If they were perfect, they would not need pruning; but the fact is there is much of original inbred sin remaining in the best of God's people, so that whenever the sap within them is strong for the production of fruit, there is a tendency for that strength to turn into evil, and instead of good fruit, evil is produced. It is the strength of the tree, and the richness of the sap that makes the branch produce too much wood so that it needs pruning. The gardener desires to see that strength in clusters, but alas! instead it runs into wood.

Now, observe that in a Christian when the sap comes into him to produce confidence in God, through the evil that is in him, it often produces confidence in himself, and he who should be strong in faith becomes strong in carnal security. When the sap would produce zeal, how very frequently it turns into rashness, and instead of zeal with knowledge, fanaticism is brought forth! Suppose the sap flows to produce self-examination; then very generally unbelief is the outgrowth, and instead of the man doubting himself, he begins to doubt his Lord. How often have I seen even the joy of the Lord turned into pride, and when the man should rejoice in Christ Jesus, he has begun to rejoice in himself, to grow proud and say, "What a fine experience I possess!"

That love that we ought to bear towards our neighbors, how apt is that to run into love of the world and carnal complacency towards its evil ways! The gentleness that I praised just now often turns to a silly compliance with everybody's whim; and meekness, which is a fruit of the Spirit, how often that becomes an excuse for holding your tongue, when you ought boldly to speak! The fact is, it is very difficult to keep ourselves, when we are in a flourishing state, from producing wood instead of grapes. God grant us grace to keep us from this evil; and I do not know how the grace can come except by his judicious pruning.

I say the fruit-bearing branches are not perfect because they bear a great deal that is not fruit, and, moreover, not one of them bears as much fruit as it ought to. I do not agree with Mr. Wesley's opinion about perfection. It is very difficult to see how he could have done more than he did, but I do not doubt that even *he* felt that he might have been more like his Lord. None of the Lord's people with whom I ever came into communion have dared to think themselves perfect; and if they had said so, and proved it, I would have rejoiced to think that there were such people, but would have greatly sorrowed to find that I belong to a very different order of beings myself; for *in me (that is, in my flesh,) dwelleth no good thing* (Romans 7:18). The Master is bringing us upon our way to bring forth more fruit, but as yet, the fruit-bearing branches are not perfect.

Therefore, we are taught, in the second place, that *pruning is the lot of all the fruitful saints.* You may escape it if you are not fruitful; you will be cut off, you will not be pruned, but all the fruit-bearing saints must feel the knife. Observe Abraham, Isaac, and Jacob – had not those patriarchs their trials? Moses and David, Jeremiah and Daniel – who among those escaped? Though they honored their Master much, who of them escaped without the pruning knife? And if you come to the saints of the New Testament, surely the flame was seven times hotter with regard to them than with regard to the elder brethren. How does the Lord prune his people, then? It is generally said by afflictions, but I question if that could be proved as it stands; it needs explanation. It is generally thought that our trials and troubles purge us, but I am not sure of that; they certainly are lost upon some. Our Lord tells us what it is that prunes us. "Now," says he, in the third verse of the chapter, *Now ye are clean [or pruned] through the word which I have spoken unto you.*

It is *the word* that prunes the Christian, it is the truth that purges him; the Scripture, made living and powerful by the Holy Spirit, effectively cleanses the Christian.

"What then does affliction do?" you ask. Well, if I may say so, affliction is the handle of the knife; affliction is the grindstone that sharpens up the Word; affliction is the dresser that removes our soft garments, and lays bare the diseased flesh, so that the surgeon's lance may get at it. Affliction makes us ready to feel the Word, but the true pruner is the Word in the hand of the great Husbandman. Sometimes when you lay stretched out upon the bed of sickness, you think more upon the Word than you did before; that is one great thing. In the next place, you see more the applicability of that Word to yourself. In the third place, the Holy Spirit makes you feel more, while you are thus laid aside, the force of the Word than you did before.

Ask that affliction may be sanctified, beloved, but always remember there is no more tendency in affliction in itself to sanctify us than there is in prosperity; in fact, the natural tendency of affliction is to make us rebel against God, which is quite opposite to sanctification. It is the Word coming to us while in affliction that purges us; it is God the Holy Spirit laying home divine truth, and applying the blood of Jesus, and working all his divine energy in the soul; it is this that prunes us, and affliction is only the handle of the knife, or what if I say the ladder that the gardener takes to reach the vine, so that he may prune it the better!

Now, it may be that some of us have been afflicted a great deal and have not been pruned. I know some people who have been very poor, and I do not see that they are any better for it. I know some others who have been very sick, and I have never heard that they have been improved. Alas! some people are of such a character that if they were stricken until their whole head were sick, and their whole heart faint, they would not be benefited; if they were beaten until they were all bruises and putrefying sores, they would still go on to rebel, for these things only provoke them to a greater hatred against the Most High. We must be pruned, but it must be by the Word, through affliction.

Now, *the object in this pruning is never to condemn.* God does not purge his children with a view to visit them punitively for sin; he chastises, but he cannot punish those for whom Jesus Christ has been already punished.

You have no right to say, when a man is afflicted, that it is because he has done wrong; on the contrary, *every branch that beareth fruit, he purgeth it.* Only the branch that is good for something gets the pruning knife. Do not say of yourselves, or of other people, "That man must have been a great offender, or he would not have met with such a judgment."

That is nonsense. Who was a holier man than Job, but who was brought lower than he was? Why, the fact is, it is because the Lord loves his people that he chastens them, not because of any anger that he has towards them. But learn, beloved, especially those of you under trial, not to see an angry God in your pains or your losses, or your crosses; but instead thereof, see a Husbandman who thinks of you as a branch whom he estimates at so great a rate that he will take the trouble to prune you, which he would not do if he had not a kind consideration towards you.

The real reason is that more fruit may be produced, which I understand to mean more in *quantity.* A good man, who feels the power of the Word pruning him of this and that indulgence, sets to work, in the power of the Holy Spirit, to do more for Jesus. Before he was afflicted, he did not know how to be patient. He learns it at last – a hard lesson. Before he was poor, he did not know how to be humble, but he learns that. Before the Word came with power, he did not know how to pray with his fellows, or how to speak to sinners, or how to lay himself out for usefulness; but the more he is pruned, the more he serves his Lord. More fruit in *variety* too, may be intended.

One tree can only produce one kind of fruit usually, but the Lord's people can produce many kinds, as we have already seen; and the more they are pruned the more they will produce. There will be all kinds of fruits, both new and old, that they will lay up for their beloved. There will be more in *quality* too. The man may not pray more, but he will pray more earnestly; he may not preach more sermons, but he will preach them more thoroughly from his heart, with a greater spiritual fervor. It may be that he will not be more in communion with God as to time, but it will be a closer communion; he will throw himself more thoroughly into the divine element of communion, and will become more hearty in all that he does.

This is the result of the pruning that our heavenly Father gives; and if such be the result, may the Lord keep on pruning, for *what greater blessing can a man have than to produce much fruit for God?* Better to serve God much than to become a prince. He that does much for Christ shall shine as the stars forever and ever. He is glorifying God; he is blessing his fellow man; he is bringing joy into his own spirit. Oh, if on bended knee we might seek but one favor, it seems to me that we would not ask for the wisdom that Solomon craved, but that we would petition for this – that we might bring forth much fruit, that so we might be Christ's disciples.

To conclude, our text invites meditation.

I will hint at the points on which it invites our thoughts. It suggests to every unconverted person here this one question. It seems that it is not very easy for the righteous to be saved: *If the righteous scarcely be saved, where shall the ungodly and the sinner appear?* (1 Peter 4:18). If the branches in Christ that bear no fruit are taken away, what must become of the Sabbath breakers, the despisers of God, the atheists, the drunkards, the impure, the dishonest, the blasphemers? I raise the question – solve it! Let it burn into your soul!

Secondly, *what a mercy it is to the believer that it is pruning him and not cutting him off!* Ah, let the knife be very sharp, let the Word throw us into the great deeps until we almost despair; yet, thank God, we are not cast into hell! Dear friends, your prayer should be: "Lord, let thy Word cut deeply into me. Do not let the preacher mince matters with me. Deliver him from sewing pillows under my armholes, and lulling me to sleep. Lord, I would be faithfully dealt with! I put the proud flesh before you. Cut it out, so that the wound heals not so as to be worse when healed than it was when it was a running sore." What a mercy it is not to be cut off! Ah, Christian, you are desponding and doubting today, while the Word is searching you, but you might have been in hell! Think of that. You are poor, or you are full of pain, but you might have been driven from the presence of God. How can you, as a living man, complain, whatever God may place upon you?

In the next place, it would be well to *think how gently the pruning has been done with most of us* up until now, compared with our barrenness. I wonder that the Lord has not cut us around much more. He who has a deep-seated disease requires sharp medicine; and when the sore runs deep, the doctor must cut deep too. With all the rust that is on us, I wonder that we are not filed more. There is so much alloy, it is marvelous that we are not more often put into the fire. O Spirit of God, you have to do hard work with some of us, but still we bless you, for your gentleness has been manifested very graciously. How tenderly have you dealt with our frail dust, O God of love!

Again, *how earnestly we ought to seek for more fruit.* If this is what God seeks after, we should be after it as well. If he often goes the length of pruning the vine, although he does not love to do it, for he does not afflict willingly, or grieve the children of men for nothing, then let us agree with God, and seek to yield more fruit.

How concerned should every one of us be to be effectively and truly one with Christ! I ought to have said that the whole gist of the text lies in the words, *in me, in me, in me* (emphasis added)! You see, if a man is not in Christ at all, why then, of course there is no hope of any sort; and then, when he is in Christ, there comes the question, Is he in Christ by living faith, by real trust? Has he the faith of God's elect? Has he been born again from above? Is he a spiritual grace-taught soul? Let this be the question that shall rest upon our minds.

I would that this morning my text might be sweet to you; sweet, I say, because if for the moment it seems bitter, the end is sweetness. Faithful are the wounds of such a friend as Jesus. If he has wounded any of you, it is not to drive you from him, but to make you cling the closer to him. Have you never learned that, when you feel the most humbled, the most afraid, the most full of sin, the most conscious of your own imperfection, the best thing to do is to cling to Christ all the more? "Well, Lord, if I have been the most cursed hypocrite that ever lived, I will come to you now. If up to this moment I have been deceived, and have not had a grain of true faith, nor a single one of the fruits of the Spirit, yet here I am, a poor wicked sinner, I to the fountain fly; a naked sinner, I wrap your righteousness around my loins; a poor sin-sick, lost sinner, I look up to you on yonder cross, and I do believe that you can save me. From the very jaws of death, and out of the belly of hell, do I cry unto you, and you will hear me."

O sinners and saints, come to Christ again, whether you are his experientially, or are strangers to him, come to him now, for still the gospel bell rings out sweetly, *Whosoever **will**, let him take the water of life freely* (Revelation 22:17, emphasis added). O God, grant us grace to come now afresh, and his be the praise! Amen, and Amen.

Chapter 4

Without Christ – Nothing

Without me ye can do nothing. (John 15:5)

This is not the language of a man of ordinary mold. No saint, no prophet, no apostle would ever have addressed a company of faithful men and said to them, *Without me ye can do nothing.* Had Jesus Christ been, as some say, a good man, and nothing more, such language as this would have been unseemly and inconsistent. Among the virtues of a perfect man we must certainly reckon modesty, but this from a mere man would have been shamelessly immodest. It is impossible to imagine that Jesus of Nazareth, had he not been more than man, could ever have uttered the sentence, *Without me ye can do nothing.*

My brethren, I hear in this sentence the voice of that divine person without whom was not anything made that was made. The majesty of the words reveals the deity of him that uttered them. The "I am" comes out in the personal word *me,* and the claim of all power unveils the Omnipotent. These words mean deity or nothing. The spirit in which we listen to this language is that of adoration. Let us bow our heads in solemn worship, and so unite with the multitude before the throne who ascribe power and dominion and might to him that *sitteth upon the throne, and unto the Lamb* (Revelation 7:10).

In this adoring state of mind we shall be the better prepared to enter into the innermost soul of the text. I am not going to preach upon the moral inability of the unconverted, although in that doctrine I most firmly believe; for that truth did not come in our Lord's way when he uttered these words, and neither did he allude to it. It is quite true that unconverted men, being without Christ, can do no spiritual action whatever, and can do nothing that is acceptable in the sight of God; but our Lord was not speaking to unconverted men at all, nor speaking about them. He was surrounded by his apostles, the eleven out of whom Judas had been weeded, and it is to them as branches of the true Vine that he says, *Without me ye can do nothing.* The statement refers to such as are in the Vine, and even to such as have been pruned, and have for a while been found abiding in the stem, which is Christ; even in such there is an utter incapacity for holy produce if separated from Christ.

We are not called upon just now to speak upon all forms of doing, as beyond us, but of that form of it which is intended in the text. There are certain forms of doing in which men excel who know little or nothing of Christ; but the text must be viewed in its own connection, and the truth is clear. Believers are here described under the figure of branches in the Vine, and the doing alluded to must therefore be the bearing of fruit. I might render it: "Apart from me you can produce nothing – make nothing, create nothing, bring forth nothing."

The reference, therefore, is to that doing that may be set forth by the fruit of the vine branch, and therefore to those good works and graces of the Spirit that are expected from men who are spiritually united to Christ. It is of these that he says, *Without me ye can do nothing.* Our text is only another form of the fourth verse: *As the branch cannot bear fruit of itself, except it abide in the vine; no more can ye, except ye abide in me.* I am therefore going to address myself to you who profess to know and love the Lord, and are anxious to glorify his name, and I have to remind you that union with Christ is essential; for only as you are one with him, and continue to be so, can you bring forth the fruits that prove you to be truly his.

Reading again this solemn sentence, *Without me ye can do nothing,* it first of all excites in me an aspiration of hope. There is something to be *done;* our religion is to have a grand, practical outcome. I have been thinking of Christ as the Vine, and of the myriads of branches in him, and my heart has hoped for great things. From such a root what a crop must come! Being branches in him, what fruit we must produce! There can be nothing scanty or poverty-stricken in the fruit of a vine so full of sap. Fruit of the best quality, fruit in the utmost abundance, fruit unrivaled, must be borne by such a vine. That word *do* has music in it.

Yes, brethren, Jesus went about doing good, and, being in him, we shall do good. Everything about him is efficient, practical – in a word, fruit bearing; and being joined to him much will yet be done by us. We have been saved by the almighty grace of God apart from all doings of our own, and now that we are saved, we long to *do* something in return; we feel a high ambition to be of some use and service to our great Lord and Master. The text, even though there be a negative in it, yet raises in our soul the hope that before we go away and be no more, we may even here on earth do something for Christ.

Beloved, there is the ambition and hope before us of doing something in the way of glorifying God by bringing forth *the fruits of holiness, peace, and love.* We would adorn the doctrine of God our Savior in all things. By pureness, by knowledge, by long-suffering, by genuine love, by every good and holy work we would show forth the praises of our God. Apart from the Lord Jesus we know we cannot be holy; but joined unto him we overcome the world, the flesh, and the devil, and walk with garments unspotted from the world. *The fruit of the Spirit is love, joy, peace, longsuffering, gentleness, goodness, faith, meekness, temperance,* and all manner of holy conversation. For none of these things are we equal in and of ourselves, and yet by faith we say with Paul, *I can do all things through Christ which strengtheneth me* (Philippians 4:13). We may be adorned with plentiful clusters, we may cause the Savior to have joy in us that our joy may be full: great possibilities are before us.

We aspire not only to produce fruit in ourselves, but also to bear much *fruit in the conversion of others,* even as Paul desired concerning the Romans, that he might have fruit among them. In this matter we can do nothing whatever alone; but being united unto Christ we bring forth increase unto the Lord. Our Lord Jesus said, *The works that I do shall [ye] do also; and greater works than these shall [ye] do; because I go unto my Father* (John 14:12). Brethren, a hope springs up in our bosom that we may each one of us bring many souls to Jesus. Not because we have any power in ourselves, but because we are united to Jesus, we joyfully hope to bring forth fruit in the way of leading others to the knowledge of the gospel.

My soul takes fire of hope, and I say to myself, If it be so, all these branches, and all alive, how much *fruit of further blessing* will ripen for this poor world. Men shall be blessed in us because we are blessed in Christ. What must be the influence of ten thousand godly examples! What must be the influence upon our country of thousands of Christian men and women practically advancing love, peace, justice, virtue, and holiness! And if each one is seeking to bring others to Christ, what numerous conversions there must be, and how largely must the church of God be increased. Do you not know that if there were only ten thousand real Christians in the world, yet if each one of these brought one other to Christ every year it would not need twenty years to accomplish the conversion of the entire population of the globe? This is a simple sum in arithmetic that any schoolboy can work out. Certainly, it seems a small thing that each one should bring another to the Lord; and surely if we are one with him, we may hope to see it done.

So I sit me down and dream right comfortably, according to the promise: *Your young men shall see visions, and your old men shall dream dreams* (Acts 2:17). See these thousands of branches, proceeding from such a stem as Christ Jesus, and with such sap as the Holy Spirit flowing through them; why, surely, this vine must soon clothe the mountains with its vegetation, and there shall not remain a single barren rock unadorned with the blessed foliage! Then shall the mountains drop sweet wine, and all the hills shall melt. Not because of any natural fertility in the branches, but because of their glorious root, and stem, and sap, each one shall bear full clusters, and each fruitful bough shall run over the wall.

Beloved friends in Christ, have you not strong desires to see some such consummation? Do you not long to take a share in the high enterprise of winning the world to Christ? Oh, you that are young and full of spirits, do you not long to press to the front of this great crusade? Our souls long to see the knowledge of the Lord covering the earth as the waters cover the sea. It is glad tidings to us that, joined unto Christ, we can do something in this great business, something upon which the Lord will smile, something that shall rebound to the glory of his name. We are not condemned to inaction; we are not denied the joy of service, the superior blessedness of giving and of doing. The Lord has chosen us and ordained us to go and bring forth fruit, fruit that shall remain. This is the aspiration that rises in our soul; the Lord grant that we may see it take actual form in our lives.

But now, in the second place, there passes through my heart a shudder – a shudder of fear. Even though I glow and burn with strong desire, and rise upon the wing of a mighty ambition to do something great for Christ, yet I read the text, and a sudden trembling takes hold upon me. *Without me* – it is possible, then, that I may be without Christ, and so may be utterly incapacitated for all good. Come, friends, I want you to feel, even though it casts a cold chill over you, that you may possibly be *without Christ* (Ephesians 2:12). I would have you feel it in the very marrow of your bones, yes, in the center of your hearts. You profess to be in Christ, but are you so?

The large majority of those to whom I speak this morning are visible members of the visible church of Christ; but what if you should *not be so in him as to bring forth fruit?* Evidently there are branches that in a certain sense are in the vine, and yet bring forth no fruit! It is written, *Every branch in me that beareth not fruit he taketh away.* Yes, you are a member, perhaps an elder, perhaps a deacon, possibly a minister, and so you are in the Vine; but are you bringing forth the fruits of holiness? Are you consecrated? Are you endeavoring to bring others to Jesus Christ? Or is your profession a thing apart from a holy life and devoid of all influence upon others? Does it give you a name among the people of God and nothing more? Say, is it a mere natural association with the church, or is it a living, supernatural union with Christ? Let the thought go through you and prostrate you before him who looks down from heaven upon you, and lifts his pierced hand and cries, *Without me ye can do nothing.*

My friend, if you are without Christ, what is the use of carrying on that Bible class, for you can do nothing. What is the use of my coming to this pulpit if I am without Christ? What is the use of your going down into the Sunday school this afternoon if, after all, you are without Christ? Unless we have the Lord Jesus ourselves, we can hardly take him to others. Unless within us we have the living water springing up unto eternal life, we cannot overflow so that out of our midst shall flow rivers of living water.

I will put the thought another way – What if you should be in Christ, and *not so in him as to abide in him?* It appears from our Lord's words that some branches in him are cast forth and are withered. *If a man abide not in me, he is cast forth as a branch, and is withered.* Some who are called by his name, and reckoned among his disciples, whose names are heard whenever the muster roll of the church is read, do not continue in him.

My friend, what if it should happen that you are only in Christ on a Sunday, but in the world all the week? What if you are only in Christ at the Communion table, or at the prayer-meeting, or at certain periods of devotion? What if you are off and on with Christ? What if you play fast and loose with the Lord? What if you are an outside saint and an inside devil? Ah me, what will come of such conduct as this? And yet some persist in attempting to hold an intermittent communion with Christ – in Christ today because it is the Sabbath; out of Christ tomorrow because it is the market, and obedience to Christ might be inconvenient when they buy and sell. This will not do. We must be so in Christ as to be always in him, or else we are not living branches of the living Vine, and we cannot produce fruit. If there were such a thing as a vine branch that was only occasionally joined to the stem, would you expect it to yield a cluster to the husbandman? So neither can you if you are off and on with Christ. You can do nothing if there be not constant union.

One year when I was traveling towards my usual winter resting place, I stopped at Marseille, and there was overtaken by great pain. In my room in the hotel I found it cold, and so I asked for a fire. I was sitting in a very desponding mood, when suddenly the tears came to my eyes as if struck with a great sorrow. I shall never forget the thoughts that stirred my heart. The porter came in to light the fire. He had in his hand a bundle of twigs. I called to him to let me look at it. He was about to push it into the stove as fuel with which to kindle the fire. As I took the bundle into my hand, I found it was made of vine branches – branches that had been cut off now that the pruning time had come. Ah me, I thought, will this be my portion? Here I am, away from home, unable to bear fruit, as I love to do. Shall I end with this as my portion? Shall I be gathered for the fire?

Those vine shoots were parts of a good vine, no doubt – branches that once looked fair and green; but now they were fuel for the flame. They had been cut off and cast off as useless things, and then men gathered them and tied them in bundles, and they were humbly thrust into the fire. What a picture! There goes a bundle of ministers into the fire! There is a bundle of elders! There's another bundle of deacons, a bundle of church members, a bundle of Sunday school teachers! *Men gather them, and cast them into the fire, and they are burned.*

Dear brothers and sisters, shall this be the lot of any of us who have named the name of Christ? Well did I say that a shudder may go through us as we listen to those words: *Without me.* Our end without Christ will be terrible indeed. First, no fruit; then no life; and at last no place among the saints, no existence in the church of God. Without Christ we do nothing, we are nothing, we are worse than nothing. This is the condition of the heathen now, and it was our own condition once; God forbid that we should find it to be our condition now – *without Christ, having no hope* (Ephesians 2:12)! Here is grave cause for heart searching, and I leave the matter with you to that end.

Having come so far in our second topic, under the third I behold a vision of total failure. *Without me,* says the text, *ye can do nothing –* you can produce nothing. The visible church of Christ has tried this experiment a great many times already, and always with the same result. Separated from Christ, his church can do nothing that she was formed to do. She is sent into the world upon a high enterprise, with noble aims before her, and grand forces at her disposal; but if she could cease from communion with Christ, she would become wholly incapable.

Now what are the outward signs of any community being apart from Christ? Answer, first, it may be seen in *a ministry without Christ in its doctrine.* This we have seen ourselves. Woe become the day that it is so! History tells us that not only in the Roman Catholic Church and the Anglican church, but also among the Nonconformist churches, Christ has been at times forgotten. Not only among Unitarians, but also among Presbyterians, Methodists, Baptists, and all around, Jesus has been dishonored. Attempts have been made to do something without Christ as the truth to be preached.

Ah me, what folly it is! They preach up intellectualism, and hope that this will be the great power of God; but it is not. "Surely," say they, "novelties of thought and refinements of speech will attract and win! The preachers aspire to be leaders of thought; will they not command the multitude and charm the intelligent? Add music and architecture, and what is to hinder success?" Many a young minister has given up his whole mind to this – to try and be exceedingly refined and intellectual; and what has he done with these showy means? The sum total is expressed in the text – *nothing. Without me ye can do nothing.* What emptiness this folly has created. When the pulpit is without Christ, the pews are soon without people.

I knew a chapel where a notable preacher was to be heard for years. A converted Jew coming to London to visit a friend set out on Sunday morning to find a place of Christian worship, and he chanced to enter the chapel of this notable preacher. When he came back, he said that he feared he had made a mistake. He had entered into a building that he hoped was a Christian place of assembly; but as he had not heard the name of Jesus all the morning, he thought perhaps he had fallen in with some other religionists. I fear that many modern sermons might just as fairly have been delivered in a Muslim mosque as in a Christian church. We have too many preachers of whom we might complain, *They have taken away my Lord, and I know not where they have laid him* (John 20:13).

Christianity without Christ is a strange thing indeed. And what comes of it where it is held up to the people? Why, by and by there are not enough people to support the ministry; empty benches are plentiful, and the thing gets pretty nearly wound up. Blessed be God for it! I am heartily glad that without Christ these pretended ministers cannot prosper. Leave Christ out of the preaching and you shall do nothing. Only advertise it all over London, Mr. Baker, that you are making bread without flour; put it in every paper – "Bread without flour" – and you may soon shut up your shop, for your customers will hurry off to other tradesmen.

Somehow there is a strange prejudice in people's minds in favor of bread made of flour, and there is also an unaccountable prejudice in the human mind that makes men think that if there be a gospel it must have Christ in it. A sermon without Christ as its beginning, middle, and end is a mistake in conception and a crime in execution. However grand the language, it will be merely much ado about nothing if Christ be not there. Alas, and I mean by "Christ" not merely his example and the ethical precepts of his teaching, but also his atoning blood, his wondrous satisfaction made for human sin, and the grand doctrine of "Believe and live." If "life for a look at the Crucified One" be obscured, all is dark; if justification by faith be not set in the very forefront in the full blaze of light, nothing can be accomplished. Without Christ in the doctrine you shall do nothing.

Furthermore, without acknowledging always *the absolute supremacy of Christ* we shall do nothing. Jesus is much complimented nowadays, but he is not submitted to as absolute Lord. I hear many pretty things about Christ from men who reject his gospel. "Lives of Christ" we have in any quantity. Oh, for one that would set him forth in his glory as God, as head of the church and Lord of all. I should greatly like to see a "Life of Christ" written by one who knew him by communion with him and by reverently sitting at his feet. Most of the pretty things about Jesus that I read nowadays seem to have been written by persons who have seen him through a telescope at a great distance, and know him "according to Matthew," but not according to personal fellowship. Oh, for a "Life of Christ" by Samuel Rutherford or George Herbert, or by some other sweet spirit to whom the ever-blessed One is as a familiar friend.

Certain modern praises of Jesus are written upon the theory that, on the whole, the Savior has given us a religion that is tolerably suited to the enlightenment of the current century, and may be allowed to last a little longer. Jesus is commended by these critics, and somewhat admired as preferable to most teachers; but he is by no means to be blindly followed. It is fortunate for Jesus that he commends himself to the "best thought" and ripest culture of the period; for, if he had not done so, these wise gentlemen would have exposed him as being behind the times. Of course they have every now and then to rectify certain dogmas of his, especially ones such as justification by faith, or atonement, or the doctrine of election – these are old-fashioned things that belong to an older and less enlightened period, and therefore they adapt them by tearing out their real meaning.

The doctrines of grace, according to the infallible critics of the period, are out of date – nobody believes them now, and so they dismiss old-fashioned believers as non-existent. Christ is rectified and squared, and his garment without seam is taken off, and he is dressed out in proper style, as by a West End clothier; then he is introduced to us as a remarkable teacher, and we are advised to accept him as far as he goes. For the present, the wise ones tolerate Jesus, but there is no telling what is to come; the progress of this age is so astonishing that it is just possible we shall before long leave Christ and Christianity behind.

Now, what will come of this foolish wisdom? Nothing but delusions, mischief, infidelity, anarchy, and all manner of imaginable and unimaginable ills. The fact is, if you do not acknowledge Christ to be all, you have virtually left him out, and are without him. We must preach the gospel because Christ has revealed it. *Thus saith the Lord* is to be our logic. We must preach the gospel as ambassadors delivering their message, that is to say, in the King's name, by an authority not their own. We preach our doctrines not because we consider them to be convenient and profitable, but because Christ has commanded us to proclaim them. We believe the doctrines of grace not because the enlightenment of the age sets its wonderful blessing upon them, but because they are true and are the voice of God. Age or no age has nothing to do with us. The world hates Christ and must hate him. If it would boldly denounce Christ, it would be to us a more hopeful sign than its deceitful Judas kiss.

We keep simply to this – the Lord has said it, and we care not who approves or disapproves. Jesus is God and head of the church, and we must do what he bids us, and say what he tells us. If we fail in this, nothing good will come of it. If the church gets back to her loyalty, she shall see what her Lord will do; but without Christ as absolute Lord, infallible Teacher, and honored King, all must be failure even to the end.

Go a little further: you may have sound doctrine, and yet you can do nothing unless you have Christ *in your spirit.* I have known all the doctrines of grace to be unmistakably preached, and yet there have been no conversions for this reason: they were not expected and scarcely desired. In former years many orthodox preachers thought it to be their sole duty to comfort and confirm the godly few who because of great perseverance found out the holes and corners in which they prophesied. These brethren spoke of sinners as people whom God might possibly gather in if he thought fit to do so, but they did not care much whether he did so or not. As to weeping over sinners as Christ wept over Jerusalem; as to offering to invite them to Christ as the Lord did when he stretched out his hands all the day long; as to lamenting with Jeremiah over a perishing people, they had no sympathy with such emotions, and feared that they smacked of Arminianism.

Both preacher and congregation were cased in a hard shell, and lived as if their own salvation was the sole design of their existence. If anybody did grow zealous and seek conversions, right away they said he was indiscreet or conceited. When a church falls into this condition, it is, as to its spirit, *without Christ*. What comes of it? Some of you know by your own observation what does come of it. The comfortable corporation exists and grows for a little while, but it comes to nothing in the long run; and so it must: there can be no fruit bearing where there is not the spirit of Christ as well as the doctrine of Christ. Unless the spirit of the Lord rests upon you, causing you to agonize for the salvation of men even as Jesus did, *ye can do nothing*.

But above all things we must have Christ with us in the power of *his actual presence*. Do we always think of this – *Without me ye can do nothing*? We are going out this afternoon to teach the young; shall we be quite sure to take Christ with us? Or on the road shall we suddenly stop and say, "I am without my Master, and I must not dare to go another step"? The abiding consciousness of the love of Christ in our soul is the essential element of our strength. We can no more convert a sinner without Christ than we could light up new stars in the sky. Power to change the human will, power to enlighten the intellect as to the things of God, and to influence the mind as to repentance and faith, must come entirely from the Most High. Do we feel that? Or do we put our thoughts together for an address, and say, "Now, that is a strong point, and that will produce effect," and do we rest there? If so, we can do nothing at all.

The power lies with the Master, not with the servant; the might is in the hand, not in the weapon. We must have Christ in these pews and in these aisles, and in this pulpit, and Christ down in our Sunday school, and Christ at the street corner when we stand up there to talk of him, and we must feel that he is with us even to the end of the world, or we shall do nothing.

We have, then, before us a vision of total failure if we attempt in any way to do without Christ. He says, *Without me ye can do nothing.* It is in the *doing* that the failure is most conspicuous. You may *talk* a good deal without him; you may hold congresses, and conferences, and conventions; but *doing* is another matter. Without Jesus you can *talk* any quantity; but without him you can *do* nothing. The most eloquent discourse without him will be all a bottle of smoke. You shall lay your plans, and arrange your machinery, and start your schemes; but without the Lord you will do nothing. An immeasurable cloudland of proposals and not a spot of solid doing large enough for a dove's foot to rest on – such shall be the end of all!

You may have all the money that generosity can lavish, all the learning that your universities can supply, and all the oratory that the most gifted can lay at your feet; but *without me,* says Christ, *ye can do nothing.* Fuss, flare, fireworks, and failure – that is the end of it. *Without me ye can do nothing.* Let me repeat those words again: *Do nothing. Do nothing,* and the world dying around us! Africa in darkness! China perishing! Hindustan sunk in superstition, and a church that can do nothing! No bread to be handed out to the hungry, and the multitudes fainting and dying! The rock to be struck and the water of life to leap out for the thirsty, but not a drop forthcoming, because Jesus is not there.

Ministers, evangelists, churches, salvation armies – the world dies for lack of you, and yet *ye can do nothing* if your Lord is away. The age shall advance in discovery, and men of science shall do their little best, but you shall do *nothing* without Christ, absolutely nothing! You shall not proceed a single inch upon your toilsome way, though you row until the oars snap with the strain; you shall be drifted back by winds and currents unless you take Jesus into the ship. Remember that all the while the great Husbandman is watching you, for his eye is on every vine branch. He sees that you are producing no grapes, and he is coming around with that sharp knife of his, cutting here and there! What must become of you who produce nothing? It makes one's very soul to curdle within him to think that we should live to do nothing.

Yet I fear that thousands of Christians get no further than this. They are not immoral, dishonest, or profane; but they do nothing. They think of what they would like to do, and they plan and they propose; but they *do* nothing. There are buds in plenty, but not a single grape is produced, and all because they do not get into that vital, overflowing, effective communion with Christ that would fill them with life, and constrain them to bring forth fruit unto the glory of God. There is a vision, then, of the failure all along the line if we try to do without Christ.

But now, fourthly, I hear a voice of wisdom, a still, small voice that speaks out of the text, and says to us who are in Christ, *Let us acknowledge this.* Down on your knees, bow your mouths in the dust and say, "Lord, it is true: without you we can do nothing, nothing whatever that is good and acceptable in the sight of God. We have not ability of ourselves to think anything of ourselves, but our ability is of God." Now, do not speak thus, as if you paid a compliment that orthodoxy requires you to make; but from the depths of your soul, struck with an absolute self-despair, admit the truth unto God. *To will is present with me; but how to perform that which is good I find not* (Romans 7:18). Lord, I am a good-for-nothing do-nothing, a fruitless, barren, dry, rotten branch without you, and this I feel in my inmost soul. Be not far from me, but energize me by your presence.

Next, *let us pray.* If without Christ we can do nothing, let us cry to him so that we may never be without him. Let us with strong crying and tears plead for his abiding presence. He comes to those who seek him: let us never cease seeking. In conscious fellowship with him, let us plead that the fellowship should be unbroken forevermore. Let us pray that we may be so knit and joined to Jesus that we may be one spirit with him, never to be separated from him again. Master and Lord, let the life floods of your grace never cease to flow into us, for we know that we must be thus supplied or we can produce nothing. Brethren, let us have much more prayer than has been usual among us. Prayer is appointed to convey the blessings God ordains to give; let us constantly use the appointed means, and may the result be ever increasing from day to day.

Next, *let us personally cleave to Jesus.* Let us not attempt a life of separation, for that would be to seek the living among the dead. Do not let us depart from him for a single minute. Would you like to be caught at any one second of your life in a condition in which you could do nothing? I must confess I would not like to be in that state – incapable of defense against my enemies, or of service for my Lord. If an awakened one should come before you under distress of mind, and you should feel quite incapable of doing any good to him, what a sad perplexity. Or if you did not *feel* incapable, and yet should really be so, and what if you should therefore talk on in a religious way, but know no power in it; would it not be a sad thing? May you never be in such a state that you would be a do-nothing, with opportunities afforded and yet without strength to utilize them! If you are divided from Christ you are divided from the possibility of doing good; cling, therefore, to the Savior with your whole might, and let nothing take you off from him, no, not even for an hour.

Heartily submit yourselves, also, dear friends, to the Lord's headship and leadership, and ask to do everything in his style and way. He will not be with you unless you accept him as your Master. There must be no quarrel about supremacy, but you must yield yourself up absolutely to him, to be, to do, or to suffer according to his will. When it is wholly so, he will be with you, and you shall do everything that is required of you. Wonderful things will the Lord perform through you when once he is your all in all. Will we not have it so?

Once more, *joyfully believe in him.* Though without him you can do nothing, yet with him all things are possible. Omnipotence is in that man who has Christ in him. Weakness itself you may be, but you shall learn to glory in that weakness because the power of Christ rests upon you if your union and communion with Christ are continually kept up. Oh, for a grand confidence in Christ! We have not believed in him yet up to the measure of the hem of his garment; for even that faith made the sick woman whole. Oh, to believe up to the measure of his infinite deity! Oh, for the splendor of the faith that measures itself by the Christ in whom it trusts! May God bring us there, and then shall we bring forth much fruit to the glory of his name.

And now, lastly, while I was listening to my text as a child puts a shell to its ear and listens until it hears the deep sea rolling in its windings, I heard within my text a song of content. *Without me ye can do nothing.* My heart said, "Lord, what is there that I want to do without you? There is no pain in this thought to me. If I can do without you, I am sorry to possess so dangerous a power. I am happy to be deprived of all strength except that which comes from you. It charms, it exhilarates, and it delights my soul to think that you are my all. You have made me penniless as to all wealth of my own, that I might dip my hand into your treasury; you have taken all power away from every sinew and muscle of mine, that I may rest on your bosom." *Without me ye can do nothing.*

Be it so. Brethren, are you not all agreed? Do you wish to have it altered, any of you who love his dear name? I am sure you do not; for suppose, dear friends, we could do something without Christ; then he would not have the glory of it. Who wishes that? There would be little crowns for our poor little heads, for we would have done something without him; but now there is one great crown for that dear head that once was girded with thorns, for all his saints put together cannot do anything without him. The goodly fellowship of the apostles, the noble army of martyrs, and the triumphant host of the redeemed by blood, all put together, can do nothing without Jesus. Let him be crowned with majesty who *worketh in [us] both to will and to do of his good pleasure.* For our own sakes, for our Lord's sake, we are glad that it is so. All things are more ours by being his; and if our fruit is his rather than our own, it is nonetheless all the more ours. Is not this rare music for a holy ear?

I feel so glad that without Christ we can do nothing, because I fear that if the church could do something without Christ, she would try to live without him. If she could teach the Sunday school and bring the children to salvation without Christ, I am afraid Christ would never go into a Sunday school again. If we could preach successfully without Jesus, I suspect that the Lord Jesus Christ would seldom stand on high among the people again. If our Christian literature could bless men without Christ, I am afraid we would set the printing press going, and never think about the Crucified One in the matter. If there could be work done by the church without Jesus, there would be rooms into which he would never be invited, and these would soon become a sort of Bluebeard's chambers, full of horror. A something that we could do without Christ! Why, the mass of the church would get to working that machinery tremendously, and all the rest would be neglected, and so it is a blessed thing for the whole church that she must have Christ everywhere.

Without me ye can do nothing. As I listened to the song within these words I began to laugh, and I wonder if you will laugh too. It was to myself I laughed, like Abraham of old. I thought of those who are going to destroy the orthodox doctrine from off the face of the earth. How they boast of the decline and death of old-fashioned evangelism. I have read once or twice that I am the last of the Puritans; the race is all dying out. To this I object: I am willing to be esteemed last in merit, but not last as ending the race. There are many others who are steadfast in the faith. They say our old theology is decaying, and that nobody believes it. It is all a lie; but wise men say so, and therefore we are bound to consider ourselves obsolete and extinct. We are, in their esteem, as much out of date as antediluvians would be if they could walk down our streets. Yes, they are going to quench our coal and blot us out from Israel. Newspapers and reviews and the general intelligence of the age all join to dance upon our graves. Put on your nightcaps, you good people of the evangelical order, and go home to bed and sleep the sleep of the righteous, for the end of you has come.

Thus say the Philistines, but the armies of the Lord think not so. The adversaries exult exceedingly, but Christ is not with them. They know very little about him. They do not work in his spirit, nor tout him, nor extol the gospel of his precious blood, and so I believe that when they have done their little best it will come to nothing. *Without me ye can do nothing.* If this be true of apostles, how much more true of opposers! If his friends can do nothing without him, I am sure his foes can do nothing against him. If they who follow his steps and lie in his bosom can do nothing without him, I am sure his adversaries cannot, and so I laughed at their laughter and smiled at their confusion. I laughed, too, because I recollected a story of a New England service when the pastor one afternoon was preaching in his own solemn way, and the good people were listening or sleeping, as their minds were inclined. It was a substantial edifice wherein they assembled, fit to outlive an earthquake. All went on peacefully in the meetinghouse that afternoon until suddenly a lunatic sprang up, denounced the minister, and declared that he would at once pull down the meetinghouse around their ears. Taking hold of one of the pillars of the gallery, this newly announced Samson repeated his threat. Everybody rose; the women were ready to faint; the men began to rush to the door; and there was danger that the people would be trodden on as they rushed down the aisles. There was about to be a great tumult; no one could see the end of it, when suddenly one cool brother sitting near the pulpit produced a calm by a single sentence. "Let him try!" was the stern sarcasm that hushed the tempest.

Even so today the Enemy is about to disprove the gospel and crush out the doctrines of grace. Are you distressed, alarmed, astounded? So far from that, my reply to the adversary's boast that he will pull down the pillars of our Zion is this only – Let him try! Amen.

Chapter 5

The Secret of Power in Prayer

If ye abide in me, and my words abide in you, ye shall ask what ye will, and it shall be done unto you. (John 15:7)

The gifts of grace are not enjoyed all at once by believers. Coming unto Christ, we are saved by a true union with him; but it is by abiding in that union that we further receive the purity, the joy, the power, and the blessedness that are stored up in him for his people. See how our Lord states this when he speaks to the believing Jews in the eighth chapter of this gospel, in the thirty-first and thirty-second verses: *Then said Jesus to those Jews which believed on him, If ye continue in my word, then are ye my disciples indeed; and ye shall know the truth, and the truth shall make you free.* We do not know all the truth at once: we learn it by abiding in Jesus. Perseverance in grace is an educational process by which we learn the truth fully. The emancipating power of that truth is also gradually perceived and enjoyed. *The truth shall make you free.* One bond after another snaps, and we are free indeed.

You who are young beginners in the divine life may be cheered to know that there is something better still for you; you have not yet received the full recompense of your faith. As your hymn puts it – "It is better on before." You shall have happier views of heavenly things as you climb the hill of spiritual experience. As you abide in Christ you shall have firmer confidence, richer joy, greater stability, more communion with

Jesus, and greater delight in the Lord your God. Infancy is harassed by many evils from which manhood is exempt; it is the same in the spiritual as in the natural world.

There are these degrees of attainment among believers, and the Savior here incites us to reach a high position by mentioning a certain privilege that is not for all who say that they are in Christ, but for those only who are *abiders* in him. Every believer should be an abider, but many have hardly earned the name as yet. Jesus says, *If ye abide in me, and my words abide in you, ye shall ask what ye will, and it shall be done unto you.* You have to live with Christ to know him, and the longer you live with him the more will you admire and adore him; yes, and the more will you receive from him, even grace for grace.

Truly he is a blessed Christ to one who is but a month old in grace; but these babes can hardly tell what a precious Jesus he is to those whose acquaintance with him covers nearly half a century! Jesus, in the esteem of abiding believers, grows sweeter and dearer, fairer and more lovely day by day. Not that he improves in himself, for he is perfect; but that as we increase in our knowledge of him, we appreciate more thoroughly his matchless excellencies. How glowingly do his old acquaintances exclaim, *Yea, he is altogether lovely* (Song of Solomon 5:16)! Oh, that we may continue to grow up into him in all things who is our Head, that we thus may prize him more and more!

I call your earnest attention to our text, begging you to consider with me three questions. First, *What is this special blessing? Ye shall ask what ye will, and it shall be done unto you.* Secondly, *How is this special blessing obtained? If ye abide in me, and my words abide in you.* Then, thirdly, *Why is it obtained in this way?* There must be a reason for the conditions laid down as needful to obtaining the promised power in prayer. Oh, that the anointing of the Holy Spirit that abides on us may now make this subject very profitable to us!

What is this special blessing? Let us read the verse again. Jesus says, *If ye abide in me, and my words abide in you, ye shall ask what ye will, and it shall be done unto you.*

Observe that our Lord had been warning us that, severed from him, we can do nothing, and, therefore, we might naturally have expected that he would now show us how we can do all spiritual acts. But the text does not run as we should have expected it to run. The Lord Jesus does not say, "Without me you can do nothing, but, if you abide in me, and my words abide in you, you shall do all spiritual and gracious things." He does not now speak of what they should themselves be enabled to do, but of what should be done unto them: *It shall be done unto you.* He says not, "Strength shall be given you sufficient for all those holy doings of which you are incapable apart from me." That would have been true enough, and it is the truth that we looked for here; but our most wise Lord improves upon all parallelisms of speech, and improves upon all expectancies of heart, and says something better still. He does not say, "If you abide in me, and my words abide in you, you shall do spiritual things," but rather, *Ye shall ask.* By prayer you shall be enabled to do; but before all attempts to do, *ye shall ask.* The choice privilege given here is a mighty prevailing prayerfulness. Power in prayer is very much the gauge of our spiritual condition; and when that is secured to us in a high degree, we are favored as to all other matters.

One of the first results, then, of our abiding union with Christ will be *the certain exercise of prayer: Ye shall ask.* If others neither seek, nor knock, nor ask, you, at any rate, shall do so. Those who keep away from Jesus do not pray. Those in whom communion with Christ is suspended feel as if they could not pray; but Jesus says, *If ye abide in me, and my words abide in you, ye shall ask.* Prayer comes spontaneously from those who abide in Jesus, even as certain Oriental trees, without pressure, shed their fragrant gums. Prayer is the natural out-gushing of a soul in communion with Jesus. Just as the leaf and the fruit will come out of the vine branch without any conscious effort on the part of the branch, but simply because of its living union with the stem, so prayer buds, and blossoms, and fruits out of souls abiding in Jesus.

As stars shine, so do abiders pray. It is their use and their second nature. They do not say to themselves, "Now it is the time for us to get to our task and pray." No, they pray as wise men eat, namely, when the desire for it is upon them. They do not cry out as under bondage, "At this time I ought to be in prayer, but I do not feel like it. What a weariness it is!" but they have a glad errand at the mercy seat, and they rejoice to go upon it. Hearts abiding in Christ send forth prayers as fires send out flames and sparks. Souls abiding in Jesus open the day with prayer;

prayer surrounds them as an atmosphere all day long; at night they fall asleep praying. I have known them even to dream a prayer, and, at any rate, they are able joyfully to say, *When I awake, I am still with thee* (Psalm 139:18). Habitual asking comes out of abiding in Christ. You will not need an urging to pray when you are abiding with Jesus; he says, *Ye shall ask,* and, depend upon it, you will.

You shall also feel most powerfully *the necessity of prayer.* Your great need of prayer will be vividly seen. Do I hear you say, "What! When we abide in Christ, and his words abide in us, have we not already attained?" Far are we, then, from being satisfied with ourselves; it is then that we feel more than ever that we must ask for more grace. He that knows Christ best, knows his own necessities best. He that is most conscious of life in Christ is also most convinced of his own death apart from Christ. He who most clearly discerns the perfect character of Jesus will be most urgent in prayer for grace to grow like him. The more I see to be in my Lord, the more I desire to obtain from him, since I know that all that is in him is put there on purpose that I may receive it.

Of his fulness have all we received, and grace for grace (John 1:16). It is just in proportion as we are linked to Christ's fullness that we feel the necessity of drawing from it by constant prayer. Nobody needs to prove to an abider in Christ the doctrine of prayer, for we enjoy the thing itself. Prayer is now as much a necessity of our spiritual life as breath is of our natural life: we cannot live without asking favors of the Lord. *If ye abide in me, and my words abide in you, ye shall ask,* and you shall not wish to cease from asking. He has said, *Seek ye my face,* and your heart will answer, *Thy face, Lord, will I seek* (Psalm 27:8).

Note next, that the fruit of our abiding is not only the exercise of prayer, and a sense of the necessity of prayer, but it also includes *liberty in prayer: Ye shall ask what ye will.* Have you not been on your knees at times without power to pray? Have you not felt that you could not plead as you desired? You wanted to pray, but the waters were frozen up and would not flow. You said mournfully, "I am shut up and cannot come forth." The will was present, but not the freedom to present that will in prayer. Do you, then, desire liberty in prayer, so that you may speak with God as a man speaks with his friend? Here is the way to it: *If ye abide in me, and my words abide in you, ye shall ask what ye will.*

I do not mean that you will gain liberty as to mere fluency of utterance, for that is a very inferior gift. Fluency is a questionable endowment, especially when it is not accompanied by weight of thought and depth of feeling. Some brethren pray by the yard; but true prayer is measured by weight, and not by length. A single groan before God may have more fullness of prayer in it than a fine speech of great length. He that dwells with God in Christ Jesus, he is the man whose steps are enlarged in intercession. He comes boldly because he abides at the throne. He sees the golden scepter stretched out, and hears the King saying, *Ask what ye will, and it shall be done unto you.* It is the man who abides in conscious union with his Lord who has freedom of access in prayer. Well may he come to Christ readily, for he is in Christ, and he abides in him. Attempt not to seize this holy liberty by excitement, or presumption; there is but one way of really gaining it, and here it is – *If ye abide in me, and my words abide in you, ye shall ask what ye will.* By this means alone shall you be enabled to open your mouth wide, that God may fill it. Thus shall you become Israels, and as princes you will have power with God.

This is not all. The favored man has the privilege of *successful prayer. Ye shall ask what ye will, and it shall be done unto you.* You may not do it, but it shall be done unto you. You long to bear fruit: ask, and *it shall be done unto you.* Look at the vine branch. It simply remains in the vine, and by remaining in the vine the fruit comes from it; it is *done unto* it. Brother in Christ, the substance of your being, its one object and design, is to bring forth fruit to the glory of the Father. To gain this end you must abide in Christ, as the branch abides in the vine.

This is the method by which your prayer for fruitfulness will become successful: *It shall be done unto you.* Concerning this matter, *ye shall ask what you will, and it shall be done unto you.* You shall have wonderful power with God in prayer, insomuch that before you call, he will answer, and while you are yet speaking, he will hear. *The desire of the righteous shall be granted* (Proverbs 10:24). To the same effect is the other text: *Delight thyself also in the Lord: and he shall give thee the desires of thine heart* (Psalm 37:4). There is a great breadth in this text: *Ye shall ask what ye will, and it shall be done unto you.* The Lord gives the abider *carte blanche.* He puts into his hand a signed check, and permits him to fill it up as he wills.

Does the text mean what it says? I never knew my Lord to say anything he did not mean. I am sure that he may sometimes mean more than we understand him to say, but he never means less. Mind you, he does not say to all men, "I will give you whatever you ask." Oh no, that would be an unkind kindness. But he speaks to his disciples and says, *If ye abide in me, and my words abide in you, ye shall ask what ye will, and it shall be done unto you.* It is to a certain class of men who have already received great grace at his hands – it is to them he commits this marvelous power of prayer.

O my dear friends, if I may covet earnestly one thing above every other, it is this: that I may be able to ask what I will of the Lord, and have it. The man who prevails in prayer is the man to preach successfully, for he may well prevail with man for God when he has already prevailed with God for men. This is the man to face the difficulties of business life; for what can baffle him when he can take all to God in prayer? One such man as this, or one such woman as this in a church, is worth ten thousand of us common people. In these we find the aristocracy of the skies. In these are the men in whom is fulfilled God's purpose concerning man, whom he made to have dominion over all the works of his hands. The stamp of sovereignty is on the brows of these men: they shape the history of nations, they guide the current of events through their power on high. We see Jesus with all things put under him by the divine purpose, and as we rise into that image, we also are clothed with dominion, and are made kings and priests unto God.

Behold Elijah, with the keys of the rain swinging at his girdle; he shuts or opens the windows of heaven! There are such men still alive. Aspire to be such men and women, I implore you, that to you the text may be fulfilled. *Ye shall ask what ye will, and it shall be done unto you.*

The text seems to imply that if we reach this point of privilege, this gift shall be a perpetuity: *Ye shall ask,* you shall always ask; you shall never get beyond asking, but you shall ask successfully, for *ye shall ask what ye will, and it shall be done unto you.* Here we have the gift of *continual prayer.* Not for the week of prayer, not during a month's conference, nor upon a few special occasions shall you pray prevailingly; but you shall possess this power with God as long as you abide in Christ, and his words abide in you. God will put his omnipotence at your disposal: he will put forth his power and might to fulfill the desires that his own Spirit has worked in you. I wish I could make this jewel glitter before the eyes of all the saints until they cried out, "Oh that we had it!"

This power in prayer is like the sword of Goliath: wisely may every David say, *There is none like that; give it me* (1 Samuel 21:9). This weapon of all-prayer beats the Enemy, and, at the same time, enriches its possessor with all the wealth of God. How can he lack anything to whom the Lord has said, *Ask what ye will, and it shall be done unto you*? Oh, come, let us seek this blessing. Listen, and learn the way. Follow me, while by the light of the text I point out the path. May the Lord lead us in it by his Holy Spirit!

The privilege of mighty prayerfulness – how is it to be obtained? The answer is: *If ye abide in me, and my words abide in you.* Here are the two feet by which we climb to power with God in prayer.

Beloved, the first line tells us that we are to *abide in Christ Jesus our Lord.* It is taken for granted that we are already in him. May it be taken for granted in your case, dear friend? If so, you are to abide where you are. As believers we are to remain tenaciously clinging to Jesus, and livingly knit to Jesus. We are to abide in him by always trusting him, and him only, with the same simple faith that joined us to him at the first. We must never admit any other thing or person into our heart's confidence as our hope of salvation, but rest alone in Jesus as we received him at the first. His deity, his manhood, his life, his death, his resurrection, his glory at the right hand of the Father – in a word, himself – he must be our heart's sole reliance. This is absolutely essential. A temporary faith will not save; an abiding faith is needful.

But abiding in the Lord Jesus does not only mean trusting in him; it also includes our yielding ourselves up to him to receive his life, and to let that life work out its results in us. We live *in* him, *by* him, *for* him, and *to* him when we abide in him. We feel that all our separate life is gone: *For ye are dead, and your life is hid with Christ.* We are nothing if we get away from Jesus; we would then be withered branches, and fit only to be cast into the fire. We have no reason for existence except that which we find in Christ, and what a marvelous reason that is! The vine needs the branch as truly as the branch needs the vine. No vine ever bore any fruit except upon its branches. Truly it bears all the branches, and so bears all the fruit; but yet it is by the branch that the vine displays its fruitfulness.

Thus are abiding believers needful to the fulfillment of their Lord's design. Wonderful thing to say, but the saints are needful to their Savior! *[The church] is his body, the fulness of him that filleth all in all* (Ephesians 1:23). I want you to recognize this, that you may see your blessed responsibility, your practical obligation to bring forth fruit, so that the Lord Jesus may be glorified in you. Abide in him. Never remove yourself from your consecration to his honor and glory. Never dream of being your own master. Be not the servant of men, but abide in Christ. Let him be the object, as well as the source, of your existence.

Oh, if you get there, and stop there in perpetual communion with your Lord, you will soon realize a joy, a delight, a power in prayer such as you never knew before. There are times when we are conscious that we are in Christ, and we know our fellowship with him; and oh, the joy and the peace that we drink from this cup! Let us abide there. *Abide in me,* says Jesus. You are not to come and go, but to abide. Let that blessed sinking of yourself into his life, the spending of all your powers for Jesus, and the firm faith of your union with him remain in you evermore. Oh, that we might attain to this by the Holy Spirit!

As if to help us to understand this, our gracious Lord has given us a delightful parable. Let us look through this discourse of the vine and its branches. Jesus says, *Every branch that beareth fruit, he purgeth it.* Take care that you *abide in Christ when you are being purged.* "Oh," says one, "I thought I was a Christian, but alas! I have more troubles than ever: men ridicule me, the devil tempts me, and my business affairs go wrong."

Brother, if you are to have power in prayer you must take care that you abide in Christ when the sharp knife is cutting everything away. Endure trial, and never dream of giving up your faith because of it. Say, *Though he slay me, yet will I trust in him* (Job 13:15). Your Lord warned you when you first came into the Vine that you would have to be purged and cut closely; and if you are now feeling the purging process, you must not think that some strange thing has happened to you. Rebel not because of anything you may have to suffer from the dear hand of your heavenly Father, who is the Husbandman of the vineyard. No, but cling to Jesus all the more closely. Say, "Cut, Lord, cut to the heart if you will; but I will cling to you. To whom should we go? You have the words of eternal life." Yes, cling to Jesus when the purging knife is in his hand, and so *ye shall ask what ye will, and it shall be done unto you.*

Take care, also, that *when the purging operation has been carried out you still cleave to your Lord.* Notice the third verse and the beginning of the fourth verse: *Now ye are clean through the word which I have spoken unto you. Abide in me, and I in you.* Abide after cleansing where you were before cleansing. When you are sanctified, abide where you were when first justified. When you see the work of the Spirit increasing in you, do not let the devil tempt you to boast that now you are somebody, and need not come to Jesus as a poor sinner, and rest in his precious blood alone for salvation. Abide still in Jesus. As you kept to him when the knife cut you, keep to him now that the tender grapes begin to form. Do not say to yourself, "What a fruitful branch I am! How greatly I adorn the Vine! Now I am full of vigor!" You are nothing and nobody. Only as you abide in Christ are you one bit better than the waste wood that is burned in the fire. "But do we not make progress?" Yes, we grow, but we abide: we never go an inch further, we abide in him; or, if not, we are cast forth, and are withered. Our whole hope lies in Jesus at our best times as well as at our worst. Jesus says, *Now ye are clean through the word which I have spoken unto you. Abide in me, and I in you.*

Abide in him *as to all your fruitfulness. As the branch cannot bear fruit of itself, except it abide in the vine; no more can ye, except ye abide in me.* "Here, then, I have something to do," cries one. Certainly, you have, but not apart from Jesus. The branch has to bear fruit; but if the branch imagines that it is going to produce a cluster, or even a grape, out of itself alone, it is utterly mistaken. The fruit of the branch must come forth out of the stem. Your work for Christ must be Christ's work in you, or else it will be good for nothing. I pray you, see to this. Your Sunday school teaching, your preaching, or whatever you do must be done in Christ Jesus. Not by your natural talent can you win souls, nor by plans of your own inventing can you save men. Beware of homemade schemes. Do for Jesus what Jesus bids you to do. Remember that our work for Christ, as we call it, must be Christ's work first, if it is to be accepted by him. Abide in him as to your fruit bearing.

Yes, abide in him *as to your very life.* Do not say, "I have been a Christian man now twenty or thirty years, I can do without continued dependence upon Christ." No, you could not do without him if you were as old as Methuselah. Your very being as a Christian depends upon your still clinging, still trusting, and still depending; and this he must give you, for it all comes from him, and him alone. To sum it all up, if you want that splendid power in prayer of which I spoke just now, you must remain in loving, living, lasting, conscious, practical, and abiding union with the Lord Jesus Christ; and if you get to that by divine grace, then you shall ask what you will, and it shall be done unto you.

But there is a second qualification mentioned in the text, and you must not forget it – *and my words abide in you.* How important, then, are Christ's words! He said in the fourth verse, *Abide in me, and I in you,* and now as a parallel to this, it is: *If ye abide in me, and my words abide in you.* What then, are Christ's words and himself identical? Yes, practically so. Some talk about Christ being the Master, but as to doctrine, they do not care what his Word declares. So long as their hearts are right towards his person, they claim liberty of thought. Alas, but this is a mere deception. We cannot separate Christ from the Word, for, in the first place, he is the Word, and, in the next place, how dare we call him Master and Lord and do not the things that he says, and reject the truth that he teaches. We must obey his precepts or he will not accept us as disciples.

Especially that precept of love, which is the essence of all his words. We must love God and our brethren; yes, we must cherish love to all men, and seek their good. Anger and malice must be far from us. We must walk even as he walked. If Christ's words abide not in you, both as to belief and practice, you are not in Christ. Christ and his gospel and his commands are one. If you will not have Christ and his words, neither will he have you nor your words; but you shall ask in vain, you shall by and by give up asking, and you shall become as a withered branch. Beloved, I am convinced of better things of you, and things that accompany salvation, though I thus speak.

Oh, for grace to pass through these two-leaved gates, these two golden doors! *If ye abide in me, and my words abide in you.* Push through the two, and enter into this large room – *Ye shall ask what ye will, and it shall be done unto you.*

It is my last work to try to show why this privilege should be so obtained. This extraordinary power of prayer, why is it given to those who abide in Christ? May what I have to say encourage you to make the glorious attempt to win this pearl of great price! Why is it, that by abiding in Christ, and having his words abide in us, we get to this liberty and prevalence in prayer?

I answer, first, *because of the fullness of Christ.* You may very well ask what you will when you abide in Christ, because whatsoever you may require is already lodged in him. Good Bishop Hall worked out this thought in a famous passage. I will give you the substance of it. Do you desire the grace of the Spirit? Go to your Lord's anointing. Do you seek holiness? Go to his example. Do you desire pardon of sin? Look to his blood. Do you need deadening of sin? Look to his crucifixion. Do you need to be buried to the world? Go to his tomb. Do you want to feel the fullness of a heavenly life? Behold his resurrection. Would you rise above the world? Observe his ascension. Would you contemplate heavenly things? Remember his session at the right hand of God, and know that he *hath raised us up together, and made us sit together in heavenly places.*

I see clearly enough why the branch gets all it wants while it abides in the stem, since all it wants is already in the stem, and it is placed there for the sake of the branch. What does the branch want more than the stem can give it? If it did want more, it could not get it, for it has no other means of living but by sucking its life out of the stem. O my precious Lord, if I want anything that is not in you, I desire always to be without it. I desire to be denied a wish that wanders outside of yourself. But if the supply of my desire is already in you for me, why should I go elsewhere? You are my all; where else should I look? Beloved, *it pleased the Father that in him should all fulness dwell* (Colossians 1:19), and the good pleasure of the Father is our good pleasure also: we are glad to draw everything from Jesus. We feel sure that, ask what we will, we shall have it, since he has it ready for us.

The next reason for this is *the richness of the Word of God.* Catch this thought: *If . . . my words abide in you, ye shall ask what ye will, and it shall be done unto you.* The best praying man is the man who is most believingly familiar with the promises of God. After all, prayer is nothing but taking God's promises to him, and saying to him, "Do as you have said." Prayer is the promise utilized. A prayer that is not based on a promise has no true foundation. If I go to the bank without a check, I need not expect to get money; it is the "order to pay" that is my power inside the bank, and my warrant for expecting to receive. You who have Christ's words abiding in you are equipped with those things that the Lord regards with attention. If the Word of God abides in you, you are the man that can pray, because you meet the great God with his own words, and thus overcome omnipotence with omnipotence. You put your finger down upon the very lines, and say, "Do as you have said." This is the best praying in all the world.

O beloved, be filled with God's Word. Study what Jesus has said, what the Holy Spirit has left on record in this divinely inspired Book, and in proportion as you feed on the Word, and are filled with the Word, and retain the Word in your faith, and obey the Word in your life – in that proportion you will be a master man in the art of prayer. You have acquired skill as a wrestler with the covenant angel in proportion as you can plead the promises of your faithful God. Be well instructed in the doctrines of grace, and let the Word of Christ dwell in you richly, that you may know how to prevail at the throne of grace. Abiding in Christ, and his words abiding in you, are like the right hand and the left hand of Moses, which were held up in prayer, so that Amalek was struck, Israel was delivered, and God was glorified.

Let us go a little further. You still may say you do not quite see why a man who abides in Christ, and in whom Christ's words abide, should be allowed to ask whatever he wills, and it shall be done unto him. I answer you again: it is so, because *in such a man as that there is a predominance of grace that causes him to have a renewed will, which is according to the will of God.* Suppose a man of God is in prayer, and he thinks that such and such a thing is desirable, yet he remembers that he is nothing but a babe in the presence of his all-wise Father, and so he bows his will, and asks as a favor to be taught what to will. Though God bids him to ask what he wills, he shrinks and cries, "My Lord, here is a request that I am not quite clear about. As far as I can judge, it is a desirable thing, and I will it; but Lord, I am not fit to judge for myself, and therefore I pray you, give not as I will, but as you will." Do you not see that, when we are in such a condition as this, our real will is God's will? Deep down in our hearts we *will* only that which the Lord himself wills; and what is this but to ask what we will, and it is done to us?

It becomes safe for God to say to the sanctified soul, *Ask what ye will, and it shall be done unto you.* The heavenly instincts of that man lead him rightly; the grace that is within his soul thrusts down all covetous lusting and foul desires, and his will is the actual shadow of God's will. The spiritual life is master in him, and so his aspirations are holy, heavenly, and godlike. He has been made a partaker of the divine nature; and as a son is like his father, so now in desire and will he is one with his God. As the echo answers to the voice, so does the renewed heart echo the mind of the Lord. Our desires are reflected beams of the divine will: you shall ask what you will, and it shall be even so.

You clearly see that the Holy God cannot pick up a common man in the street, and say to him, "I will give you whatsoever you will." What would he ask for? He would ask for a good drink, or permission to enjoy himself in evil lust. It would be very unsafe to trust most men with this permission. But when the Lord has taken a man, and has made him new, has revived him into newness of life, and has formed him in the image of his dear Son, then he can trust him!

Behold, the great Father treats us in our measure as he treats his Firstborn. Jesus could say, *I knew that thou hearest me always,* and the Lord is educating us to the selfsame assurance. We can say with one of old, "My God will hear me." Do not your mouths water for this privilege of prevailing prayer? Do not your hearts long to get at this? It is by the way of holiness, it is by the way of union to Christ, it is by the way of a permanent abiding in him, and an obedient holding fast of his truth, that you are to come to this privilege. Behold the only safe and true way. When once that way is really trodden, it is a most sure and effective way of gaining substantial power in prayer.

I am not quite done. A man will succeed in prayer *when his faith is strong;* and this is the case with those who abide in Jesus. It is faith that prevails in prayer. The real eloquence of prayer is a believing desire. *All things are possible to him that believeth* (Mark 9:23). A man abiding in Christ with Christ's words abiding in him, is notably a believer, and consequently very successful in prayer. He has strong faith indeed, for his faith has brought him into vital contact with Christ, and he is therefore at the source of every blessing, and may drink to his full at the well itself.

Such a man, once more, will also possess *the indwelling of the Spirit of God.* If we abide in Christ, and his words abide in us, then the Holy Spirit has come and taken up his residence in us; and what better help in prayer can we have? Is it not a wonderful thing that the Holy Spirit himself makes intercession for the saints according to the will of God? *The Spirit itself maketh intercession for us with groanings which cannot be uttered* (Romans 8:26). What man knows the mind of a man except the spirit of a man? The Spirit of God knows the mind of God, and he works in us to will what God wills, so that a believing man's prayer is God's purpose reflected in the soul as in a mirror. The eternal decrees of God project their shadows over the hearts of godly men in the form of prayer.

What God intends to do he tells unto his servants by inclining them to ask him to do what he himself is resolved to do. God says, "I will do this and that"; but then he adds, *I will yet for this be enquired of by the house of Israel, to do it for them* (Ezekiel 36:37). How clear it is that if we abide in Christ, and his words abide in us, we may ask what we will! For we shall only ask what the Spirit of God moves us to ask; and it would be impossible that God the Holy Spirit and God the Father should be at cross-purposes with one another. What the one prompts us to ask, the other has assuredly determined to bestow.

I struck out a line just now to which I must return for a single moment. Beloved, do you not know that when we abide in Christ, and his words abide in us, the Father looks upon us with the same eye with which he looks upon his dear Son? Christ is the Vine, and the Vine includes the branches. The branches are a part of the Vine. God, therefore, looks upon us as part of Christ – members of his body, of his flesh, and of his bones. Such is the Father's love to Jesus that he denies him nothing. He was obedient to death, even the death of the cross; therefore does his Father love him, as the God-man Mediator, and he will grant him all his petitions. And is it so, that when you and I are in real union with Christ, the Lord God looks upon us in the same way as he looks on Jesus, and says to us, "I will deny you nothing; *ye shall ask what ye will, and it shall be done unto you*"? So do I understand the text.

I call your attention to the fact that in that fifteenth chapter, the ninth verse, which I did not read this morning, it says thus: *As the Father hath loved me, so have I loved you.* The same love that God gives to his Son, the Son gives to us; and therefore we are dwellers in the love of the Father and of the Son. How can our prayers be rejected? Will not infinite love have respect unto our petitions? O dear brother in Christ, if your prayers succeed not at the throne, suspect that there is some sin that hinders them; your Father's love sees a necessity for disciplining you this way. If you do not abide in Christ, how can you hope to pray successfully? If you pick and choose his words, and doubt this, and doubt that, how can you hope to succeed at the throne? If you are willfully disobedient to any one of his words, will not this account for failure in prayer?

But abide in Christ, and take fast hold upon his words, and be altogether his disciple, and then shall you be heard by him. Sitting at Jesus' feet, hearing his words, you may lift up your eyes to his dear face, and say, "My Lord, hear me now," and he will answer you graciously. He will say unto you, *I have heard thee in a time accepted, and in the day of salvation have I succored thee* (2 Corinthians 6:2). *Ask what ye will, and it shall be done unto you.* Oh, for power at the mercy seat!

Beloved friends, do not hear this message, and then go away and forget it. Do try to reach this place of boundless influence. What a church we would be if you were all mighty in prayer! Dear children of God, do you want to be half starved? Beloved brethren, do you desire to be poor, little, puny, and drooling children who will never grow into men? I pray you, aspire to be strong in the Lord, and to enjoy this exceedingly high privilege. What an army would you be if you all had this power with God in prayer! It is within your reach, you children of God! Only abide in Christ, and let his words abide in you, and then this special privilege will be yours. These are not tedious duties, but they are in themselves a joy. Go in for them with your whole heart, and then you shall get this added to you, that you shall ask what you will, and it shall be done unto you.

Unhappily, to a portion of this congregation my text says nothing at all; for some of you are not even in Christ, and therefore you cannot abide in him. O sirs, what shall I say to you? You seem to me to miss an utter heaven even now. If there were no hell hereafter, it is hell enough not to know Christ now, not to know what it is to prevail with God in prayer, not to know the choice privilege of abiding in him, and his words abiding in you. Your first matter is that you believe in Jesus Christ to the saving of your souls, yielding your souls to his cleansing, your lives to his government. God has sent him forth as a Savior; accept him. Receive him as your Teacher; yield yourself up to him as your Master. May his gracious Spirit come and do this work upon you now; and then, after this, but not before, you may aspire to this honor.

First of all – *You must be born again.* I cannot say to you as you are now, "Grow," because you will only grow into a bigger sinner. However much you may be developed, you will only develop what is in you; and that is, the heir of wrath will become more and more the child of evil. You must be made anew in Christ. There must be an absolute change, a reversal of all the currents of nature, a making you a new creature in Christ Jesus; and then you may aspire to abide in Christ, and let his words abide in you, and the consequent power with God in prayer shall be yours.

Gracious Lord, help us this morning. Poor creatures as we are, we can only lie at your feet. Come yourself, and uplift us to yourself, for your mercy's sake! Amen.

Chapter 6

The Candle

Neither do men light a candle, and put it under a bushel, but on a candlestick; and it giveth light unto all that are in the house. Let your light so shine before men, that they may see your good works, and glorify your Father which is in heaven. (Matthew 5:15-16)

Our Savior was speaking of the influence of his disciples upon their fellows, and he first of all mentioned that secret but powerful influence that he describes under the figure of salt: *Ye are the salt of the earth* (Matthew 5:13). No sooner is a man born unto God than he begins to affect his fellow man with an influence that is rather felt than seen. The very existence of a believer operates upon unbelievers. He is like a handful of salt cast upon flesh; he has a savor in himself, and this begins to penetrate those who are in contact with him. The unobserved, and almost unconscious, influence of a holy life is most effective to the conserving of society and the prevention of moral corruption. May there be salt in every one of us, for *salt is good* (Mark 9:50). Have salt in yourselves, and then you will become a blessing to all those around you.

But there is around every true Christian a manifest and visible influence that he is bound to exercise, and this our Lord sets forth under the figure of light: *Ye are the light of the world. A city that is set on an hill cannot be hid* (Matthew 5:14). In any case, the genuine Christian will exercise the silent and unseen salting influence upon those who come into immediate contact with him; but let him also labor to possess the second, or illuminating influence, that covers a far larger area, and deals more with real life; for salt is for dead flesh, and light is for living men. *Let your light so shine before men, that they may see your good works, and glorify your Father which is in heaven.* Saltiness and light are the power of a Christian.

I do not believe that any man will give forth light if he has not first received salt; and yet some have a measure of salt who are none too liberal with their light. May God grant you grace to balance the inward and the outward. May we have the conserving salt and the diffusive light. Our thoughts will now run towards light-giving, and I pray that I may be helped to move the more retiring and less active among us to exert their influence upon others to a greater extent; to crown the silent testimonies of their humble faith by an outspoken witness-bearing for their Lord and Savior. All who have salt will now be urged to show their light.

The figure that our Savior uses is a simple one, borrowed from the Eastern tent and house. He speaks of a candle, or, more accurately, of a lamp. We should read the passage – "Neither do men light a lamp, and put it under a bushel, but on the lampstand; and it giveth light unto all that are in the house." I shall use the figure both in its Eastern and in its Western dress, and sometimes we will make a lamp of it and sometimes a candle. Perhaps we shall see all the better with both a lamp and a candle; and, though we may confuse the metaphor, we shall not confuse anybody's mind upon the important truth that it sets forth.

Three things are in the text. The first is *the lighting*, the second is *the placing,* and the third is *the shining.* The first two are both intended to produce the third. May he who alone can create light illuminate our minds while dwelling on his Word.

First let us consider the lighting. *Neither do men light a candle.* What is this lighting up of the souls of men? They are without light by nature, *having the understanding darkened, being alienated from the life of God through the ignorance that is in them* (Ephesians 4:18). What, then, is this lighting?

It is, first of all, *a divine work.* God began his creating work of old by saying, *Let there be light,* and there was light (Genesis 1:3). And as in the old creation so in the new, the first thing that God works in the heart of man is light: *The entrance of thy words giveth light* (Psalm 119:130). Well did David say, *The Lord is my light and my salvation* (Psalm 27:1). The Holy Spirit enlightens the understanding, so that the man perceives the desperateness of his own condition, and his inability to win salvation by his own works. The Lord pours light into the soul, so that Christ is seen by faith, and at the sight of him the heart catches fire, and light takes hold upon the inner man, so that he not only *sees* light but also *has* light. The light not only shines *upon* the heart, but also *from* the heart. *Ye were sometime darkness* (Ephesians 5:8) – not only in the dark, but darkness itself – *but now are ye light in the Lord;* so not only do you have light from the Lord, but you also *are* light, your souls having caught the flame.

The Holy Spirit alone can accomplish this work. No human being will ever have light within himself until God who spoke the decree at creation shall by the selfsame word create light in the soul. The apostle Paul says of all the saints, *God, who commanded the light to shine out of darkness, hath shined in our hearts, to give the light of the knowledge of the glory of God in the face of Jesus Christ* (2 Corinthians 4:6).

This lighting is *a separating* work. When this light comes, it separates a man from those around him who are as the darkness. It does not take him away from his surroundings, it does not shut him up in a monastery, but the separation is complete; for to set a division between a candle and the darkness, all that is needed is to light it. The tiniest spark will by its very existence be distinguished from the darkness. There is no need to label light to prevent its being confounded with the darkness, and there is no need for it to sound a trumpet before itself, saying, "Here am I." What fellowship has light with darkness? No sooner comes the light into a man's heart than he is separate from those who are around about him, called by the grace of God by a vocation that at once sets a difference between the called ones and the rest of the sons of men. The darkness could not have created the light, for it does not even comprehend it; *the light shineth in darkness; and the darkness comprehended it not* (John 1:5).

Those that are round about the Christian man cannot make him out, for his *life is hid with Christ in God*. At his conversion they perceive that a strange alteration has come over him, and, as Dr. Watts says, they "gaze and admire, and hate the change"; but they know no more about it than owls do of the sun. At first they set the change down to sadness, until the man's experience flashes into delight, and then they call it fanaticism or a kind of madness, a sort of twist of the mind. Oh, blessed twist! Would God that those who know it not could be twisted after the same fashion! It is the kindling of the candle, so that where all was darkness before, there may now be the heavenly light.

The darkness, though it does not understand or love the light, is nevertheless compelled to yield to it; for the battle between light and darkness is short and decisive. Up to the measure of the light is the measure of its conquest. Though only a few beams should irradiate the eastern sky, yet so far the arrows of the sun have pierced the heart of the night; and as that light shall glow into high noon, all traces of darkness must fly before it.

Beloved, if God has given light to us, he has put within us a principle that shall go forth conquering and to conquer. Let the darkness be as dense as that which plagued the Egyptians, yet must it yield to light. A conflict is to be expected, but a conquest is guaranteed. We must not dream that the darkness will put forth its black arms to embrace our light; nor may we imagine that it will come cowering at the foot of our candlestick and ask to make an association with us. Light cannot dwell side by side with the darkness, making covenant with that, for it is written, *God divided the light from the darkness. And God called the light Day, and the darkness he called Night* (Genesis 1:4-5), thus giving to each its own distinguishing name, that none might confound them. No man shall ever be able to mingle the two: they are and must be forever distinct.

To the end of time there shall be two seeds, the heirs of light and the children of darkness, and these two cannot be one. The light shall war with the darkness until the eternal light has fully risen and reached its zenith, and then the earth shall be filled with the light of the glory of God. until then, you children of light, see to it that you have no fellowship with the unfruitful works of darkness. This lighting up of the candle takes place at rebirth, and you perceive it in enlightenment, conviction, and conversion. The question is: Have you ever been lit, dear friend? Have you ever received that divine light? Have you ever felt the touch of the heavenly torch of the Word by which light has come to you, and now dwells within you, so that you yourself have become a light, and are shining to the glory of God?

Furthermore, this light-giving is *a personal work to every man* who is the subject of it. The text says, *Let **your** light so shine before men* (emphasis added). When a man lights a candle, the light does not belong to the candle originally; but when once the candle has accepted the flame, the light becomes the candle's own light, and the candle begins to shine by its own light. So, beloved, the grace of God, the light from heaven, must come to each one of us individually from the divine hand, and we must personally receive it. Light is not inherent in any one of us, and therefore it must be bestowed. Its bestowal necessitates a personal acceptance. It is not bestowed upon us as part of a nation or family.

In its enlightening operations grace does not deal with men in the sum, but with each man by himself. Sin is personal, and so must grace be. We are individually in the darkness, and must be individually kindled into light. One by one each man must accept the light, permitting it, as it were, to kindle upon him, so that the very wick of his being, that innermost life that goes through the very center of his nature, shall embrace the flame and begin to burn with it. There must be an individual appropriation of the light, so that to each one of you it becomes your own. *Let **your** light so shine before men.* Do not deceive yourselves with the notion of national Christianity or hereditary Christianity; the only true religion is personal godliness. We cannot light these candles by the pound at a time, nor heap up lamps in a pile and light them in a mass. We have nowadays wonderful lights, which can be all lit in an instant by a single touch of electricity; but even then, each one of the lights has to receive a flame for itself, which becomes all its own. There is no way by which individuality can be destroyed and men saved *en masse.*

In each man the light is peculiar and distinct. The light that burns in one true minister of Christ is the same that shines forth from another, and yet *one star differeth from another star in glory:* Peter is not John, Paul is not James, Whitfield is not Wesley. You shall examine the whole range of God's lamps and candlesticks, and you shall not find two exactly alike. Many artists exhaust themselves and then repeat themselves, but God is inexhaustibly original; no two touches of his pencil are the same.

Light is one, and its glory is one, and yet there is one glory of the sun, and another glory of the moon, and another glory of the stars. There is a difference in the lights of various oils and gases, and so there is in your light, my brother, and my light. It is very possible that you would like to put my candle in order; you may do so if you can, but do not snuff me out. Your own light is, however, your main concern, and you had better ask for special grace that it may not fail. Your light is distinct from mine, as distinct as your life is from mine, though in another sense it is true that your spiritual light is one with all the light that ever shone in this world. There is in the lighting a personal appropriation of the divine flame, and afterwards a personal and distinct sending forth of the sacred light in the individual's own way. Look well to this, lest you be mistaken, and suppose yourselves to be lighted from heaven when you are the mere will-o'-the-wisps of delusion.

I like our translators reading the word *candle – Neither do men light a candle,* for nowadays a candle is the smallest of all lights. We almost despise a candle in these days of the electric light; yet small lights are useful, and tiny lamps have their sphere. God has many small lights; in his great house he has candles as well as stars, and he would not have even a small light wasted. Even the most twinkling ray of light is of God's kindling. Think of that, you who cannot do more than talk to a child or give away a tract for love of his dear name. You are a little light, but if the Lord has given you even a spark of the sacred fire, he means that you should shine. In this world there are many lights, but none too many.

We could not spare the sun, and it would be a calamity if the smallest star were quenched. We cannot spare those modern inventions that so cheer us by turning our city's night into day; but I know we would miss even the glowworm from its dewy haunt in the quiet lane. We cannot afford to lose a ray of light in this misty, foggy, clouded sky of ours. The church and the world need all the light that has been vouchsafed, and much more. I, therefore, would press upon all my brethren and sisters here who may happen to have but one talent the necessity of their putting it out to interest. Your light, my friend, may be but a mite rushlight, but you must not hide it, for all lights are of God, and are sent with a kind and gracious purpose by the great Father of lights.

Note further, that lighting *is a work that needs sustaining.* While lighting is a process performed in a moment, it is also, as a matter of fact, prolonged; for the lamp needs to be trimmed, and it would be ill to light a lamp and leave it to itself. The lamp must have fresh oil from time to time, since by shining it consumes its fuel. Do not any of you, therefore, think if you can fix upon a certain time and say, "I was converted then," that you may live as you like afterwards. God forbid!

The saints prove their conversion by their perseverance, and that perseverance comes from a continual supply of divine grace to their souls. Judge yourselves, then, by this, not so much whether on a certain special occasion you were turned from darkness to light, but are you still *light in the Lord*? Have you oil in your vessels with your lamps? Are you looking unto Jesus? It was well that you looked once, but are you still looking? For that is the great thing.

Remember, it is a present business – looking. It is well that you came to Jesus, but that is merely the beginning; it is *to whom coming,* coming continually, *as unto a living stone* (1 Peter 2:4). Our lungs must have, as we all know, fresh supplies of air. It will profit me nothing that I breathed yesterday; I am dead unless I breathe today. We must have constant food: you ate yesterday, but could you without hunger and weakness go without food today? We continually need to be built up as to our bodies, and it is just the same with our souls, and if we neglect this, if we imagine that something done twenty years ago is all that is needed, we shall make a great mistake. There must be the frequent trimming of the lamp, which is, in effect, a continuation of the lighting.

Once again, let me say that this work of lighting is a work that, when it is done upon a man, *consecrates him entirely to the service of light-giving.* A candle once lit, if it continues lit, will be all consumed in giving light. It is what it was made for – not to be laid by in a glass case and looked at, but to be burned away. Blessed is the man who can say, "My zeal has consumed me." You will say that in the case of the lamp the lamp itself is not consumed. No, but it is consecrated to the one purpose of lighting the house, and it contains the supply of oil by which the flame is fed. The whole of the lamp, whether it be of gold or silver or clay, or whatever it may be, is dedicated to the one purpose of giving light; and if God ever comes and lights you, my dear brother, you are henceforth separated from all other purposes, and appointed to the one calling. You may be a great many other things according to your human calling, but these must be subordinate. I wish that some men kept earthly things much more subordinate than they do.

The first thing in a Christian is his Christianity. The chief business of one whom God has called is that he should live as the elect of God. Look at Christ Jesus; he was a carpenter, but I confess I seldom think of him as such. Rather, it is as the Savior of men, and the servant of God that he comes before my mind. Even thus a Christian man ought so to live if he be a carpenter that the Christian swallows up the carpenter; and if he be a businessman, or a man of letters, or an orator, he ought so to live that the most conspicuous fact about him is that he is a Christian. He is a lamp, and his one business is to shine. You may use a candle for many purposes. I saw a man grease a saw with one the other day, and another made his boots fit for walking in the snow in like manner; but still these are not the objects for which a candle is designed. It has missed the object of its existence if it does not give light.

I suppose on occasions you might use a lamp for a weight, or for some other purpose; but it would not be the suitable instrument for any purpose except that of giving light. Everything is best when fulfilling its proper purpose. Have you ever seen a swan out of water? How ungainly is his walk! What a cumbersome bird he seems to be! But see him on the water. What a fine model for a ship! What grace! What beauty! So it is with the Christian: his beauty is best seen in his proper element; give him any other aim and he is awkward and uncomely. When seeking to instruct and save his fellow man, he is where God would have him, and then all the lines of creating wisdom, and all the beauties of divine grace are manifested in him. Let us take care then about this lighting, that it be a lighting from above, that it be a lighting such as makes the light our own, and that it be a lighting that takes possession of us, and consecrates us entirely, and is perpetually sustained by the visitation of the Spirit of God. So much on that first point.

We will now, in the second place, consider the placing. *Neither do men light a candle, and put it under a bushel.* It is a great point, this placing of a man – it may hide his light or send it further astray. The chief matter is the lighting him, and getting him to have light to give;

but the next most important thing is where to put him when he is lit. Some men, when they first find Christ, are in the wrong place altogether. How can a lamp shine if it be dropped into a river? After the conversion of certain persons their removal becomes necessary. It is significant that when God called Abraham, he did not let him stop in Ur of the Chaldees, and the place for Abraham to shine was not even in Haran; but he had to get into the chosen country and wander as a shepherd prince, for only there and in that character could Abraham shine to the glory of God.

Most men will be wise to stay where they are and shine, but others must undergo a great change of position before they will be able to scatter their light to the extent that the Lord intends for them. That may account, my friend, for your having more trouble since you were converted than you ever had before. You have been left to lie still until now, but you are needed, and so you are fetched out from your hiding. It did not matter where you were when you gave no light, for you were just as well behind a box or in a closet as anywhere else; but now that you are lit, you must be put on a lampstand, and therefore you are undergoing processes of providence that are somewhat painful to you. Our placing, whether it has necessitated removal or not, is largely done by the providence of God: one man is placed here and another there, and it is well for us to look at our position from this point of view. God puts us where we can best serve his cause and bless our age.

If you had your choice, perhaps, if you had to be a streetlamp, you would like to be a lamp in Hyde Park, to shine upon the nobles who pass that way. But the poor souls want lights far more down that blind alley, down that den of a court, where wild Irish are quarreling, or drunkards are murdering their wives. He that loves God, if he had his choice, might sooner choose to shine in the worse place than in the better. "Oh, that I lived in the midst of a warmhearted church!" says one. If you are an earnest, thoroughgoing man, I am glad that you are placed in that dreary village where the people are pretty nearly starved for spiritual life. "What," cries one, "glad that I have to suffer so much?" No, not for that, but because if you are a strong man, you will not suffer, but you will make other people suffer; that is to say, you will make it hard for the minister, and the deacons, and the church to remain in their wretched condition of lukewarmness. I hope you will be the means of arousing them, and bringing them nearer to Christ.

How often a place that appears undesirable will become desirable if we regard it in this light. Providence puts us where we can give the most light, and if our lamp is set up in the midst of darkness, where else should it be? This tabernacle reminds me of those frames of wheels, filled with lamps, that are used at our railway stations. Here we have scores of lamps all burning together, and when first one and then another is dropped through the roof into a carriage and whisked away along the line, though it be to Australia, or America, or India. I am sorry to lose you, but I am glad that you are going where you will do more good than you will do here. Why should you not be scattered abroad like the first believers? Why should not the candles be carried where the darkness is? Why should we keep up an everlasting illumination upon this particular spot, just to gladden our own eyes, instead of lending light to all the world? It is ours to say to others, "There is a candle, let it shine in your houses," or "Here is a lamp, set it up in your tents, that God may bless you thereby."

But though I have thus spoken of Providence, a good deal of our placing is in our own hands. There are ways of placing yourselves – for instance, that mentioned in the text – that may be as ruinous to our influence as if a candle were placed under a bushel; or you can put yourself in a place of advantage, as when a lamp is set upon a lampstand.

First, note the word in *the negative – Neither do men . . . put it under a bushel.* A bushel is a good and useful article. In almost every Eastern house there was a corn measure, here called a *bushel,* though it did not generally measure much more than a peck. This measure was commonly in every house because they ground their own corn, and so were generally dealing with the neighbors. That useful corn measure to me represents the pursuits of ordinary life – the proper and natural avocations of the household. Many men and women hide the candle that God has lit under the bushel of business and domestic cares. But you ask, Is not a housewife to be a housewife? Certainly, but not so much a housewife as to conceal her godliness. Is not the laboring man to work with his hands? Certainly, but not so much to work for the bread that perishes as to miss life eternal. Is not the man of business to give his best attention thereto? Of course he is, but he must see to it that he does not lose his own soul or injure the souls of others. Keep your bushel, nobody asks you to burn it; but do keep it in its place. Subordinate all worldly things to the glory of God. Permit not your possessions or your desires, your pleasures or your cares, to act as a bushel hiding God's light. This happens with a great many. I must ask conscience to be so kind as to preach for you for a minute or two. Will you look at home, dear friends, and see where you place your business and your religion? Which is uppermost? Which is foremost? Is religion your business, or is business your religion? Does your candle shine upon the bushel, or does the bushel hide the candle? I will not dwell upon the question, because it will be well for you to answer it in quiet, each man for himself.

I know how a minister can put his light under a bushel – he can be a mere official and perform service, being nothing more than a performer. The worst thing to do with the gospel is to *parsonificate* it. As soon as we preach as mere officials, we have lost all power; we must speak as men to men. A brother minister one day said to me, "The moment I shut the pulpit door I shut out my natural self." This will never do. A man must be all there when he is serving God, and if ever he is himself, it must be in preaching. We can also cover the candle by using hard words, words that are not hard for educated people, but yet are hard for the bulk of our listeners. We can also use technical creed words, such as we might use in the classroom or in the discussion hall, and these may conceal our meaning from the people.

I know some Christians who put their light under a bushel by being excessively bashful and shamefaced. They are not so dreadfully shy when five-pound notes are to be made; but if anything is to be said for Christ, then they blush and stammer. Oh, that they could overcome this hindrance. Others put their light under a bushel by inconsistency: they do not act as Christians should act, and when people see their bad works, they do not glorify God. God forbid that in the house our darkness should be more conspicuous than our light. Some, I fear, cover their light under the bushel of indifference: they do not seem to care how things go with the cause and kingdom of Christ. They look well to the state of their flocks and herds, but for the house of the Lord they have small concern. I pray you, dear friends, do not hide your light in any way. Let not your lawful callings, your relationships, your sicknesses, your literary pursuits, or your personal sorrows become so exaggerated as to conceal the divine light within your soul.

The text is, however, *positive*. Put yourself on a candlestick or on a lampstand. What must that be? A candlestick is an appropriate exhibitor of the light, and each man should make an appropriate confession of his faith. The best way is prescribed in God's Word. It is written, *He that believeth and is baptized shall be saved.* Take care that when you have faith, you declare it in the ordained manner; for he that with his heart believes and with his mouth makes confession of him shall be saved. O lamp, do not say, "I will shine, but I will lie upon the floor and do it." No, your place is on the stand that is provided. Dear Christian friend, join the church so that you may be placed where you will be in order with the arrangements of the divine household.

A lampstand should also be something that makes the lamp sufficiently visible. If you do not come out and diffuse your light willingly and cheerfully, it is very likely that the master of the house will fetch you out. Providence will arrange that the light shall not be hidden. See what the Lord did for his church years ago; he allowed her to be persecuted into publicity. What a lampstand was found for Christianity in the martyrdoms of the Colosseum, in the public burnings by pagans and Roman Catholics, and in all the other modes by which believers in Christ were forced into flame. When there was no printing press, when there were scarce opportunities of making the gospel public compared with those of today, the Lord caused his witnesses to stand before rulers and kings, and there publish in the most public places the word of his salvation.

Persecution built the lighthouse, and the divine love set up aloft the burning and shining light of sacred truth. You may find that God will make such a candlestick for you. You shall be forced into testimony in your family by the opposition of those around you unless you take other and happier methods. We ought to be valiant for the truth, and speak of it with all carefulness, but without limitation.

I long for the day when the precepts of the Christian religion shall be the rule among all classes of men, in all transactions. I often hear it said, "Do not bring religion into politics." This is precisely where it ought to be brought, and set there in the face of all men as on a candlestick.

I would have the cabinet and the members of parliament do the work of the nation as before the Lord, and I would have the nation, either in making war or peace, consider the matter by the light of righteousness. We are to deal with other nations about this or that upon the principles of the New Testament. I thank God that I have lived to see the attempt made in one or two instances, and I pray that the principle may become dominant and permanent. We have had enough of clever men without conscience; let us now see what honest, God-fearing men will do.

But we are told that we must study "British interests," as if it were not always to a nation's truest interest to do righteousness. "But we must carry out our policy." I say, No! Let the policies that are founded on wrong be cast like idols to the moles and to the bats. Stand to that most admirable of policies – *As ye would that men should do to you, do ye also to them likewise* (Luke 6:31). Whether we are kings, or queens, or prime ministers, or members of parliament, or crossing sweepers, this is our rule if we are Christians.

Yes, and bring religion into your business, and let the light shine in the factory and in the countinghouse. Then we shall not have quite so much china clay in the fabric by which to cheat the foreigner, nor shall we see cheap and nasty articles described as of best quality, nor any other of the dodges in trade that everybody seems to practice nowadays. You tradespeople and manufacturers are very much one like the other in this: there are tricks in all trades, and one sees it everywhere. I believe everybody to be honest until he is found out; but whether there are any so incorruptible that they will never be found absent, this witness does not say, for I am not a judge.

Do not put your candle under a bushel, but let it shine, for it was intended that it should be seen. Religion ought to be as much seen at our own table as at the Lord's Table. Godliness should as much influence the House of Commons as the Assembly of Divines. God grant that the day may come when the mischievous division between secular and religious things shall no more be heard of, for in all things Christians are to glorify God, according to the precept, *Whether therefore ye eat, or drink, or whatsoever ye do, do all to the glory of God* (1 Corinthians 10:31).

Our time has gone, but I must detain you a little while I speak upon the shining: *Let your light so shine before men.*

When a candle shines it is because it cannot help it. Shining is the natural result of possessing light, and I want you, dear brethren, to exert a holy influence upon others, because the grace of God is really in you. Some men make desperate attempts to *appear* good, but they would be far more successful if they would seek to *be* good. Grace must be in a man as a living fountain, and then rivers of living water will flow from him. The natural result of a renewed heart is a renewed life, and the natural result of a renewed life is that men see it and glorify God.

Shining, however, is not altogether a thing of necessity so as to forbid our attention to it, for the text demands care from us. *Let your light so shine.* I must ask the printer to put the two letters *s* and *o* in very large capitals. "Let your light SO shine" – let it so shine that men *may see your good works, and glorify your Father which is in heaven.* You will not shine in the best manner, though you may have grace in your heart, unless you abound in prayerful, watchful, and earnest care. You must guard heart and lip and hand, or your light will not *so* shine before men as could be desired. Your light will need trimming. Neglect it not.

The shining that comes from the Christian is here described as *good works*. Good talk is very well, but it takes a great deal of talk to light a room. Good works are the *splendor,* the light of God. What works are good works? I would answer – upright actions, honest dealings, sincere behavior. When a man is scrupulously true, and sternly faithful, all right-minded persons admit that his works are good works. Good works are works of love, unselfish works, works done for the benefit of others and the glory of God. Deeds of charity, kindness, and brotherly love are good works, as are also careful attendance to duty, and all service honestly done, together with all courses that promote the moral and spiritual good of our fellow man. Works of devotion in which you prove that you love God and his Christ, that you love the gospel, that you desire to spread the kingdom of Christ – these may not be so highly valued by ordinary people, but they are exceedingly good works. Let these good and true things abound in you, and shine out from you; do them not out of excessive display, but do them nevertheless without shame.

Good works, like the shining of a candle, have good effects. A candle cheers the gloom. What a comfort it is when you have long been wandering in the dark to spy out a twinkling candle in a cottage window!

A candle directs and guides men, and by its illumination it instructs them. In its light they see, discern, and discover. He who acts teaches. The man who lives Christianity preaches it. He is the truest evangelist whose life brings glory to God and goodwill to men.

But note, it is said that *it giveth light unto all that are **in the house*** (emphasis added), so that when we are lit from on high, we are first to shine at home. It is not abroad alone that we should make our Christianity known, but chiefly at the fireside, to those who are *in the house.* Some have a very little house, they live in a couple of rooms with a small family; let them take care that they have grace enough to make a few thoroughly happy, which is not always the easiest thing in the world. Others have a large family; may they have grace enough to influence the whole. A few have large workshops, and employ many hands, and these ought to exercise a holy influence over all their workfolks. Some of us are preachers of the gospel, and have a large house in which to shine; we shall need more of the oil of grace than others so that we may give light to the whole of our house, and that grace is to be had. The whole world is a house in which the church is the candle; and, therefore, the members of the church should so shine, each one in his place, that the whole world shall be filled with the knowledge of the glory of God.

The text says that the candle gives light to *all* that are in the house. Some professing Christians give light only to a part of the house. I have known women who are very good to all but their husbands, and these they nag from morning to night, so that they give no light to them. I have known husbands who are so often out at meetings that they neglect home, and thus their wives miss the light. I have known masters who are utterly indifferent about their servants, and mistresses who quite forget to seek the good of their maids. If our light be in good order, it will illuminate the parlor and the kitchen, the drawing room and the scullery, shining upon all that are in the house. Candles do not shed all their light either that way or this, but they shine in all directions. A Christian should be an all-around man, blessing all, both great and small, who come in contact with him.

The object of our shining is not that men may see how good we are, nor even see us at all, but that they may see grace in us and God in us, and cry, "What a Father these people must have." Is not this the first time in the New Testament that God is called our Father? Is it not unusual that the first time it peeps out should be when men are seeing the good works of his children? The fatherhood of God is best seen in the holiness of saints. When men see that light is good, they bless the source of that light, and seeing that it comes from the Father of lights, they glorify his name.

I have had to hasten over all this, but I pray God to make it nonetheless effective for the stirring up of every Christian here to use all the light he has. It is a dark world, and it seems to get darker, for the emissaries of Satan are going about thirsting to quench every light. Look well to your lamps, look well to your lamps, you virgin souls. Trim well the flame, and go you forth even into the black night to meet the Bridegroom. Lift high your torches into the very face of darkness, and make men see that God the Father is still in the midst of his people.

The Venerable Bede, when he was interpreting this text, said that Christ Jesus brought the light of Deity into the poor lantern of our humanity, and then set it upon the candlestick of his church so that the whole house of the world might be lit up thereby. So indeed it is. The reason why there is light in the church is that those who are in the dark may see. Churches do not exist for themselves, but for the world at large. Have you thought of this, you professing Christians? You are blessed so that you may be a blessing. Take heed that you behave right. You go to Christ's wedding feast, and you are glad to hear that he turns water into wine, and you are ready to bless him that he has kept the best wine until now. But oh, you servants of God, remember what is said: *Draw out now, and bear* (John 2:8). These are your orders. There is the God-made wine – *Draw out now, and bear.* Receive from Christ's fullness, and distribute to others.

Neglect not your duty as servants at your Lord's great feast. Your Master has taken the bread, and has blessed and broken it, and then he has given it to you. Is that the end of the process? Do you stand there and munch your own personal morsel with a miserable self-satisfaction? No, if you be indeed disciples of Christ, you will remember that the next words are: *and the disciples to the multitude. And they did all eat* (Matthew 14:19-20). Break then your bread among the hungry that surround you. Take the whole loaf of Christ, and rightly divide and distribute it, and you shall have as much left as at the first; yes, more, for you shall gather of the fragments many baskets full. Only see to it that you freely give what you have freely received, lest hoarded manna breed corruption, lest a canker come upon your hoarded gold and silver, and lest your very souls grow moldy even to reeking rottenness before God, because you have not drawn out your souls unto the hungry, nor sought to teach those who are perishing for lack of knowledge.

The Baptist Missionary Society will enable you to teach the heathen. Take a share in it. There, make the collection! Do your best!

Chapter 7

The Eye and the Light

*No man, when he hath lighted a candle, putteth it in a
secret place, neither under a bushel, but on a candlestick, that they which come in may see the light. The light
of the body is the eye: therefore when thine eye is single,
thy whole body also is full of light; but when thine eye is
evil, thy body also is full of darkness. Take heed therefore that the light which is in thee be not darkness. If
thy whole body therefore be full of light, having no part
dark, the whole shall be full of light, as when the bright
shining of a candle doth give thee light.* (Luke 11:33-36)

In this parable, our Lord Jesus Christ is the light. Some saw his brightness, and were even dazzled by it, as was that woman who cried, *Blessed is the womb that bare thee, and the paps which thou hast sucked* (Luke 11:27). The malicious saw not his light, but even dared to credit his miracles to the Prince of Darkness. Others professed to see so little light in him that they demanded a sign from heaven. Our Lord's constant answer was to go shining on. He was meant to be observed, even as a lamp is intended to be seen. A lamp is not lit to be placed in a cellar, nor to be hidden under a bushel; a lamp is lit on purpose so that all who come into the house may see the light. Even so, our Lord Jesus Christ could not be hidden. In the narrow circle of the Holy Land, he shone so clearly that Gentiles came to the brightness of his rising.

Yet, to make him seen to the ends of the earth, he needed to be set on the lampstand. He was lifted up by crucifixion, and immediately he was further raised by resurrection. He was lifted up from earth to heaven at his ascension, and in another sense he was set on high by the descent of the Holy Spirit and the widespread ministry of his servants. Our Lord was thus taken from under the bushel of the obscurity that attached to his humble origin, brought away from the dark cellar of the despised Jewish nation, and set out in the open, where Greek and Roman, Barbarian and Scythian, might rejoice in his light. It is our duty to keep his name and his truth ever before the world, waiting for the time when every eye shall see him on the throne of his glory.

Our Lord would have all men behold the light of his gospel; for the text says *that they which come in may see the light*. Whosoever comes into the church, or even into the world, should be met with this lamp; for this gospel is to be preached to every creature under heaven. The mighty deeds of his salvation were not done in a corner: they are for worldwide observation. He that has eyes to see let him see. If you do not see Jesus, it is not because he has hidden himself in darkness, but because your eyes are blinded. The light that streams from the face of Jesus is meant for human eyes. The moderated brightness of the Mediator's glory suits those eyes, which are bidden to look to him and live. Light is not for the rich, the wise, and the strong, but for men as men. The doctrines of our Lord Jesus Christ are not meant to be the monopoly of a few learned doctors; they are the common inheritance of those who labor and are heavy-laden. As the morning breaks for all weary, watching eyes, so shines the light of the glorious gospel for all who sit in darkness and long for the light of God.

Beloved, the great thing to be desired is that the light that is so freely given forth by the Lord Jesus may become light within our souls. There he stands, as the lamp placed upon the lampstand, conspicuous to all; but we need that the light outside in the room may become light inside, within the soul. Nothing more truly needs light than our inner man. We are, by nature, as a lantern with the candle blown out. Whether we will believe it or not, by nature we are in a thick Egyptian night. Well says the apostle: *Ye were sometimes darkness*. Much is said about the light of conscience, but in many this is but a glimmering slender candle whose beams are "not light, but darkness visible." The light of nature is dimmed by so many surroundings, and has so little oil to sustain it, that it leads no man to eternal life, unless there be added to it light from above – the light of grace, the clear shining of the Holy Spirit.

Light is absolutely essential to spiritual life. Ignorance is not the mother of devotion, but of superstition. Knowledge, grace, and truth are the nurses of true faith. The light of God is needful to the life of God. We must know Christ, we must be illuminated by his Holy Spirit, we must have fellowship with the Father's truth, or else we are dead as well as dark. Light within we must have, or the light outside will not benefit us. Upon that subject we will speak at this time. May God grant us the light of his Spirit; for it would be idle for us to try to explain the action of light while we ourselves are in darkness. Shine within, O Holy Spirit, that we speak not of theory, but of actual experience!

First, we will consider *how the light enters. The light of the body is the eye: therefore when thine eye is single, thy whole body also is full of light.* Secondly, we shall note *how this light may be perverted. When thine eye is evil, thy body also is full of darkness. Take heed therefore that the light which is in thee be not darkness.* In conclusion, we shall observe *how the light acts within. If thy whole body therefore be full of light, having no part dark, the whole shall be full of light, as when the bright shining of a candle doth give thee light.*

First, then, consider how the light enters the soul. Into the body the light enters through the eye. A man without an eye might as well be without the sun, so far as light is concerned. The eye is as needful as the lamp, if a man is to see. The most brilliant light that ever has been invented, or ever can be discovered, will be of no use to the person who has no eye; therefore it is true: *The light of the body is the **eye*** (emphasis added). It is most important to attend to that which is the eye of the inner man; for in vain does Christ himself shine if his light cannot enter our souls. The condition of the eye of the mind is of the utmost importance: our light or our darkness will depend upon it. The eye of the soul may be viewed as the understanding, the conscience, the motive, or the heart. It would not be possible to confine it to any one of these names.

I venture to call it "the intent of the mind," or, if you will, "the aim of the heart," the honesty of the understanding. When God has given a man a true intent to see the light of the gospel, he has in that honest intent furnished him with an eye for the heavenly light. If the Holy Spirit makes us truly willing to know the truth, he has cleared the mental eye. The worst of it is that men have no will to see the light of God; their foolish heart is darkened, and therefore they do not understand, but altogether misrepresent the doctrine of the Lord Jesus. The battle of grace is with man's unwillingness to see those truths against which he is naturally hostile. If a man wills to see the honest truth, and submits himself to the enlightenment of the Holy Spirit, he will not be left in darkness. When a man does not want to see, he cannot see; when he is determined not to learn, when truth is unpalatable to him, when he designedly twists it from its meaning, then his eye is diseased, and the light is hindered from its due effect.

Many things darken the eye of the soul. One of the most common is *prejudice*. The man conceives that he has light already. His father, his grandfather, his great-grandfather, and previous generations were brought up in a certain religion, and therefore it must be right. Whether the lamp gives light or not is not the question; it is the family lamp, and he will have no other. He will not inquire; he is quite sure, and wants no evidence. When the light of God comes to him, he at once repels it. He cannot be disturbed, and therefore he will not hear, nor read, nor consider the matter; he is satisfied to let things be as they are. The very supposition that he may be wrong he regards as an insult, maliciously invented by an uncharitable mind. What is to be done with one so blindfolded? Are there not many such?

Sloth, too, is a great blinder of the eye. It draws down the eyelid, and shuts out the fight by the spirit of slumber. The man does not care what the gospel is or is not. Like Pilate, he asks, *What is truth?* (John 18:38), but he never waits for an answer. It is too much trouble to some people to think, to search the Scriptures, and to pray. They have no heart for a process so troublesome. "No," says the person engrossed in the present concerns of this world, "I have other fish to fry. I go my way to my farm, and to my merchandise. Let graceless bigots fight about creeds and the like; it matters not one jot what a man believes." Thus do many abide in the blackest darkness, because it is too much trouble to open the shutters and draw up the blinds. Ah me! how dark are they who prefer a lazy ease to the light of God!

The light is often shut out by *gross error.* I cannot go over the list of the favorite errors of the present hour, for that list has grown too long for one day's reading. Deceptively taught in selected phrases, cunningly supported by a dreamy science, and adorned with certain great names, errors come to us nowadays as respectable forms of thought. Falsehoods that we heard of when we were children – but only heard of them as awful heresies, long ago decayed and thrown into the limbo of worthless and mischievous imaginations – these are now refashioned, freshened up with touches of bright color, and brought out as advanced ideas.

When any of these are permitted to occupy the mind, as they so commonly do nowadays, the old gospel is no longer seen, because the eye is inflamed by the incoming of a foreign and irritating substance. Can it be that what was true a hundred years ago is not true now? Can it be that the gospel that saved souls in the days of the apostles cannot save souls now? Is it so, that some men are wiser than God, and are qualified to sit in judgment upon prophets and apostles? Surely, judicial blindness has happened to this generation; the chaff of their own folly has darkened their eyes, and Christ is hidden from them.

One thing darkens the eye more than any other, and that is *the love of sin.* Nine times out of ten, allowed sin is the cataract that darkens the mental eye. Men cannot see truth because they love falsehood. The gospel is not seen because it is too pure for their loose lives and lewd thoughts. Christ's holy example is too severe for the worldly; his Spirit is too pure for lovers of carnal pleasure. When people reject the doctrines of the gospel, they also tolerate slackness of morals, and give predominance to the customs of the world. How can men see, when sin has pricked the very eyeballs of the mind? *How can ye believe,* said Christ, *which receive honour one of another?* (John 5:44).

The love of worldly honor prevented the Pharisees from believing in the lowly Messiah. When sin, like a handful of mud, seals up the eye, you need not wonder that the man becomes an agnostic, a doubter, a quibbler. To have a clear eye one must have a clean heart. The pure in heart shall see God, and therefore the pure in heart see God's truth so as to appreciate it and delight in it. Oh, that the Spirit of God may wash the filth out of our eyes, that we may walk in the light, as God is in the light.

Pride, too, is a great darkener of the soul's eye. When a man admires himself, he never adores God. He that is taken up with the conceit of his own righteousness will never see the righteousness of Christ. If you believe yourself to be pure, you will never prize the blood that cleanses from all sin. If you believe yourself to be already perfect, you will not prize the Holy Spirit, the Sanctifier. No man cries for grace until he perceives his own need of it. If, therefore, we be puffed up with the notion that we are rich and increased in goods, we shall never see the riches of grace that are treasured up in Christ Jesus. The light of God dwells not with human self-sufficiency. A man's own shadow is very often the means of keeping him in the dark.

Self-seeking, in every form, is a sad cause of obscuring the light of the soul. Self-seeking, in the grosser form of covetousness, makes men grope in the daytime. The glitter of gold is injurious to the eye. How could Judas see the beauty of Christ when he saw such value in the thirty pieces of silver? How can a man set store by a future heaven when a present fortune is heaven enough for him? Wealth repays its worshippers with blinded eyes. Self does the same when it appears as ambition, desire of honor and respect, or a wish to have a finger in one's own salvation. The proud desire to share the glory of our salvation with free grace prevents the entrance of the light of God. Self, in the form of magnifying the nobility of human nature, extolling the grandeur of our common humanity, and all that, is a very blinding thing. How can a man that has his eye upon self have any sight for Jesus? Of all anti-christs, self is the hardest to overcome. It is written, *He must increase, but I must decrease* (John 3:30); but if proud self will not endure a decrease, how can I see Christ increasing? There is no room for him in my heart. Appreciation of self leads to depreciation of the Lord Jesus.

Multitudes are kept in darkness through *fear of men*. They dare not see. They feel bound to think as the fashion goes – and there is a fashion of opinions as well as of coats and bonnets. If you resolve to hold fast the faith once delivered to the saints you will be regarded as antiquated, and you will be as much pointed out for your faith as you would be for your dress if you should walk down the street in the costume of the reign of Queen Elizabeth. To many it would be a great sin to be peculiar. They never think for themselves; in fact, they are mentally shiftless. They ask their way of a certain person supposed to be a deeper student than themselves; of him they inquire what they ought to believe, disbelieve, praise, or blame. I remember well a man who never knew whether he liked a sermon until he had asked a certain wise, old gentleman whether it was a good one or not; he had no home-grown judgment, he imported his ideas. His brains, for safekeeping, were placed in another person's head. This is a very convenient thing, and saves a good deal of headache; but it has its drawbacks.

Some persons put all their thinking out, and have it done for them by the dozen. But he that would have God's light knows that it comes not to the coward who fears the frown of a mortal, and makes man his god. God could have given to the crowd a common judgment, and have left us to be guided by a central authority, if he had thought it right so to do; but having given to each individual an understanding, he expects us to use it, and to an honest personal use of understanding he gives the light. The eye of the sparrow or of the ant may be very small, yet it sees the great light if it be a healthy and clear eye. Pray, then, for grace, that you may search out for yourselves the truth of God, free from the fear of man that brings a snare. Let us never inquire, *Have any of the rulers or of the Pharisees believed?* (John 7:48). Whether the rulers have or have not believed, let us follow the Lamb to whatever place he goes, and rejoice in that pure light that flows from him.

God save you, dear friends, from having your eye injured by any of the mischiefs I have mentioned. There are legions more of these blinding things; may grace guard you from them! May God give you a "single eye," by which is meant an eye that does not look at two things at a time – a mind that is free from sinister motives, and from anything that would cause you to choose falsehood rather than truth, and wrong rather than right. God grant that we may have a desire to be right, a resolute plan to know the truth as it is in Jesus, and to feel and act in sincere conformity with that! Oh, to be sincere, simplehearted, child-like, and true! We want neither great genius nor sparkling wit, but we need an unsophisticated mind; for so the light gets entrance into the soul through the Spirit of God.

Secondly, let us consider how the light may be perverted. Some men might have light enough, but their eye is in such an evil condition that the light is turned into darkness. I suppose that in the natural world light could not actually become darkness; but in the spiritual kingdom it is certainly so. *When thine eye is evil, thy body also is full of darkness. Take heed therefore that the light which is in thee be not darkness.* Hear, my brethren, and take heed.

A man has heard the gospel of free grace and dying love; he has heard a message full of love concerning the forgiveness of sin, and pardon bought with blood, and freely given to him that believes. The doctrine of justification by faith has been clearly explained to him. He believes firmly in these great evangelical truths, and calls them glorious and precious. But he draws an inference from this teaching that is ruinous to his soul. He considers that, after all, sin is of small consequence, and he may indulge in it freely, for God is merciful, and grace is infinite. At some time or other he will repent and believe in Jesus, and then he will be set right, however flagrantly he may have offended. God is gracious, and therefore he may be sinful. God freely forgives, and therefore he may recklessly offend. This is to turn light into darkness. Such turning of the grace of God into foulness is disgraceful. Words cannot set forth the hideous ingratitude of such a depraved argument. We may justly say of a man who thus turns light into darkness, "His damnation is just." Yet no doubt there are many such who silently, in their own hearts, draw from the goodness of God a license to sin.

Ah, my friend! If your eye be in this condition, the more freely we preach to you the gospel of the grace of God, the more surely will you go from sin to sin. This is terrible. O false hearts! What shall I do with you? You make me wish to be dumb, lest I minister to your condemnation. In the lowest hell you are digging for yourselves a deeper hell; you use the promises of mercy as the instruments of your own destruction. What! Can you hang yourselves nowhere but on the cross? Can you drown yourselves nowhere but in the waters of Siloah? What has come to you, that you are so infatuated as to find your death in the gospel that is ordained for life?

Let me set before you another form of this evil. A man perceives the great value of the means of grace, but he goes further and misuses them. Having been brought up religiously, he has a deep respect for the ministers of God's house, for the services of the sanctuary, and especially for the two ordinances that Christ has established in his church – baptism and the Lord's Supper. He reverences the Sabbath and the

THE EYE AND THE LIGHT

inspired Word, and the church and all its sacred ministries. But it may be that he proceeds from a due regard of these things to a superstitious trust in them, making of them what God has never made of them; thus his light becomes darkness. He regards attendance at public worship as a substitute for inward religion: he looks upon membership with a church as a certificate of salvation. He may be so foolish as to speak of baptism as an ordinance whereby he was made a member of Christ, and a child of God; and of the Lord's Supper as a saving ordinance, or even as a sacrifice for the living and the dead.

When instructive symbols are perverted into instruments of priest-craft, the light is turned into darkness. By multitudes, in these days, aids to faith are degraded into the machinery of superstition. The church, which is our mother and nurse, is made into an antichrist, and men look to her for salvation instead of looking wholly and alone to the Lord Jesus Christ. Outward modes of worship and instruction may be very beneficial, but if they are allowed to usurp the confidence of the soul, they may bring about disease and death. When a man's religion becomes his destruction, how sure is that destruction!

I have known many who have gone another way. They have said, "I care very little about the shape or form of religion. A sincere spirit is everything. *The letter killeth, but the spirit giveth life.*" Such a man professes to clutch at the soul of things, but I have seen him grow indifferent in creed and licentious in life. He believes everything to have some measure of truth in it; every evil practice to have some good point about it. This is a poisonous atmosphere for any man to breathe. Hear him talk, if you would see how the worse can be made to seem the better. Nothing to him is fixed truth, nor even settled right. He is like the chameleon, which takes its color from the changing light around it. This he calls "liberty," but assuredly it is not the liberty by which Christ makes men free. Say, rather, it is the light of charity turned into the darkness of indifference. How great is this darkness! How many are deceived by it! After all, there is light and there is darkness, and they are not the same thing. There is truth, taught of God, and there is a lie, which is the devil's own; and these will never sit at the same table. There is a blessing for the preacher of the truth; but if any man preaches another gospel, for him there is a curse that none can reverse.

I have also seen this light turned to darkness in the case of the student who has gathered great knowledge, and enrolled himself among the learned. He begins to criticize. Do not condemn him for that; he judges very properly at first, and he criticizes things that ought to be criticized, but he does not stop there. Once having his critical faculties aroused, he is like a boy with a new knife: he must cut something or other. Nothing comes in his way more often than the Scriptures, and he must have a cut at them. He whittles at Genesis; he makes a gash in Deuteronomy; he halves Isaiah; he takes slices out of the Gospels; and he cuts the Epistles into slivers. You see, he has so sharp a knife that he must use it. By and by, from a critic he advances to an irreverent faultfinder, and from that to an utter unbeliever, hard in the mouth and stiff in the neck. His light has blinded him. He has taken his own eye to pieces that he might study its anatomy, and henceforth the light will be of no more use to him than to the dead.

We have seen the light turned to darkness in a further sense; hear and understand. There is a blessed light called the full assurance of faith: the more we have of it the better. Blessed is that man who never doubts his God, who hangs with holy confidence upon the eternal promise and the unchangeable covenant, and is never perplexed through unbelief. He walks in the light of God, and enjoys divine fellowship. But I have seen something very similar to this holy confidence that has been before the Lord a very different matter.

Assurance has been counterfeited by presumption. The man has taken for granted that he is a child of God when he is not, and he has appropriated privileges that are none of his. He has supposed himself to be in the covenant when he has neither part nor lot in the matter; and without repentance, without the new birth, and without saving faith, he has dared to boast of those sacred securities that belong only to the heirs of grace, sanctified in Christ Jesus. Dreadful is the case of the man who has presumed to hope for heaven while living an ungodly life; boasting of freedom from all fear, when, indeed, he was destitute of all hope.

I have also seen the light turned to darkness in quite another manner. Sweet and soft is the light of holy fear: it is as the twilight of the evening. It is a light that comes from God, when a man is afraid to sin, when he fears lest he should grieve the Spirit of God, when he trembles lest in anything he should stray from the teaching of his heavenly Father. But then this light may be corrupted into despicable dread, despondency, and despair. Introspection, or looking within, may degenerate into a morbid habit: under its influence, the soul may refuse to look to Christ, and may enshroud itself in the gloom of remorse. Truth may be distorted until it takes a most alarming shape, and the soul, in sullen despair, refuses to be comforted, refuses to believe in the Son of God.

Do you wonder that our Lord seemed to hold up his hands in astonishment as he said, *If therefore the light that is in thee be darkness, how great is that darkness!* (Matthew 6:23). If that which should lead misleads, how misled you will be! If your better part turns out to be evil, how evil must you be! See to it then, dear friends, as before the living God, that you have a clear eye, and that the light of Christ comes streaming into your soul in all its glorious purity and power.

I close by coming to the third and most important point: how the light acts when it comes within. If the eye be right, healthy, and clear, there is no laborious work for that eye to do to obtain the light. When the sun is shining, if you wish for light, you simply open your eyes, and you have light at once. You do not have to rub the eye, or work it into some unusual position. Let the outward light come to the eye, and at once it enters it, and conveys an image to the mind. When the eye is healthy, it takes pleasure in the light, and with delight conveys the image of things external to the mind within.

If the Lord, in his great grace, has made your eye healthy, so that you desire only to know the truth, and to be yourself true, then without toil you will perceive truth, and the image thereof will readily appear before your mind. The light is willing enough to enter when the window of the soul allows its admission. When that light comes in, you will know it. No man passes from his natural darkness into heavenly light without being aware that a great change has taken place. Beloved, I will try to show you how the holy light acts when it enters our nature!

When it first comes in *it reveals* much that was before unperceived. If a room has been long shut up, and kept in darkness, the light has a startling effect. You may have hurried through that room with a candle, but you never stayed to look, and therefore did not notice the state of things. The room did not strike you as being very unpleasant, though it smelled a little stale and rusty; but now that you have pulled back the shutters and drawn up the blinds, the light has made the mold and dust very manifest. That black festoon of spiders' webs; those insects that hurry out of the light; that all-encrusting dust – these had been overlooked. The room cannot be permitted to remain in such a state. What a change is demanded! All hands are summoned to clean out the den, and turn it into a healthy chamber fit to be inhabited.

The light of heaven reveals a thousand sins, and causes their removal. The first effect of the light of God in the soul is painfully unpleasant; it makes you loathe yourself, and almost wish that you had never been born. Things grow worse and worse to our consciousness as the light shines more and more. Beloved, we wish it to be so. We would have no part kept in the dark. We would have every idol discovered and broken, every secret chamber of imagery exposed to the sun, and then destroyed. Is it not so? Do you wish to keep the light from any one part of your nature? Do you not much rather desire that the light should search you through and through, and lay bare all the deceitfulness of the heart, and all the falseness of the depraved mind?

As that light continues to enter, *it gradually illuminates* each faculty of the mind. The will, by nature, prefers the darkness: the man claims the right to act as he pleases, and to give no reasons for his waywardness. When the light of God enters the soul, the Lord Jesus becomes altogether lovely, and then the sacred light falls on the proud will, and the man sees that it is evil and perverse, and he cries, "O Lord Jesus, not my will, but yours be done." This same light falls on the outward life that is ruled by the will, and the conduct and conversation become bright with the light of love. The judgment feels the inner illumination, and decides according to the law of truth and righteousness. With the judgment the delight is lit up also, and the heart rejoices in the law of the Lord.

The light is poured in upon the conscience, and now that poor, half-blinded thing issues edicts and gives forth verdicts that are according to the oracles of God. What a difference between a natural conscience and a conscience instructed by God, and enlightened by his Word! There remains much more to be done in this direction than many of us suspect. We may be living unconsciously in evils for which our consciences have never once accused us. Godly men, in old time, persecuted those who differed from them, and thought it a duty to do so; they even called toleration a crime. The best of men owned Negro slaves, and were not conscious of wrong. When Mr. Whitefield left certain Negroes to the Orphan House, he did not dream that he was violating the rights of man; in fact, he was very careful for their present and future welfare. Conscience does not tolerate slavery now.

Do you not think that a great enlightenment has taken place upon the drink question? Is not similar light needed as to war, as to wage-paying and wage-earning, and a thousand other things? It is a happy thing that we have received a light that will shine brighter and brighter unto the perfect day. There is nothing hidden within us that this light will not manifest; and so, as one by one we see our imperfections, we shall cry for grace to remove them, and thus we shall grow in holiness through the grace of God.

This same light, falling on the memory, awakens repentance for our faults and gratitude for God's goodness. Shining on our thoughts, it makes them sparkle with the beauty of holiness; shining upon our emotions, it makes them flash and glow with love to God and heavenly things. A soul is a fine object when thus lit up! The holy light falls on our motives, and unveils the secret heart of all our actions. You do right, but this light shows you why you do right. You are a friend to man, but why? You are a Christian professor, but are you sincere? The light makes short work with that which did not flow from a pure motive. This light falls also on the spirit in which a deed was done, and here much is seen that some would rather not see.

Did you ever have the light of God brought to bear upon your imagination? Imagination is the playroom of the soul. Here many a man considers that he is without law. "Surely," says he, "thought is free." The man gloats over sins that he would fear to commit; he finds a pleasure in thinking over lusts that his circumstances compel him to avoid. In the dark chambers of imagination, the heart commits adulteries, murders, thefts, and all manner of evil acts. When the light falls here, the man shudders as he learns that as he thinks in his heart, so he is. He trembles as he perceives that the fond imagination of sin is sin. Then is the floor of imagination purged, and the foul dust and chaff are driven into the fire. Inclination then gleams in the light of

God, and imagination, washed in the brass basin, sings songs on her stringed instruments unto the God of her salvation who has brought her out of darkness into his marvelous light.

Brethren, we need the light to shine in upon our tempers. We know some Christian people who will not let you mention their tempers; they have taken out a license to be as arrogant as they like, on the ground of "it is their constitution." "No," they say, "I cannot help being passionate. My mother was a very quick-tempered woman, and I am naturally in that way. There's no help for it." Let the light in upon that unseemly thing. If what you say is true, write it down in black and white that you are an unruly vixen, and must be so all your life. What! Do you not like it? If it is true, let the light in upon it. Let it be known to your own self and to others that you are a mad dog, and that there is no curing you. Are you angry with me for suggesting it? I am only taking you at your word. Do not say, "I cannot help having a bad temper." Friend, you must help it. Pray God to help you to overcome it at once, for either you must kill it, or it will kill you. You cannot carry a bad temper into heaven. They will have none of your passions in the Father's house above. Let in the light of Christ's love on it, and the vile thing will be made to die. It is a night bird; it cannot bear the light of grace and love.

Live near to Jesus, and his compassion will destroy your evil passion. Try it.

Your desires, your hopes, your fears, your aspirations should all be set in the light, and what a joy it will be when they all glitter in it! "No part dark" – what a wonderful condition! Some professing Christians appear to have a little light in the upper rooms; they have notions in their heads, and ideas on their tongues, but alas! the first floor is dark, very dark. From their common conversation the light of God is absent. Enter at the door, and you cannot see your way into the passage, or up the stairs; the light is up aloft, but not in the dwelling rooms.

Oh, for light in the region of the heart! Oh, for light upon the household talk, and the business conversation! From attic to cellar may the whole houses of our humanity be lit up! This is the true work of grace, when the whole man is brought into the light, and no part is left to languish in the darkness. Then are we the children of light, when we abide in the light, and have no fellowship with darkness. Then is the distinction seen between Israel and Egypt; for while all Egypt sat in a darkness that might be felt, in the land of Goshen there was light.

Where this light comes it gives *certainty;* we cease to doubt, and we know whom we have believed. With this comes *direction;* we see our way, and how to walk in it. We pursue a plain path, and are no more in a maze. *This is the way, walk ye in it* (Isaiah 30:21) is sounded in our ears as the light reveals to us the narrow way that leads to life eternal.

This fight, when it dwells in the heart, *brings good cheer* with it. Darkness is sad, light brings delight. Did you never travel by a train that passed through a tunnel, but was destitute of a single lamp? Somebody has struck a match, and lit a candle, and all eyes have turned towards him. In a small way he was a benefactor: all eyes are glad of light. Oh, what a sweet thing is the light of the Holy Spirit to one that has been long in the darkness of ignorance, sorrow, and despair!

A poor boy who was put down in the coal mine to close a door after the coal wagons had passed by was forced to sit there all alone, hour after hour, in the dark. He was a gracious child; and when one said to him, "Are you not weary with sitting so long in the dark?" he said, "Yes, I do get tired; but sometimes the men give me a bit of candle, and when I get a light I sing." So do we. When we get a light we sing. Glory be to God, he is our light and our salvation, and therefore we sing. O child of God, when your eye is clear, and the light of God fills every part of your being, then you sing, and sing again, and feel that you can never be done singing on earth, until you begin singing in heaven.

The text has perplexed many a learned reader; and therefore you will not wonder that I confess that it has puzzled me many times. See what it says: *If thy whole body therefore be full of light, having no part dark, the whole shall be full of light.* Is not this saying the same thing? The Holy Spirit would not use a needless repetition of a word, nor utter a commonplace, self-evident thing. Yet we must not go beyond what the text says. It seems to me that our Lord wished us to feel that he could say nothing better in praise of a soul in which there was no part dark than what he had said; namely, *the whole shall be full of light.*

Some have thought that he meant that by being lit within we shall be full of light to others. That is a great truth, but our Lord does not say so here; for he compares our inward light to a candle that shines on ourselves: *as when the bright shining of a candle doth give thee light.* He refers to our own personal comfort. When a room is thoroughly well lit up in every corner, it has a joyous splendor. One looks around and feels content and satisfied. So, when the whole nature is filled with the light of God, we have sweetness and light to the full, and heaven seems to have begun below. It is inexpressibly delightful, luxuriously blessed, to dwell in the full light of God when there is no concealment and no love of evil. When once the sun thus shines full on me, I would cry with Joshua, *Sun, stand thou still* (Joshua 10:12).

This inner light will make us shine before others. It is the only shining we should seek. A clean lantern with a lighted candle in it makes no noise, and yet it wins attention: the darker the night, the more it is valued. There never was a time in which true inner light was more needed than now. May the Lord impart it to each one of us, and then we shall shine as lights in the world! The Lord God bring this light to you, and fill you with it; and unto his name shall be the glory! You do not have to work for the light, you have only to receive it. Then shall your profiting be known unto all men when it is true profiting to your own character. God bless you, for the Lord Jesus' names sake. Amen.

Chapter 8

The Two Builders and Their Houses

*Therefore whosoever heareth these sayings of mine, and
doeth them, I will liken him unto a wise man, which built
his house upon a rock: and the rain descended, and the
floods came, and the winds blew, and beat upon that house;
and it fell not: for it was founded upon a rock. And every
one that heareth these sayings of mine, and doeth them not,
shall be likened unto a foolish man, which built his house
upon the sand: and the rain descended, and the floods came,
and the winds blew, and beat upon that house; and it fell:
and great was the fall of it.* (Matthew 7:24-27)

These were the closing words of our Savior's most famous Sermon on the Mount. Some preachers concentrate all their powers on an effort to conclude with a fine thing called a peroration, which, being interpreted, means a blaze of rhetorical fireworks, in the glory of which the speaker subsides. They certainly do not have the example of Christ in this discourse to warrant them in the practice. Here is the Savior's peroration, and yet it is as simple as any other part of the address. There is an evident absence of all artificial oratory. The whole of his mountain sermon was intensely earnest, and that earnestness was sustained to the end, so that the closing words are as glowing coals, or as sharp arrows of the bow.

Our Lord closes not by displaying his own powers of public speaking, but by simply and affectionately addressing a warning to those who, having heard his words, would remain satisfied with hearing, and would not go forth and put them into practice. As according to usual experience a preacher warms to his subject as he advances, and becomes more intense as he nears his final sentences, we are bound to give the more earnest heed to the words that are now before us, with which the Lord of all preachers concluded his memorable discourse.

Jesus had been saying many things, but these are two words to which I think he specially alluded when he said, *Whosoever heareth these sayings of mine, and doeth them, I will liken him unto a wise man.* The first of these words was, *Enter ye in* (Matthew 7:13), and the second was, *Beware* (Matthew 7:15). Our Lord had spoken of the *strait gate,* of the "narrow way," and of the few who travel it, and his urgent admonition was, *Enter ye in.* It was not "Learn ye all concerning it, and then be satisfied"; not "Find fault with the travelers and the road"; not "Seek to enlarge the gate and widen the way"; but *Enter ye in.* Be obedient to the gospel, believe its testimony concerning Jesus; enter into fellowship with its mysteries, receive its blessings, be travelers along its road. *Enter ye in.* He who hears of the way to heaven but enters not into it is a foolish man; he who hearing of the strait gate presses to enter in is a wise man.

Afterwards our Lord added the other admonition: *Beware. Beware,* says he, *of false prophets;* and after having dwelt for a while on that, he added in other words: "Beware of false professions." Of false prophets beware, for they may delude you; they may bring before you a salvation that will not save, a mere mirage that looks like the pure, cooling, refreshing stream, but that only mocks your thirst. Beware of all teaching that would lead you away from the one Savior of the souls of men. And then he adds, "Beware of false professions," however loudly they make you cry, *Lord, Lord.* You may have in company with these professions the loftiest gifts, such as casting out devils; and the greatest abilities, such as only prophets possess; but they shall not help you.

In that day when the Master shall only accept into his marriage feast the companions of his warfare on earth, he will say to those who have not done the Father's will, *I never knew you: depart from me, ye that work iniquity* (Matthew 7:23). These are two of the sayings of Christ, and they are comprehensive of almost all he ever said: *Enter ye in* and *Beware.* Take heed that you do them as well as hear them.

We shall now proceed to the Master's parable, and will you please notice, first of all, the two builders.

The wise man and the foolish man were both engaged in precisely the same vocation, and to a considerable extent achieved the same purpose. Both of them undertook to build houses, both of them persevered in building, and both of them finished their houses. The likeness between them is very considerable. *They were equally impressed with the need of building a house.* They perceived the necessity of shelter from the heavy rains, they were equally desirous of being shielded from the floods and screened from the wind. The advantage of a house to dwell in was evident to both.

Even thus, at this period, we have a large number in the congregation who are impressed with the conviction that they need a Savior. I am delighted to find that there is a stir among my audience, and I trust it is a movement of God's Holy Spirit; and as a result very many of you feel deeply that you need a refuge from the wrath to come. You now admit that you must be forgiven, justified, born again, and sanctified, and your desires are fervent; for all of this I am deeply grateful, but also deeply anxious. You are in crowds desirous of becoming builders, and although some are wise and some foolish, up to this present time we can see no difference in you; for you seem to be equally convinced that you need eternal life and a good hope for the world to come. Nor does the likeness end here, for the two builders were both equally *resolved to obtain what they needed* – a house; and their determination was not in words only, but also in deeds, for they both resolutely set to work to build.

In the same way there are among us at this hour many who are resolved that if Christ is to be had, they will have him; and if there is such a thing as salvation, they will find it. They are very earnest, intensely earnest, and though some of them will fail, and some of them succeed, yet up to this point they are both alike, and none but he who searches all hearts can discern the slightest difference. I look with sadness upon the two pilgrims, with their faces zealously turned Zionward, and I sigh as I wonder which one will find the Celestial City, and which will join with Formalist and Hypocrisy, and perish on the dark mountains.

We are glad to hear of yearning hearts and resolute determinations, but alas, all is not grain that grows in wheatfields, and all is not gold that glitters. Appearances are very, very hopeful, but appearances are often deceptive. There may be a deep sense of need, and there may be a determined resolution to get that need supplied; and yet out of two seekers, one may find and the other may miss, and one may be foolish and the other may be wise.

These two builders seem to have been *equally well skilled in architecture.* The one could build a house without receiving any more instruction than the other. I do not find that there was a halt or a pause on the part of either because he could not turn an arch or fix a truss. Evidently, they were both skilled workmen, well acquainted with their art. So it is with many here. They know as far as the theory goes what the plan of salvation is, as well as I do. Yet, where the knowledge is the same, the ultimate result may vary; two men may be equally well instructed in the Scriptures, yet one of them may be wise and the other foolish. To know what faith is, what repentance is, what a good hope in Christ is, may all be yours, and yet it may but increase your misery forever. *If ye know these things, happy are ye if ye do them* (John 13:17). It is not the hearer, but the doer of the Word that is blessed. Knowledge puffs up; love alone builds up.

My dear friends, I am most earnest that those of you who are desiring to find everlasting life in Christ I may not be content with anything short of a true, deep, and real work of grace in your hearts, for no clearness of head knowledge, no natural earnestness of purpose or eagerness of desire can save you; without an interest in ChIJesus you are lost to all eternity. *Ye must be born again;* you must be brought into vital union with the living Savior, or your hopefulness will end in overwhelming destruction.

Once more, *these two builders both persevered and finished their structures.* The foolish man did not begin to build and then cease his work because he was not able to finish; but, as far as I know, his house was finished with as much completeness as the other, and, perhaps, furnished quite as well. If you had looked at the two structures, they would have seemed equally complete from basement to roof, and yet there was a great difference between them in a most essential point. Even thus, alas! many persevere in seeking salvation until they imagine that they have found it; they abide for years in the full belief that they are saved; they cry, "Peace, peace," and write themselves down among the blessed, and yet a fatal error lies at the base of all their religion; all their hopes are vain, and their lifework will prove to be a terrible failure.

The builders are much alike up to this point, but yet in reality they are as wide as the poles apart from each other both in work and in character. The one builder is wise, the other foolish; the one superficial, the other substantial; the one grandiose, the other sincere. The wise man's work was honest work where men's eyes could not judge it. The other's work was only well worked above ground; there was nothing of reality in the hidden parts, and therefore in due time the first builder rejoiced as he saw his house outlive the storm, while the other with his house was swept away to total destruction.

Thus much upon the two builders; let us now think upon their two houses.

One chief apparent difference between the two edifices probably was this, *that one of them built his house more quickly than the other.* The wise man had to spend a portion of his time in underground work. Luke tells us that he dug deep, and laid his foundation on a rock. Now that rock-blasting, that carving and cutting of the hard granite, must have consumed days and weeks. The foolish builder had not this delay to encounter; the sand was all smooth and ready for him; he was able to commence at once to lay his courses of brick, and raise the walls with all rapidity. But all haste is not good speed, and there be some who travel too fast to hold.

Unsound professing Christians are often very rapid in their supposed spiritual growth. They were yesterday unconverted, today they become believers, tomorrow they begin to teach, the next day they are made perfect. They appear to be born of full stature, and equipped at all points like Minerva, when, according to the fable, she leaped from the brain of Jupiter. They come up in a night, And alas! too often, like Jonah's plant, they perish also in a night. Now I raise not a question concerning the genuine character of sudden conversions. I believe that sudden conversions are among the best and truest forms of conversion.

Take, for instance, that of the apostle Paul. But still there are among those who profess to have been suddenly converted a sadly numerous company who answer to the description I have just given, for they build very, very quickly, much too quickly for the masonry to be well constructed and lasting. It may be that some mourner is lamenting bitterly that he makes very slow progress in grace. "I have been seeking God in prayer," says one, "these months. I have been humbled and broken down under a sense of sin for weeks, and have only as yet had now and then a glimpse of hope, when I have been able to turn my eye to the crucified Savior. I have as yet few consolations, and many doubts. I willingly would have the full light of love in my heart, but the dawning is slow in breaking."

Well, friend, you are building slowly, but if it be surely, you shall have no cause to regret that deep digging. Little cause will you have to mourn that it took you longer to arrive at peace than it did your hasty friend, if your peace shall last you to eternity, while his hope shall be a possession in cloudland, driven away by the wind.

Of the two houses, one was built, I doubt not, *with far less trouble than the other.* Digging foundations in hard rocks, as I have said, takes time, but it also involves labor. Oftentimes did that wise builder pause to wipe the sweat from his brow; oftentimes did he retire to his bed worn-out with his day's work, and yet there was not a stone appearing above the soil. His neighbor, opposite, had run up the walls, had reached the gable, was almost about to put on the roof before there was scarcely a foot above the ground of the wise builder's structure. "Ah," said he of the sandy foundation, "your toil is needless, and you have nothing to show for it. See how quickly my walls have risen, and yet I don't slave as you do. I take things easily; I neither bore myself nor the rocks, and yet see how my house springs up, and how neat it looks! Your old-fashioned ways are absurd. You dig and hammer away down below there as if you meant to pierce the center. Why not use your common sense, and go ahead as I do? Away with your sighing and groaning; do as I do, and rejoice at once. Anxiety will kill you."

After this fashion are truly awakened souls, like "lamps despised of those who are at ease." One man jumps, as it were, into peace, and boasts himself secure; whether he is correct or not in his confidence, he does not pause to question; he is too comfortable to have time to inquire into that matter. The estate is fair, why worry about the title deeds? The feast is rich, why wait for the wedding garments? If a doubt should arise, the carnally secure man ascribes it to Satan, and puts it aside, whereas it is his own conscience and the warning voice of heaven that bid him to take heed and be not deceived. The prayer for the Lord to search and try his heart and his mind he never sincerely offers. Such a man does not like self-examination, and cannot endure to be told that there must be fruits suitable for repentance. He takes things at guesswork, comes to rash conclusions, and shuts his eyes to disagreeable facts. He dreams that he is rich and increased in goods, whereas he is naked, and poor, and miserable.

Alas, what a waking will be his! His more serious companion aroused at the same time is, on the other hand, far more reserved and self-distrustful; when he prays, his heart groans before God, yet he fears he does not pray right, and never rises from his knees contented with himself. He is not quite so soon satisfied about the reality of his faith as the other. "Perhaps," says he, "after all it is not the faith of God's elect." He examines himself whether he be in the faith. He trembles lest he should have the form of godliness without the power. He is afraid of shams and counterfeits, and is for buying gold tested in the fire. "As for my repentance," says he, "am I sure it is a real loathing of sin as sin, or did I only shed a tear or two under the excitement of a revival service? Am I sure that my nature is renewed by the work of the Holy Spirit, or is it mere reformation?"

You see this second man has much exercise of soul; he labors to enter into rest, lest by any means he should seem to come short of it. He has many strivings, many anxieties, many searchings of heart because he is sincere and fears being deceived. From him the kingdom of heaven suffers violence, he finds the gate wide and the way narrow, and that the righteous scarcely are saved.

Be thankful, dear friend, if you are among this second class, for these are the true sons of God, and heirs of immortality. Your house costs you more to build, but it will be worth the cost. O beware of wearing the sheep's clothing without the sheep's nature; beware of saying, *Lord, Lord,* while you are the servant of sin. Beware of acquiring fictitious religion, borrowing your experience from biographies, picking up godliness secondhand from your mothers and fathers, and friends and acquaintances. Whatever it may cost you in heartbreak and agony, see to it that the sure foundation is reached, and the house is so built that it will endure the trials that will inevitably test it. I would willingly saturate my speech with tears, so weighty and so needful do I feel this caution to be, both to myself and to you.

I should think that, in the course of time, although the foolish builder built with so much less cost, and so much more rapidly, *his walls would be liable to very ugly settlements.* For walls that have no foundation, but are piled up on the sand, would every now and then gape wide with hideous cracks; and stones would start here, and timbers would slip there, and cement and plugging would be much required. What work for daubers and plasterers to make the ruinous fabric look like decent masonry! Very likely when a settlement was covered up in one place, another would happen in the next wall; for with such a foundation it would be hard to keep the structure well together, and in the long run I would not wonder but what it would cost the foolish builder more pains to keep up his wretched edifice than it did the wise builder who labored so hard with his foundation at the start.

Mark you well, that mere formal religion and hypocrisy in the end become a very difficult affair to maintain. The man has to struggle hard to patch up his reputation, propping it up with new lies, and bolstering it with fresh claims. At one time an unrenewed will rebels fiercely, and he has to pretend resignation to affliction; next an unconquered lust demands indulgence, and he has to conceal the sin with more double-distilled deceit; the form of prayer becomes irksome, and he has to screw himself up to the horrible farce, and meanwhile his outward life is always on the verge of a slip, and he fears detection. One way or another he is continually afraid, like a thief at-large who fears that the police will find him. At every puff of wind his habitation threatens to tumble around his ears. He half wishes after all that he had taken the trouble to dig a foundation on the rock, but with desperate resolve he puts from him the voice of caution, and will have none of its rebuke.

O dear friend, rest assured that truth, after all, is the cheapest and easiest in the long run. Your goldlike surface, your varnish, your paint, your hypocrisy soon wear off, while the reality is at no expense for beautifying. Even as a matter of consideration for this life, it will be harder in the long run to keep up the grandiose than to maintain the true; and then in the latter case you have God at your back, while he abhors everything unreal. I beg you to see to it that you do not plaster your walls with untempered mortar, lest they not only come down with a crash when you most need to shelter behind them, but also even now they begin to show alarming signs of decay.

The higher the foolish man built, the harder work he had to keep it upright, for of course every tier of bricks that he laid made the weight the greater, and caused the sand to give way. The nearer to heaven the builder went, the sooner his wall bowed to its fall. A man who only makes it his aim to be thought a respectable man by attending a place of worship may manage pretty well to keep up such a low wall even without a foundation; another man who joins a worldly church – a church that makes no claim of purity – can also succeed with ease; but if he joins a church of Jesus Christ that carefully seeks to preserve purity in its membership, he has hard work to live up to the standard required of him.

Suppose, yet further, that he should become a deacon or an elder, and he is devoid of grace. His higher aim will cost him more by far, for there are more to look at him, and there is more required of him. Now he prays in public, now he speaks a word of instruction to inquirers, and what distresses and extremities the poor man is driven to, how constantly out of his own mouth is he condemned. "Why," says he in his heart, "I know nothing about these things in my soul, and yet I have to speak and act as if I were taught of God." If he becomes a preacher, he is in a still more pitiful plight; what hard work must it be, then, to keep up the character! When the tower rises tier upon tier, upon so frail a base, it leans like the Tower of Pisa, and unlike that odd structure, it threatens to come down with a crash. By and by such a worthless thing falls in utter ruin, and its elevation helps to hasten the catastrophe. So, my dear friends, the more spirituality you aim at, and the more useful-ness you strive for, the worse for you, unless you have a good founda-tion to begin with, in true sincerity and real faith. So bad is the course of unsound religion, that the further you go in it the worse it becomes.

The main difference, however, between the two houses did not lay in these cracks and settlements, nor in the cheapness or rapidity of the building – *it lay out of sight, underground.* It was all a matter of foundation. How many there are who suppose that if a thing is out of sight it may as well be out of mind! Who do you think is likely to dig down and see what the foundations are? "Well," says one, "I see no need for being overly precise; I do not believe in being so particular. What nobody sees cannot signify." Many subscribe to the graceless song –

> For faith and grace let foolish zealots fight;
> He can't be wrong whose life is in the right.

"You pay twenty shillings in the pound, attend a place of worship, take the sacrament, be charitable, and say your prayers, and never trouble about anything further" – that is the popular notion. "What is the use of fretting about your heart? That is all transcendental nonsense. What can it signify?" That is how the foolish builder comforted himself, and he doubtless sneered at the wise builder as a poor miserable creature who was righteous in too great a degree, and melancholy. Outward appearance is everything with men, but it is nothing with God. The essential difference between the true child of God and the mere professing Christian is not readily to be discovered, even by spiritual minds; but the Lord sees it. It is a secret, mysterious something that the Lord prizes, for he *knoweth them that are his.* He separates between the precious and the vile. He puts away the pretenders as rubbish, but he permits no sincere heart to be destroyed.

What, then, is this important matter? I answer, it is just this. Beloved friend, if you would be built on a rock, see to it that you have *a true sense of sin.* I do not say that a sense of sin is a preparation for Christ, and that we ought to push men back from the gospel until they feel their sin; but I do believe that wherever there is true faith in Jesus, there goes with it a deep abhorrence of sin. Faith without remorse is a dead and worthless faith. When I meet with professing Christians who talk lightly of sin, I feel sure that they have built without a foundation. If they had ever felt the Spirit's wounding and killing sword of conviction, they would flee from sin as from a lion or a bear.

Truly forgiven sinners dread the appearance of evil as burned children dread the fire. Superficial repentance always leads to careless living. Faith that was never moistened with repentance never brings forth the flowers of holiness. Pray earnestly for a broken and contrite heart. Remember, it is the remorseful spirit that God is pleased with. Do not believe that you can have ground for rejoicing if you never saw reason for lamenting. The promised comfort is only secured to those who have been mourners. (See Matthew 5:4.)

Next to this, seek for *real faith*. Many things that men call faith are not the precious faith of God's elect. Sincere trust in Jesus Christ is counterfeited in a thousand ways, and often imitated so accurately that only by rigid self-examination shall you discover the cheat. You must lie flat upon Christ, the Rock; you must depend entirely upon him, all your hope and all your trust must be in him. If you believe with the heart, and not nominally, you are safe, but not otherwise. You must have true repentance and real faith, or you are foolish builders.

Furthermore, seek an *ornamented experience of divine truth*. Ask to have it burned into you. Why is it that people give up the doctrines of grace if they fall in with eloquent advocates of free will? Why is it they renounce the orthodox creed if they meet with smart reasoners who contradict it? Because they have never received the Word in the power of the Holy Spirit so as to have it sealed in their hearts. I tremble for our churches now that false doctrine is rife, because I fear that many are not established in the truth. I pray the Lord for you, my dear flock, that you may know the truth by being taught of the Lord, for then you will not be led astray. The thieves and robbers will come, but as Christ's sheep you will not hear them. It is one thing to have a creed; it is quite another thing to have the truth graven upon the tablets of the heart. Many fail here because truth was never experimentally made their own.

Pray, moreover, that your *faith may produce personal holiness*. Do not believe yourself to be saved from sin while you are living in sin. If you can find pleasure in the lusts of the flesh, you are no child of God. If you are given to drunkenness – and, mark you, many professing Christians are, only they drink at home and are not seen in the streets – how does the grace of God dwell in you? If you delight in idle songs, and frequenting of places of vain amusement, you need not be long in weighing yourself, for you are found deficient already. If you were renewed in the spirit of your mind, you would no more love these things than an angel would. There must be a newborn nature implanted, and where there is not this exemplified in holiness of life, you may build ever so high and chatter ever so loudly about your building, but still it is a poor, miserable shanty after all, and will fall in the last hurricane.

Lack of depth, lack of sincerity, lack of reality in religion – this is the poverty of our times. Lack of an eye to God in religion, lack of sincere dealing with one's own soul, neglect of using the lancet with our hearts, neglect of the search warrant that God gives out against sin, carelessness concerning living upon Christ; much reading about him, much talking about him, but too little feeding upon his flesh and drinking of his blood – these are the causes of tottering professions and baseless hopes.

Thus have I tried to open up the parable, and I have not intended to discourage any sincere soul; rather, my aim has been to say to you, "Make your calling and election sure. Build on Christ's love, sincerity, desire, the work of the Holy Spirit, and be not deceived."

So now I come, in the third place, to notice the common trial of the two houses.

Whether your religion be true or not, it will be tested; whether it be chaff or wheat, the fan of the Great Winnower will surely be brought into operation upon all that lies on the threshing floor. If you have dealings with God, you have to deal with a *consuming fire* (Hebrews 12:29). Whether you be really or nominally a Christian, if you come near to Christ, he will refine you as silver is refined. Judgment must begin at the house of God, and if you dare to come into the house of God, judgment will begin with you. By the way, let us note that if there are such trials for those who profess to be Christians, what will become of you who make no profession? If the righteous scarcely be saved, where will the ungodly and the wicked appear? If judgment begins with the house of God, what will the end be of them that believe not? Terrible thought!

Trials will come to profession, whether it be true or false. If I do not mistake the reference in the text to rain, flood, and wind, these trials will be of three sorts at least. The rain typifies *afflictions from heaven*. God will send you adversities like showers, tribulations as many as the drops of the dew. Between now and heaven, O professing Christian, you will feel the pelting storm. Like other men, your body will be sick, or if not, you shall have trouble in your house; children and friends will die, or riches will take to themselves wings, and fly like an eagle towards heaven. You must have trials from God's hand, and, if you are not relying on Christ, you will not be able to bear them. If you are not, by real faith, one with Jesus Christ, even God's rain will be too much for you.

But there will also arise *trials from earth – the floods came.* In former days the floods of persecution were more terrible than now, but persecution is still felt; and if you are a professing Christian, you will have to bear a measure of it. Cruel mockings are still used against the people of God. The world no more loves the true church today than it did in the olden times. Can you bear slander and reproach for Jesus? Not unless you are firmly rooted and grounded. In the day of temptation and persecution the rootless plants of the stony ground are withered away. See to this. Then there will come *mysterious trials* typified by *the winds.* The prince of the power of the air will attack you with blasphemous suggestions, horrible temptations, or cunning insinuations. He knows how to cast clouds of despondency over the human spirit; he can attack the four corners of the house at once by his mysterious agency; he can tempt us in diverse ways at the same time, and drive us to our wits' end. Woe to you, then, unless you have something to hold by that is better than the mere sand of profession!

Where there is a good foundation trials will do no hurt, but where there is no foundation, they will frequently bring the man's profession down in ruin, even in this life. How many lose their religion at the very outset! Pliable and Christian both set out for the Celestial City, both aspiring to the crown of gold. But they fell into the Slough of Despond, and then, as one of them struggled out on the side nearest his own house, and went back to the City of Destruction, while the other endeavored bravely to reach the farther shore, the difference between the wise pilgrim and the foolish pilgrim was made manifest.

After Christians have proceeded further, they will be tested in other ways. Infidelities often test Christians, and I mean doubts about the essentials of the faith, and all its doctrines; and those that are not well cemented to the rock are easily moved to unbelief. This is the age of faithlessness, but those who are on the rock by a truthful experience are not moved.

A poor slave was once told by a friend that some man had said the

Bible was not true. Now, our poor friend had never thought anybody could doubt the Bible, but his quick way of disposing of the striking difficulty was, "Dat book not true! why, I take it into my house and I sit down and read it, and it make my heart laugh. How can it be a lie dat make my heart laugh? I was drunkard, thief, and liar, and dat book talked to me and made me a new man – dat book no lie." That is the very best proof in the world surely, at least to the man himself, if not to others. We who have had our hearts made to laugh by God's Word cannot be laughed out of our faith. We have lived on the Word and proved its truthfulness by experience, and are therefore invulnerable to all attacks, while strangers to such experience are shocked.

Where the heart is really grounded upon the truth, you will find that heresies as well as falsities have but little effect. The sound Christian is like a stone – if he is thrown into the pool of false doctrine, he may be made wet by it, but he does not receive it into his inner self, whereas the unsound professing Christian is like a sponge – he sucks it all in greedily, and retains what he absorbs.

How many there are who are tested by worldliness, and if their religion be but mere profession, worldliness soon eats the heart of it as does a canker, and they become even as others! If, however, the Christian man's heart is right with God, he comes out and is separate, and the pride of life does not entrap him.

In cases of backsliding, where there is a sound heart towards God, the backslider is soon brought back, but where the heart is rotten, the backslider goes from bad to worse. I was struck with a story of two men who were accustomed to giving exhortations at meetings, who had fallen out with each other, and one of their brethren, who grieved to think two servants of God should be at odds with each other, went to reconcile them. He called upon the first one and said, "John, I am very sorry to find you and James have quarreled. It seems a great pity, and it brings much dishonor on the church of God."

"Ah," said John, "I am very grieved too, and what grieves me most is that I am the sole cause of it. It was only because I spoke so bitterly that James took offense."

"Ah, ah," said the good man, "we will soon settle this difficulty then," and away he went to James. "James, I am very sorry that you and John cannot agree."

"Yes," he said, "it is a sad thing we don't; we ought to do so, for we are brethren. But what troubles me most is that it is all my fault. If I had not taken notice of a little word John said, there would have been an end of it." The matter, as you may guess, was soon rectified. You see there was at the bottom a true friendship between them, so that the little difficulty was soon gotten over, and so where there is a true union between God and the soul, the backsliding will soon be recovered.

To close, having thus mentioned the common trials and the effects produced in this life, let me now remind you of the different results of the trials in reference to the life to come.

In the one case, the rain descended very heavily and threatened to wash the house away, but it was built on a rock, and not only did the house stand, but also the man inside found great comfort in it. He could hear the pelting torrent beating on the roof, and he could sit and sing; when the gusts came against the windows, he would only be the more happy to think he had such a shelter. Then came the floods. They would, if they could, have sapped and undermined the foundation, but they had no effect on the granite rock, and though the wind howled around the habitation, every stone was well cemented, and all bound as with iron bands to the grand old rock, and therefore the man was safe and happy within, and above all, grateful that he had built on such a foundation. He could sit down and sing,

> Loud may the troubled ocean roar,
> In sacred peace my soul abides.

The Christian rests peacefully upon Christ. Troubles come one after another, but they do not sweep him away; they only endear to him the hope that is based upon Christ Jesus. And when at last death comes, that awful flood that will undermine everything that can be removed, it cannot find anything to shake in the wise builder's hope. He rests on what Christ has done; death cannot affect that. He believes in a faithful God; and dying cannot affect that. He believes in the covenant signed, and sealed, and ratified, and in all things ordered well. He lays hold on the *shalls* and *wills* of an unchangeable God, all sealed with the blood of the Redeemer; death cannot affect any of these.

And when the last great trumpet sounds, and the last fire that shall test every man's work of what sort it is comes forth from the throne of God, the man who in true sincerity and with real experience has laid hold on Christ is not afraid of the tremendous hour. Though the trumpet sounds exceedingly loud and long, and the dead awake, and the angels gather around the great white throne, and the pillars of heaven tremble, and the earth is dissolved, and the elements melt with fervent heat, the man of God feels that the rock on which he has built can never fail him, and the hope that grace has given him can never be removed. He smiles serenely amidst it all.

But look at the case of the man whose hope is built on the sand! He could hardly endure the trials of life; he almost fell under common temptation; he turned his coat during the hour of persecution, but sorer trials now await him. Some hypocrites have been bolstered up even in the last moments, and perhaps have never known that they were lost until they felt they were; like the rich man, of whom it is written, *In hell he lift up his eyes, being in torments* (Luke 16:23). He had never lifted up his eyes before; he did not know his condition until he actually realized it in all its misery. But most men who have come under the sound of the gospel, and made a profession, if they have been deceivers, they find it out at death, and it must be a dreadful thing to make that discovery when pain is sharp and parting is bitter.

Ah! dear friend, if you be mistaken, may you find it out now, and not on your dying couch. May your prayer be: "Lord, show me the worst of my case. If my profession has been a mistake, O let me not build up and prop up a rotten thing, but help me to build right upon the Rock of ages." Do pray that prayer, I implore you. Remember, if death should not teach you the whole truth of your case, judgment will. There will be no mistake there, and no opportunity for repentance. This fallen house was never built again; there was no salvage from the total wreck. Lost, lost, lost, there is no word to follow; for once lost, lost forever!

O dear friend, I bid you if you have a name to live and are dead, to arise from the dead, and Christ shall give you life. I pray you, if you be a seeker, be not put off with empty hopes and vain confidences. Buy the truth and sell it not. Lay hold on eternal life. Seek the true Savior and be not content until you have him, for if lost, your ruin will be terrible. Oh, *that lake!* Have you ever read the words, *Were cast into the lake of fire. This is the second death* (Revelation 20:14)? The lake of fire! and souls cast into it! The imagery is dreadful. "Ah," says one, "that is a metaphor." Yes, I know it is, and a metaphor is but a shadow of the reality. Then, if the shadow be a lake of fire, what must the reality be? If we can hardly bear to think of a *worm [that] shall not die* (Isaiah 66:24), and a *fire that never shall be quenched* (Mark 9:43), and of a lake whose seething waves of fire dash over undying and hopeless souls, what must hell be indeed?

The descriptions of Scriptures are, after all, but patronizing attitudes to our ignorance, and partial revealings of fathomless mysteries; but if these are so dreadful, what must the full reality be? Provoke it not, my friends, tempt not your God, neglect not the great salvation, for if you do, you shall not escape. Play not with your souls, be not heedless and careless of the realities of eternity; but now, even now, may God hear your prayer as you breathe it from your inmost souls, and give you truly to be washed in the precious blood, and effectively saved by him, in whom there is fullness of truth and grace. Amen.

> My God, I mark with fear
>   How many hopes decay,
> And like the foolish builder's house
>   Fall in the trial day.
>
> Perhaps amid this throng
>   Thou dost a soul espy
> Whose towering hopes are built on sand,
>   I ask, "Lord, is it I?"
>
> A thousand doubts arise,
>   I bring them all to thee;
> Am I unconsciously deceived?
>   Lord, search my heart and see.
>
> O teach me how to dig deep
>   Down to the solid rock,

That when tornadoes round me sweep
   My house may bear the shock.

Jesus, thou only art
   The sure foundation stone,
Firm as th' eternal hills art thou,
   I build on thee alone.

Cemented fast to thee
   No stone is laid in vain,
My hope defies th' assaults of hell,
   The flood, the wind, the rain.

Chapter 9

The Right Foundation

And why call ye me, Lord, Lord, and do not the things which I say? Whosoever cometh to me, and heareth my sayings, and doeth them, I will shew you to whom he is like: He is like a man which built an house, and digged deep, and laid the foundation on a rock: and when the flood arose, the stream beat vehemently upon that house, and could not shake it: for it was founded upon a rock. But he that heareth, and doeth not, is like a man that without a foundation built an house upon the earth; against which the stream did beat vehemently, and immediately it fell; and the ruin of that house was great. (Luke 6:46-49)

These parables describe two classes of hearers, but they say nothing of those who are not hearers. Their position and prospects we must infer from what is said of hearers. Our Lord Jesus Christ has come into the world to tell us of the Father's love, and never a man spoke as he spoke, and yet there are many who refuse to hear him. I do not mean those who are far away, to whom the name of Jesus is almost unknown, but I mean persons in this land, and especially in this great and highly favored city, who willfully refuse to hear him whom God has anointed to bring tidings of salvation. Our Lord Jesus is proclaimed, I was about to say, upon the housetops in this city; for even in their music halls and theaters Christ is preached to the multitudes, and at the corners of our streets his banner is lifted up; and yet there are tens of thousands to whom the preaching of the gospel is as music in the ears of a corpse. They shut their ears and will not hear, though the testimony be concerning God's own Son, and life eternal, and the way to escape from everlasting wrath. To their own best interests, to their eternal benefit, men are dead: nothing will secure their attention to their God.

To what, then, are these men like? They may rightly be compared to the man who built no house whatsoever, and remained homeless by day and shelterless by night. When worldly trouble comes like a storm, those persons who will not hear the words of Jesus have no consolation to cheer them; when sickness comes, they have no joy of heart to sustain them under its pains; and when death, that most terrible of storms, beats upon them, they feel its full fury, but they cannot find a hiding place. They neglect the housing of their souls, and when the hurricane of almighty wrath shall break forth in the world to come, they will have no place of refuge. In vain will they call upon the rocks to fall on them, and the mountains to cover them. They shall be in that day without a shelter from the righteous wrath of the Most High. Alas, that any being who wears the image of man should be found in such a plight! Homeless wanderers in the day of tempest! How my soul grieves for them! Yet, what excuse will those men invent who have refused even to know the way of salvation? What excuse can the most tender heart make for them? Will they plead that they could not believe? Yet they may not say that they could not hear; and faith comes by hearing, and hearing by the Word of God.

Oh my friend, if the Word of God comes to you, and you decline to hear it, and therefore do not believe in Jesus, but die in your sins, what is this but soul suicide? If a man dies of a disease when infallible medicine is to be had, must not his death lie at his own door? If a man perishes from hunger when bread is all around him and others feed to the full, and he will not have it, will any man pity him? Surely not a drop of pity will be yielded to a lost soul with which he may relieve the torment of his conscience, for all holy intelligences will perceive that the sinner chose his own destruction. This shall ever press upon the condemned conscience: "You knew the gospel, but you did not pay attention to it.

You knew that there was salvation, and that Christ was the Savior, and that pardon was proclaimed to guilty men, but you would not make available any time from your farm and from your merchandise, from your pleasures and from your sins, to learn how you could be saved. That which cost God so dearly you treated as a trifle."

Ah, my dear friends, may none of you belong to the non-hearing class. It is not to such that I shall this morning address myself, and yet I could not enter upon my discourse without a word of loving challenges to them. Let me part with them by quoting the warning word of the Holy Spirit: *See that ye refuse not him that speaketh. For if they escaped not who refused him that spake on earth, much more shall not we escape, if we turn away from him that speaketh from heaven* (Hebrews 12:25).

Our earnest attention will now be given to those who are hearers of the Word, and are somewhat affected by it. All hearers are builders of houses for their souls: they are each one doing something to set up a spiritual habitation. Some of these go a considerable distance in this house-building, and even crown the structure by publicly confessing Christ. They say unto him, *Lord, Lord;* they meet with his followers, and join with them in reverence to the Master's name; but they do not obey the Lord; they hear him, but they fail to do the things that he says. Therefore, they are mistaken builders, who fail in the foundation, and make nothing sure except that their house will come down around their ears. Others there are, and we trust they will be found to be many among us, who are building rightly, building for eternity, constructing a dwelling place with a basis of rock, and walls of well-built stone, of which the Lord Christ is both the foundation and the cornerstone.

I am anxious to speak at this time to those who are just beginning to build for eternity. I am indeed happy to know that there are many such among us. May the Holy Spirit bless this message to them.

Our first subject will be a common temptation with spiritual builders. A common temptation with hearers of the Word, according to the two parables before us, is to neglect foundation work, to get hurriedly over the first part of the business, and run up the building quickly. They are tempted to assume that all is done that is said to be done; to take it for granted that all is right that is hoped to be right; and then to go on piling up the walls as rapidly as possible. The great temptation, I say, with young beginners in religious life, is to deal with the foundation in a hasty manner, and treat those things lightly that are of the first importance. The same temptation comes to us throughout the whole of life, but to young beginners it is especially perilous. Satan would have them neglect the fundamental principles upon which their future hope and character are to rest, so that in a future testing hour, from lack of a solid foundation, they may yield to evil, and lose the whole of their life-building.

This temptation is all the more dangerous, first, because *these young beginners have no experience.* Even the most experienced child of God is often deceived; how much more the pilgrim who has but just entered the Wicket Gate[1]! The tested saint sometimes mistakes that for a virtue that is only a gold-plated fault, and he imagines that to be genuine which is mere counterfeit. How, then, without any experience whatever, can the mere babe in grace escape deception unless he be graciously preserved? Newly awakened and rendered serious, earnest hearts get to work in the divine life with much hurry, seizing upon that which first comes to hand, building in heedless haste, without due care and examination. Something must be done, and they do it without asking whether it is according to the teaching of the Lord. They call Jesus "Lord," but they do what others say rather than what Jesus says. Satan is sure to be at hand at such times, so that he may lead the young convert to lay in place of gospel repentance a repentance that needs to be repented of, and instead of the faith of God's elect, a proud presumption or an idle dream. For that love of God that is the work of the Spirit of God he brings mere natural affection for a minister; and he says, "There, that will do: you must have a house for your soul to dwell in. There are the materials, pile them up."

Like children at play upon the beach, the anxious heap up their sandcastles, and please themselves with that, for they are ignorant of Satan's devices. I am for this cause doubly anxious to save my beloved young friends from the deceiver. The common temptation is, instead of really repenting, to *talk about* repentance; instead of heartily believing, to *say*, "I believe," without believing; instead of truly loving, to talk of love, without loving; instead of coming to Christ, to speak about coming

---

1   The Wicket Gate in *The Pilgrim's Progress* represents Jesus Christ, the only door through which we can enter heaven (John 10:9).

to Christ, and profess to come to Christ, and yet not to come at all. The character of Talkative in *The Pilgrim's Progress* is ably drawn. I have met the gentleman many times, and can bear witness that John Bunyan was a photographer before photography was invented. Christian said of him, "He talketh of prayer, of repentance, of faith, and of the new birth; but he knows but only to *talk* of them. I have been in his family, and his house is as empty of religion as the white of an egg is of savor." We have too many such persons around us who are, as to what they say, everything that is to be desired, and yet, by what they are proven to be, are mere shams.

As tradesmen place dummies in their shops, papered and labeled to look like goods, while yet they are nothing of the sort, so are these men marked and labeled as Christians, but the grace of God is not in them. Oh, that you young beginners may be on the alert, that you be not content with the form of godliness, but are made to feel the power of it.

There is this to help the temptation too, that *this plan for the present saves a great deal of trouble.* Your mind is distressed, and you want comfort; well, it will comfort you to say, *Lord, Lord,* though you do not do the things that Christ says. If you admit the claims of Jesus to be Lord, even though you do not believe on him for salvation, and so neglect the main thing that he commands, yet you will find some ease in the admission. He bids you to repent of sin, trust his blood, love his Word, and seek after holiness; but it is much easier to admire these things without following after them in your life. To pretend repentance and faith is not difficult, but genuine godliness is heart work, and requires thought, care, sincerity, prayerfulness, and watchfulness.

Believe me, real religion is no sport. He that would be saved will find it to be no jesting matter. *The kingdom of heaven suffereth violence;* and he that is easy about the thing, and thinks it is nothing more than the magician's "Heigh, presto, done," has made a fatal mistake. *Strive,* says Christ, *to enter in at the strait gate* (Luke 13:24). The Spirit strives in us mightily, and often works us to an agony. The crown of eternal glory is not won without fighting, nor the prize of our high calling received without running; yet by just making a holy profession, and by practicing an outward form, a man imagines that the same result is produced as by seeking the Lord with his whole heart, and believing in the Lord

Jesus. If it were so, there would be a fine broad road to heaven, and Satan himself would turn pilgrim. Believe me, dear friends, this saving of trouble will turn out to be a making of trouble, and, before matters end, the hardest way will turn out to be the easiest way.

This kind of building without a foundation has this advantage to back up the temptation – *it enables a man to run up a religion very quickly.* He makes splendid progress. While the anxious heart is searching after truth in the inward parts, and begging to be renewed by grace, his exulting friend is as happy as he can be in a peace that he has suddenly obtained without question or examination. This rapid grower never asks, "Has my religion changed my conduct? Is my faith accompanied by a new nature? Does the Spirit of God dwell in me? Am I really what I profess to be, or am I but a bastard professor after all?" No, he puts aside all inquiry as a temptation of the devil. He takes every good thing for granted, and votes that all is gold that glitters. See how fast he goes! The fog is dense, but he steams through it, heedless of danger! He has joined the church; he has commenced work for God; he is boasting of his own achievements; he hints that he is perfect. But is this mushroom building safe? Will it pass muster in the last great survey? Will it stand should a tempest happen? The chimney shaft is tall, but is it safe?

Alas, there's the rub. This is the question that makes an end of much of the boasting that is all around us. It is better to tremble at God's Word than boldly to presume. It is better to be fearful, lest after all we may be castaways, than to harden one's forehead with vain confidence. When a man travels upon a wrong road, the faster he runs the farther he will go astray. Remember the advice to hasten slowly, and the old proverb that says, "The more haste the less speed." If you build quickly because you build without a foundation, your time and toil are thrown away.

How common, how deceptive is this temptation! For the young beginner, the man who is just aroused to seek the Lord will find *a great many to help him in his mistake,* should he neglect the foundation. Kind, good, Christian friends often, without a thought of doing so, help to mislead seeking souls. "Yes," they say, "you are converted," and so perhaps the person would be if all he said was true; but then it is said without feeling; it comes from the lips only, and does not come from the heart, and therefore it is ruinous to encourage him. A kindly assurance from a Christian friend may breed false confidence, if that assurance was mistakenly given. In these days we do not meet with many Christians who err by dealing too severely with converts – instead, the shot strikes the other target.

Our forefathers were possibly too suspicious and jealous; but nowadays we nearly all err in the opposite direction. We are so anxious to see everybody brought to Christ, that our wish may tend to delude us into the belief that it is so. We are so willing to cheer and comfort those who seek the Lord, that we may fall into the habit of prophesying smooth things, and thus shun everything that tends to probe and test, lest it should also discourage. Let us beware lest we cry, *Peace, peace; when there is no peace* (Jeremiah 6:14). It will be a sad thing to breed hypocrites when we were looking for converts. I have heard of one who had been into the inquiry room a dozen times, and when on another occasion she was invited to go there she said, "I really do not know why I should go, for I have been told that I was saved twelve times already, and I am not a bit better than before they told me so." It would be better to send some home weeping rather than rejoicing. Many a wound needs the lance more than the plaster. You may be comforted by well-meant assurances of tender friends, and yet that comfort may be all a lie.

I therefore warn you against any peace except that which comes from doing that which Jesus commands, or in other words, against any confidence except that which rests in Jesus only, and is accompanied by repentance, faith, and a life of obedience to your Lord.

No doubt many are encouraged in slight building by the fact that *so many professing Christians are making a fair show, and yet their building is without foundation.* We cannot shut our eyes to the fact that in all churches there are persons who have no depth of spiritual root, and we are afraid no real spiritual life. We cannot root them up, though we fear that they are tares, for we are assured that we would unavoidably root up the wheat with them, and this our Master forbids. There is nothing about their outward conduct that we could lay hold upon as a proof of their being deceivers, and yet a cold chill runs through us when we talk with them, for they have no warmth, and no life, and nothing of the Lord about them. We miss in their conversation that sweet spirituality, that holy unction, that blessed humility, which are sure to be present when men are truly familiar with the Lord, and have entered into living union with him.

People of this order mix up with us in our holy convocations, and when they come across the newly awakened ones, they talk of divine things in such an offhand and flippant manner that they do serious mischief. They speak about conversion as if it were a mere trifle, a matter as easy as kissing your hand; and so those who are hopeful, and over whom our hearts are yearning, are turned aside by them. Young people are apt to think, "So-and-so is a member of the church, and he is never very precise. If a lukewarm profession satisfies him, why should it not satisfy me?"

Ah, my dear friends, but you would not say so in business. If you knew a man was trading without capital and likely to come to bankruptcy, you would not say, "I wish to do the same." If you saw a man venturing into deep water who could not swim, and you felt sure that he would ultimately sink, you would not follow his example and be drowned too. No, no; let these frothy professing Christians be beacons to you. Get away from Mr. Talkative, lest he make you as hollow a drum as himself. Beware of loose professing Christians who are as wreckers' lights that lure men upon the rocks. Make certain your eternal life, and rid yourself of triflers.

Again, there is always at the back of all this an inducement to build without a foundation because *it will not be known, and possibly may not be found out for years.* Foundation work is quite out of sight, and the house can be built and be very useful in a great many ways, and it may stand a good while without the underground work; for houses without foundations do not tumble down at once. They will stand for years; nobody knows how long they may stay up; perhaps they may even be inhabited with comfort until the last great rainstorm. Death alone will discover some acts of deception.

Therefore, because the ill-founded house will do for the present, and can be used, and may bring immediate comfort, many people consider it economical to leave out the foundation as a needless luxury. If they are questioned as to their vital godliness, they grow angry: "What business have you to enter into my private business? Why should you meddle with the secrets of my soul?" Ah, dear friend, if we were cruel to you, and wished you to be deceived, we would hold our tongues, or speak to you with the voice of flattery; but since we love you, and since we hope to be blessed in years to come through your true and holy consecration to Christ, we are intensely earnest that you should begin right. We would have you build that which will not need to be pulled down again, work that will stand when the waters are out and the stream beats vehemently upon it. I dread that any man should perish without religion, but I dread far more that any man should perish with it, finding his faith to have been false after all.

If you do build, build what is worth building. If you must be builders for your souls, and surely you must, or else be shelterless, then take heed on what foundation you build, and be careful what you build thereon, lest after all you suffer the loss of all your labor in that last tremendous day. How sad it will seem to dwell near the gates of heaven, and spend your lives among those who are to be its future inhabitants, and then for lack of sincerity and truth to be shut out of the Celestial City. How terrible to find out by experience that there is a back way to the gates of hell even from the gates of heaven. God grant it be not so with one of us present here. O you builders, care not merely for the present, but build for death, and judgment, and eternity!

This part of our discourse is not only for young people, but also for us all – for old as well as young. Depend upon it, there is not one man among us but who has need to search himself, and see whether the foundation of his faith has been truly laid or not.

So I advance to the second step, and there we will consider a wise precaution that safe builders never forget. They dig deep, and never rest until they get a good substantial foundation. They are glad to get to the bottom of all the loose earth and to build on the rock. Let me commend this wise precaution to all of you.

Follow the text and learn to see to your *sincerity*. The Lord I says, *Why call ye me, Lord, Lord, and do not the things which I say?* May the Holy Spirit make you true to the core. Be afraid to say a word more than you feel. Never permit yourself to speak as if you had an experience of which you have only read. Let not your outward worship go a step beyond the inward emotion of your soul. If Christ be truly your Lord, you will obey him; if he be not your Lord, do not call him so. It is a great point in all your religious thoughts, beliefs, words, and actions to have the heart moving in all. It is an awful thing to make a high profession of sanctity, and yet live in the indulgence of secret sin. Such persons will listen to my observation and commend me for my faithfulness, and yet continue in their hypocrisy. This is most painful.

These men can speak the Jew's language, and yet the tongue of Babylon is more natural to them; they follow Christ, but their hearts are with Belial. Ah, Me! my soul is sick at the thought of them. Be true! Be true! If truth will carry you no further than despair, better that you stop in despair than gain hope by a lie. Do not live on fiction, profession, or presumption. Eat that which is good, and feed only upon the truth. Remember that when you build with the wood, hay, and stubble of mere notion, you are only gathering materials for your own funeral pile in that day when the fire shall devour all lovers and makers of a lie. Be true as steel! Every wise builder for his soul must mind that.

The next thing is *thoroughness*. Observe, according to our Lord, that the wise builder dug deep. You cannot do a right thing too well. Dig deep if you do dig a foundation. If it be repentance, let it be an intensely earnest repentance, including a vehement hatred of every form of sin. If you make confession before God, confess with your very soul, and not with your lips only; lay bare your spirit before the glance of Deity. If it be faith that you talk of, believe right up to the hilt. Do not go in for that kind of skeptical believing that is so common nowadays. If you believe, believe; if you repent, repent. In the purging of the soul there is nothing like sweeping out every particle of the old leaven of falsehood; and in bringing in the good things into the heart there is nothing like bringing in everything that Christ prescribes, that of his fullness we may receive not only grace, but also grace for grace, grace upon grace, all the grace that is needed. Be blunt in everything. The wise builder dug through the earth, and continued his digging until he reached the rock; and then he dug into the rock, and dug out a trench wherein he might lay his foundation, for he could not be content unless he made sure and thorough work of it. Sincerity and thoroughness are fine building materials.

Next to that add *self-renunciation,* for that is in the parable. When a man digs a deep foundation, he has much earth to throw out. So, he that builds for eternity has a great deal to get rid of. Self-trust must go at the beginning; love of sin must follow; worldliness, pride, self-seeking, all sorts of iniquity – these must be cast aside. There is very much rubbish, and the rubbish must go. You cannot make sure work for eternity without clearing away much that flesh and blood would like to retain. See to this, and count the cost.

Then must come *solid principle.* The man who is determined that if he does build he will build securely, digs down to the rock. He says, "I believe in God, he is my helper. I believe in ChIJesus, and on his atoning sacrifice and living intercession I build my eternal hopes. I also build on the doctrine of grace, for the Lord has said it – *By grace are ye saved through faith.* I build on Scripture; nothing but the confirmation of the Word will do for me." What God has said is a rock; what man teaches is mere shifting sand. What a blessed thing it is to get down to the eternal principles of divine truth! You that pick up your religion from your mothers and fathers; you that follow it because it happened to be in the family – what are you worth in the day of trouble? You are blown down like a booth, or a hut of boughs. But you that know what you believe, and why you believe it; you who, when you put your foot down, know what you are standing upon, and are persuaded that you have firm rock beneath you – you are the men who will stand fast when mere pretenders are hurled out of their place. Oh, my dear, seeking friends, fix upon true principles, and be not content with falsehood.

These truthful principles must be *firmly adhered to.* Bind your building to the rock. A house will not stand merely because it is *on* the rock; you must also get its foundation *into* the rock. The house must take a grip of the rock, and the rock must grasp the house. The more you can get the house to be a bit of the rock, and the rock, as it were, to grow up into the house, the more secure you are. It is of no use saying, "Yes, I confide in Christ, in grace, in revelation," unless your very life enters into these things, and they enter into you. Hypocrites, Job says, are stolen away in the night; so easily are they removed. The inventor of some new notion comes along, touts his new ideas, and silly souls are at once taken in by him. Christ may go, grace may go, and the Bible may go, too; their new master has them wholly in his power. We do not want such unsubstantial men; we care not for these speculating builders whose carcasses are all around us. We have had enough of castles in the air; we need true men who will stand fast like the mountains, while errors, like clouds, blow over them. Remember the huge shaft at Bradford, and how many were slain by its fall, and let it teach you to hold hard to foundational truths, and never depart from them.

The man in the second parable did not build as he should; what may I say of him? I will say three words. First, he was a man who had *nothing out of sight:* you could see all his house when you looked at it. If you can see all a man's religion at a glance, he has no religion worth having. Godliness lies most in secret prayer, private devotion, and inward grace. The wise builder had the most costly part of his house buried in the ground; but the other man showed all that he had above ground. He is a poor tradesman who has no stock but that which he puts into the window. He will not last long who has no capital. He cannot stand for long who has no backbone within. Beware of a religion of show.

Next, this man had *nothing to hold to.* He built a house, but it stood upon the loose soil. He easily dug into that, and built his house; but his walls had no holdfast. Beware of a religion without holdfasts. But if I get a grip upon a doctrine, they call me a bigot. Let them do so. Bigotry is a hateful thing, and yet that which is now accused of being bigotry is a great virtue, and greatly needed in these frivolous times. I have been inclined lately to start a new denomination and call it "the Church of the Bigoted." Everybody is getting to be so oily, so plastic, so untrue, that we need a race of hard shells to teach us how to believe. Those old-fashioned people who in former ages believed something, and thought the opposite of it to be false, were truer folk than the present time-servers.

I would like to ask the preachers of the broad school whether any doctrine is worth a man's dying for it. They would have to reply, "Well, of course, if a man had to go to the stake or change his opinions, the proper way would be to state them with much reservedness, and to be extremely respectful to the opposite school." But suppose he is required to deny the truth? "Well, there is much to be said on each side, and probably the negative may have a measure of truth in it as well as the positive. At any rate, it cannot be a prudent thing to incur the disgrace of being burned, and so it might be preferable to leave the matter an open question for the time being." Yes, and as these gentlemen always find it unpleasant to be unpopular, they soften down the hard threatenings of Scripture as to the world to come, and put a color upon every doctrine to which worldly-wise men object.

The teachers of doubt are very doubtful teachers. A man must have something to hold to, or he will neither bless himself nor others. Bring all the ships into the pool, but do not moor or anchor one of them; let each one be free! Wait for a stormy night, and they will dash against each other, and great mischief will come of this freedom. Perfect love and charity will not come through our being all unmoored, but by each having his proper moorings and keeping to them in the name of God. You must have something to hold to; but the builder in the parable had not, and so he perished.

The foolish builder had *nothing to resist outward circumstances.* On summer days his house was a favorite resort, and was considered to be quite as good as his neighbor's in all respects. Frequently he rubbed his hands and said, "I do not see but what my house is quite as good as his, and perhaps a little better; the fact is, I had a few pounds to spare that I did not bury in the ground as he did, and with it I have bought many a little ornament, so that my habitation has a finer look than his building." So it seemed; but when the torrent came raging down the mountainside, his building, having nothing with which to resist the violence of the flood, fell down at once, and not a trace of it remained when the storm had ceased. Thus do men fail because they offer no resistance to forces that drive them into sin; the great current of evil finds in them victims, and not opponents.

Thirdly, we will now gather from our text a set of arguments *urging us to take care of the foundation.* I will glance over these arguments, wishing much that I had time to enforce them. The first is this: we ought to build with a good foundation at the beginning, because otherwise *we shall not build well in any other part of the house.* Bad work in the foundation influences all the rest of the courses. In the Revised Version at the end of the forty-eighth verse, instead of *for it was founded upon a rock,* we read: *because it had been well builded.* The house was built well at the bottom, and that led the workman to put in good work all the way up, so that all through *it had been well builded.* The other man built badly underground, and did the same up to the roof. When you get into the habit of doing sloppy work in secret, the tendency is to be sloppy in public too.

If the underground part of our religion is not firmly laid upon Christ, then in the upper part there will be rotten work, half-baked bricks, mud instead of mortar, and a general dealing in a neglectful manner with everything. When a great Grecian artist was fashioning an image for the temple, he was diligently carving the back part of the goddess, and someone said to him, "You need not finish that part of the statue, because it is to be built into the wall." He replied, "The gods can see in the wall." He had a right idea of what is due to God. That part of my religion that no man can see should be as perfect as if it were to be observed by all. The day shall declare it. When Christ shall come, everything shall be made known and published before the universe. Therefore, see to it that it is fit to be thus made known.

See, again, that we ought to have good foundations when we *look at the situation whereon the house is to be built.* It is clear from this parable that both these houses were built in places not far from a river, or where streams might be expected to come. Certain parts of the South of France are marvelously like Palestine, and perhaps at the present moment they are more like what the Holy Land was in Christ's day than what the Holy Land is now. When I reached Cannes last year, I found that there had been a flood in the town. This flood did not come by reason of a river being swollen, but through a deluge of rain. A waterspout seems to have burst upon the hillside, tearing up earth, and rocks, and stones, and then hurrying down to the sea. It rushed across the railway station and poured down the street that led to it, drowning several persons in its progress. When I was there, a large hotel – I would think five stories high – was shored up with timber, and was evidently doomed; for when this stream rushed down the narrow street it undermined the lower layers of the building, and as there were no foundations at all able to bear such a test, the whole construction was rendered unsafe.

The Savior had some such case in his mind's eye. A torrent of water would come tearing down the side of the mountain, and if a house was built on the mere earth, it would be carried away directly; but if it was fastened into the rock so that it became part and parcel of it, then the flood might rush all around it, but it would not shake the walls. Beloved builder of a house for your soul, your house is so situated that one of these days there must come great pressure upon it. "How do you know?" Well, I know that the house wherein my soul lives is pitched just where winds blow, and waves rise, and storms beat. Where is yours? Do you live in a snug corner? Yes, but one of these times you will find that the snug corner will be no more shielded than the open riverside; for God so orders providence that every man has his test sooner or later. It may be that you think yourself past temptation, but the idea is a delusion, as time will show. Perhaps from the very fact that you seem quite out of the way, a peculiar temptation may come upon you. Therefore, I do pray you, because of the exposed condition of your life's building, build upon a good foundation.

The next argument is: build deep, because of the *ruin that will result from a bad foundation*. The foolish builder's house was without a foundation. Notice the words, *without a foundation*. Write down the expression, and see whether the words apply to you or not. What happened to this house without a foundation? The stream beat vehemently upon it. The river's bed had long been dry, but suddenly it was flooded, and the torrent rolled with tremendous power. Perhaps it was persecution, perhaps it was prosperity, perhaps it was trouble, perhaps it was temptation, perhaps it was prevalent skepticism, perhaps it was death. But anyhow, the flood beat vehemently upon that house, and now we read the next words – *and immediately it fell*. It did not stand a prolonged assault, it was captured at once. *Immediately it fell.* What! In a minute, all that fair profession of faith gone? *Immediately it fell.*

Why, that is the man I shook hands with the other Sunday, and called him "Brother," and he has been seen drunk! or he has been in the frivolous assembly, using unholy language! or he has become an utter doubter all of a sudden! It is sorrowful work burying our friends, but it is much more sorrowful work to lose them in this fashion; and yet so they vanish. They are gone, even as Job said, *The east wind carrieth him away, and he departeth* (Job 27:21). *Immediately* they fall, and yet we thought so highly of them, and they thought so highly of themselves. *Immediately it fell.* Their profession of faith could not endure trial, and all because it had no foundation.

Then it is added, *And the ruin of that house was great.* The house came down with a crash, and it was the man's all. The man was a distinguished professor, and therefore his ruin was all the more notable. It was a great fall because it could never be built up again. When a man dies a hypocrite, certainly there is no hope of restitution for him. By the stream the very debris of the ruined house was swept away; nothing was left. Oh men, if you lose a battle, you may fight again and win another; if you fail in business, you may start again in trade and realize a fortune; but if you lose your souls, the loss is irretrievable. Once lost, lost forever. There will be no second opportunity. Do not deceive yourselves about that. Therefore, dig deep, and lay every stone most firmly upon the foundation of rock.

For lastly, and perhaps this will be the best argument, *observe the effect of this good, sure building,* this deep building. We read that when the flood beat upon the wise man's house, the flood *could not shake it.* That is very beautiful. Not only could it not carry it away, but it also *could not shake it.* I see the man: he lost his money and became poor, but he did not give up his faith; that *could not shake it.* He was ridiculed and slandered, and many of his former friends gave him the cold shoulder, but they *could not shake it.* He went to Jesus under his great trial and he was sustained: the trial *could not shake it.* He was very sick and his spirit was depressed within him, but still he held his confidence in Christ: depression *could not shake it.* He was near to death; he knew that he must soon depart out of this world, but all the pains of death and the certainty of dissolution could not shake him. He died as he lived, firm as a rock, rejoicing as much as ever, no, rejoicing more, because he was nearer to the kingdom and to the fruition of all his hopes. The flood *could not shake it.* It is a grand thing to have a faith that cannot be shaken.

I saw one day a number of beech trees that had formed a woodland: they had all fallen to the ground through a storm. The fact was, they leaned upon one another to a great extent, and the thickness of the wood prevented each tree from getting a firm hold of the soil. They kept each other up and also constrained each other to grow up tall and thin, to the neglect of root growth. When the tempest forced down the first few trees, the others readily followed one after the other. Close to that same spot I saw another tree in the open, bravely defying the blast, in solitary strength. The hurricane had beaten upon it, but it had endured all its force unsheltered. That lone, brave tree seemed to be better rooted than before the storm. I thought, "Is it not so with professing Christians?" They often hold together, and help each other to grow up, but if they do not have a firm personal roothold, when a storm arises they fall in rows. A minister dies, or certain leaders are taken away, and there go the members by departure from the faith and from holiness.

I would have you be self-contained, growing each man into Christ for himself, rooted and grounded in love and faith and every holy grace. Then when the worst storm that ever blew on mortal man shall come, it will be said of your faith, the storm *could not shake it.* I plead with you who are now seeking Christ to take care that you build well, that you may stand long in our Zion, steadfast and unmovable. God grant it, in the name of Christ. Amen.

Chapter 10

One Lost Sheep

How think ye? if a man have an hundred sheep,
and one of them be gone astray, doth he not leave
the ninety and nine, and goeth into the moun-
tains, and seeketh that which is gone astray? And if
so be that he find it, verily I say unto you, he rejoi-
ceth more of that sheep, than of the ninety and
nine which went not astray. (Matthew 18:12-13)

This passage occurs in a discourse of our Savior against *despising one of those little ones that believe in him.* He foretells a dreadful doom for those who, in their contempt for the little ones, cause them to stumble; and he forbids that contempt by a variety of forcible arguments, upon which we cannot now dwell. There is a tendency, apparent at this present time, to think little of the conversion of individuals, and to look upon the work of the Holy Spirit upon each separate person as much too slow a business for this progressive age.

We hear grand theories of a theocracy of a kind unknown to Holy Scripture: a semi-political dominion of the Lord over masses wherein the individuals are unconverted. We listen to great swelling words about the uplifting of nations and the advancement of the race; but these lofty ideas do not produce facts, nor have they any moral power. Our "cultured" teachers, weary of the humdrum work of bringing individual souls into light, long to do it wholesale, by a far more rapid process than that of personal salvation. They are tired of the units; their great minds dwell upon "the solidarity of the race."

I am bold to assert that if ever we despise the method of individual conversion, we shall get into an unsound order of business altogether, and find ourselves wrecked upon the rocks of hypocrisy. Even in those right glorious times when the gospel shall have the freest course, and shall run the most quickly, and be the most extensively glorified, its progress will still be after the former manner of the conviction, conversion, and sanctification of individuals who shall each one believe and be baptized, according to the Word of the Lord.

I fear lest in any of you there should be even the least measure of despising the one lost sheep because of the large and philosophical methods that are now so loudly touted. I would not have you exchange the gold of individual Christianity for the base metal of Christian socialism. If the wanderers are to be brought in vast numbers, as I pray they may be, yet must it be accomplished by the bringing of them in one by one. To attempt national conversion without personal conversion is to dream of erecting a house without separate bricks. In the vain attempt to work in the sum, we may miss the practical result that would have followed working in detail. Let us settle it in our minds that we cannot do better than obey the example of our Lord Jesus, given to us in the text, and go after the one sheep that has gone astray.

Our text warns us that *we are not to despise one person, even on account of evil character.* The first temptation is to despise *one* because it is only one; the next is to despise one because that one is so little; the next, and perhaps the most dangerous form of the temptation, is to despise one because that one has gone astray. The individual is not in the right path, not obeying the law, nor reflecting credit on the church, but doing much that disturbs the spiritual, and grieves the holy; yet we are not, therefore, to despise him. Read the eleventh verse: *The Son of man is come to save that which was lost.*

In the Greek, the word *lost* is a very strong word; we may read it: "that which is destroyed." It does not mean "that which is nonexistent," as you will clearly see, but that which is destroyed as to usefulness to the shepherd, as to happiness to itself, and as to working out the intent for which it was created. If any are so effectively destroyed by sin that their existence is a greater calamity than their nonexistence would have been; if they are now dead in trespasses and sins, and even offensive in character, still we must not despise them. The Son of Man did not despise such, since he has *come to seek and to save that which was lost.*

Many a soul that has been so destroyed as to be lost to itself, lost to God, lost to his people, and lost to anything like hope and holiness, the Lord Jesus Christ has saved by his gracious power. *He values each one;* this is the lesson that I would teach this morning to the utmost of my power. May the Holy Spirit teach it also.

In considering the words of our Lord that are now before us, I beg you to notice, first, that *the Lord Jesus herein shows peculiar interest in one lost soul;* secondly, *he puts forth special exertion for the rescue of this lost one;* and thirdly, *he displays a special rejoicing when the lost one is restored.* When we have thought of all this, we shall then observe, fourthly, that *he sets us a very striking example,* herein teaching us to care for each soul destroyed by sin.

First, then, in the words before us, our Savior shows peculiar interest in one lost soul.

Note, in the commencement, that for the sake of those lost ones *our Lord assumes a special character.* The eleventh verse puts it: *The Son of man is come to save that which was lost.* He was not originally known as *the Son of man,* but as "the Son of God." Before all worlds, he dwelt in the bosom of the Father, and *thought it not robbery to be equal with God* (Philippians 2:6). But in order to redeem men, the Son of the Highest became *the Son of man.* He was born of the Virgin, and by birth inherited the innocent infirmities of our nature, and bore the sufferings falling on those infirmities. Then did he also take upon himself our sin and its penalty, and therefore died upon the cross. He was in all points made like unto his brethren. He could not be the Shepherd of men without becoming like them, and therefore the Word stooped to be made flesh. Behold the stupendous miracle of incarnation! Nothing can excel this marvel – Immanuel, God with us! *Being found in fashion as a man, he humbled himself, and became obedient unto death, even the death of the cross* (Philippians 2:8). O lost one, conscious of your loss, take heart today when the name of Jesus is named in your hearing; he is God, but he is man, and as God and man he saves his people from their sins.

Next to this, to show how Jesus values one lost soul, he *makes a very wonderful descent. The Son of man is come.* He was always known as "The Coming One"; but as to the salvation of the lost, he has actually come. For judgment he is "The Coming One" still; but for salvation we rejoice that our Savior has already come. Leaving the assemblies of the perfect, he has been here as the Friend of publicans and sinners. From being the Lord of angels, he has stooped to be *a man of sorrows, and acquainted with grief* (Isaiah 53:3). Yes, he has come, and not in vain. Those who preached the coming Savior had such a joyous message to deliver that their feet were beautiful upon the mountains, and their voices were as heavenly music; but as for us who preach that he has come, and, coming, has finished the work that he undertook to perform – surely ours is the choicest of messages.

Our Lord Jesus has completed the atoning sacrifice, and the justifying righteousness, by which lost men are saved. Happy is the preacher of such tidings, and blessed are your ears that hear them! The Good Shepherd has performed all that is necessary for the salvation of the flock that his Father has given into his hands. Beloved, let us take heart. Lost as we are, Christ has come to save us. He has come to the place of our ruin and woe. His coming and seeking will not be in vain. Brethren, how greatly ought we to value the souls of men when Jesus for their sake becomes a man, and comes into this sinful world among our guilty race that he may work the salvation of the lost!

Note, here, that *he does this for those that are still straying.* I have observed, in looking at the Greek text, that it is written, "He seeketh that which goeth astray." The Shepherd seeks while the sheep strays; he seeks it because it strays and needs seeking. Very many of the Lord's redeemed are even now going astray, and even now is the Shepherd going after them. The Savior seeks those who are even now sinning. That he should have a love for those who are repenting I can well understand, but that he should care for those who are willfully going astray is far more gracious. Jesus seeks those whose backs are towards him, who are going further and further away from the fold; herein is grace most free, most full, most sovereign. Indeed, it is so. Though you harden yourself against the Lord, though you refuse to turn at his rebuke, yet if you be his redeemed, his eye of love observes you; in all your willful wanderings he follows you. He sees you, he seeks you. Oh, that you may yield, and find that he saves you! O you that are now in the flock, think of the love of Christ for you when you were outside the fold; when you had no wish to return; when, seeing him pursuing you, you only ran the faster to escape his almighty love! Let us sing together:

> Determined to save, he watched o'er my path,
> When, Satan's blind slave, I sported with death.

Notwithstanding all my rebellion, and all my willful transgression, he still loved me with his heart, and pursued me with his Word. Oh, how we ought to love sinners, since Jesus loved us and died for us while we were yet sinners! We must care for drunkards while they still pass around the cup; swearers even while we hear them swear; and prodigals while we mourn to see them polluting our midnight streets. We must not wait until we see some better thing in them, but feel an intense interest for them as what they are – straying and lost. When the sheep is torn with the thorns of the waste places, and is sick, and worn to skin and bones with long wanderings and hungerings, we must seek its restoration, though we see in it no desire to submit itself to the Shepherd's care and rule. Such was our Savior's love for us; such be our love for lost ones.

The Shepherd takes a peculiar interest in the lost, not only as now straying, but also as *having already gone very far away.* Carefully consider these words – *if so be that he find it.* That *if* tells its own tale. The sheep had become so terribly lost that it was not likely to be found again. It had wandered into so dense a thicket, or strayed into so wild a region, that it seemed scarcely within the bounds of hope that it would ever be discovered and brought back. We do not often meet with an *if* in reference to the work of Christ, but here is one – *if so be that he find it.* This does not show weakness in the Shepherd, but shows the desperate danger for the sheep. I have often heard it said, by those who come to confess Christ, and to acknowledge his love for them, that they are struck with wonder that they, above all others, should be doing any such thing. When we sit at the Lord's Table, the feast is very wonderful; but the greatest wonder is the guest when I am there. How humbly do we each one sing,

Why was I made to hear thy voice,
And enter where there's room,
When thousands make a wretched choice,
And rather starve than come?

But it is so. The Good Shepherd is today seeking many whose salvation seems highly improbable, if not utterly impossible. Herein is love that he should go after those whose finding is by no means a certainty, nor even a probability! Very improbable, almost impossible, is the task he undertakes! Yet in such he takes a deep interest.

Moreover, those toward whom our Lord has these thoughts of love have often sinned so as to have *brought themselves into the deadliest danger. For the Son of man is come* **to save** *that which was lost* (emphasis added). Saving implies that ruin, peril, jeopardy – yes, destruction – is already in a measure present. Are not many now playing with the fire of hell? For what is that unquenchable fire but sin in its nature and results? Men are trifling on the brink of eternal woe: *Their foot shall slide in due time* (Deuteronomy 32:35). Playing with edged tools is nothing in danger compared with sporting with your lusts; and many are doing so.

Yet, despite their danger, Jesus seeks them. Do you not see those sheep heedlessly feeding near the den of the wolf? In a little time the monster will devour them. They are far away from home, and food, and rest, and safety. They have no desire to return, but they are resolved to roam yet farther from the fold. The Lord Jesus comes after such desperately deluded ones. Until you pass the iron gate the gospel will invite you to return. If you be but one inch this side of hell, love will pursue you, and mercy will follow you. Our glorious David, while a lamb still lives, is able to rescue it from the jaw of the lion, and the paw of the bear. Though, like Jonah, a soul may have descended into the deeps, and may lie out of all human reach, yet a word from Jesus can bring it up from the lowest pit. Glory be to the blessed name of the almighty Savior, for he is able to save to the uttermost. His power to save the lost is such that none are too vile for his salvation.

If we rightly consider the parable before us, we shall see that *he takes a special interest in these stray sheep because they are his own.* This man did not go after wild beasts, nor after other men's sheep; but he had a hundred sheep of his own, and when he had counted them, he missed one. The hireling, whose own the sheep are not, would have said, "We have nearly the hundred; we need not be particular about an odd one." But these hundred sheep belonged to the Shepherd himself; they were his own by choice, by inheritance, by divine gift, by glorious capture, and by costly purchase, and he could not accept ninety and nine for a hundred. *None of them is lost,* says he. *Those that thou gavest me I have kept, and none of them is lost, but the son of perdition; that the scripture might be fulfilled.* Jesus could not endure to report a loss upon the flock handed over to him by the Father. Ninety-nine is not a hundred, and the Savior will not consider it such, for well he knows that *it is not the will of your Father which is in heaven, that one of these little ones should perish* (Matthew 18:14).

Dear friends, since Jesus takes such an interest even in one stray soul, you must not think it little that you should be called to care for a single soul. Do not think that a little congregation of forty or fifty is too few to be worthy of your best efforts. Should your class, through various circumstances, get down to a very small number, do not, therefore, give it up. No, no. Value one soul more than a world's purchase. The full company of the redeemed is far from being made up as yet, and the Lord has many people in this city not yet brought to his feet; therefore, never dream of ceasing your labors. Rest not until the hour shall come,

> When all the chosen race
> Shall meet around the throne;
> Shall bless the conduct of his grace,
> And make his glories known.

Secondly, may the Spirit of God help me while I remind you that our Lord put forth special exertion to save one solitary individual.

Observe in the parable – for it is a parable, though briefly told – that we see the Shepherd *leaving happier cares.* He felt himself at home with his attached and faithful flock; they had not gone astray, and they gathered around him, and he fed them, and took pleasure in them. There is always a great deal to do with sheep: they have many diseases, many weaknesses, and many needs; but when you have an attached, affectionate flock around you, you feel at home with them. So the Great Shepherd describes himself as leaving the ninety and nine, his choice flock, the sheep that had fellowship with him, and he with them. Yes, he leaves those in whom he could take pleasure, to seek one that gave him pain. I will not dwell upon how he left the paradise above, and all the joy of his Father's house, and came to this bleak world; but I pray you remember that he did so. It was a wonderful descent when he came from beyond the stars to dwell on this clouded globe, to redeem the sons of men.

But remember, he still continually comes by his Spirit. His errands of mercy are perpetual. The Spirit of God moves his ministers, who are Christ's representatives, to forego the feeding of the gathered flock, and to seek, in their discourses, the salvation of the wandering ones, in whose character and behavior there is nothing to cheer us. My Master's heart is full of care for all that love him; he wears their names engraved on the jewels of his breastplate. But yet his heart is always going forth afar, after those who have not yet been brought to him, and after those who once were in his fold, but have gone aside and left the flock. He leaves the happy and the holy, and gives his best thoughts to the lost.

Our Lord *goes out to seek these.* It is not merely a sending forth of thought, it is also a marching forth of power. His divine grace is going forth, I trust, this day, beyond the company whom he has called by his grace, to those other sheep who are not yet of his fold, whom also he must bring in. He would not have his church expend all her care on the flock that he has led into her green pastures, but he would have her go abroad after those who are not yet in her blessed society.

According to the text, the Shepherd goes into the mountains: he goes among difficulties and dangers. He will do and dare for the saving of the lost; no hardships can daunt his mighty love. You know through what dark ravines he passed in saving men. You have heard what climbing he did after proud souls, and what voluntary descent for despairing ones. A sheep in the East is more light of foot than our sheep; it will leap like a gazelle, and climb the mountains like a goat; and so are sinners very swift in transgression, and very daring in presumption. They leap in their iniquities where the children of God would shudder to follow them even in thought. They make nothing of leaps of profanity that would curdle the blood of him that has been taught the fear of God at the feet of Jesus Christ.

Yet the Lord Jesus went after these desperadoes. What difficulties he conquered, what sufferings he endured, what mountains he leaped over, that he might seek and save! O brethren, the same heart is in him still; he goes forth continually in the preaching of the Word. With many a sigh and many a groan on the part of his chosen ministers, he goes among the mountains to seek that which has gone astray. I pray that he may accept the effort of his unworthy servant this day, and bring some lost one home by means of this message.

To show his exertion for the lost, our Lord describes himself as *seeking with persevering diligence.* He looks this way, but sees nothing. He shades his eyes with his hand, and looks steadily! He thought he saw his sheep. There is surely a living object upon the hillside! He gazes intently. No, it does not stir; it is a white rock! Possibly the lost sheep is in yonder gully! It is a long way to go, but he is so intent on his purpose that he is soon there; but the sheep is not to be seen. Where can it be? He travels on with swift foot, for he does not know what may become of his sheep while he delays. Every now and then he stops: he thinks he hears a bleating. Surely it is the voice of his sheep! He is mistaken. His love makes his ear the father of sounds that are not sounds at all. He has neither seen nor heard it these long hours, but he will continue seeking until he finds it.

The concentrated omniscience of Christ is set upon a soul that goes astray, looking after it in all its evil desires and evil emotions; watching the growth of anything that looks like repentance; and observing with sorrow the hardening of its heart. This is what our Lord is doing for those redeemed with blood, who as yet have not been carried back to the fold. He puts forth a gracious exertion of eye and mind as well as of foot and hand towards his wandering sheep.

At the end he saves – completely saves. He has not come to make the salvation of his people possible, but to actually save them. He has not come to put them in the way of saving themselves, but to save them. He has not come to half save them, but to save them altogether. When my Lord comes forth in the majesty of his sovereign grace to save a soul, he achieves his purpose, despite sin, and death, and hell. The wolf may grind his teeth, but the Shepherd is the wolf's master. The sheep itself may for a long time have wandered, and at the end may struggle against him; but he grips its feet, and throws the creature on his shoulders, and bears it home, for he is resolved to save it. The sheep is glad to be so borne, for with a touch the Shepherd molds its will to his more perfect will. His grace is the triumphant energy by which the lost one is restored.

The salvation of a single soul is a mass of miracles. I have heard of a fire that consumed the shop of a jeweler, and a number of costly treasures of gold, and silver, and precious stones were found among the ruins, caked into a conglomerate of riches. What a salvage! Such is the salvation of a single man; it is a mass of priceless mercies melted into one inestimable ingot, dedicated to the praise of the glory of his grace who makes us to be *accepted in the beloved* (Ephesians 1:6), and *saved in the Lord with an everlasting salvation* (Isaiah 45:17). When I think of the energy that is put forth by the Lord to save a single lost soul, I feel stirred in my heart, and I desire that your hearts should be stirred also, that we may put forth all our strength to go and find the Lord's lost ones. Let us cooperate with him in his great labor of seeking that which is lost. Oh, that the Holy Spirit may put such a spirit within us and keep it there!

I am compelled to pass onward somewhat hurriedly. Notice, in the third place, that our Lord feels a special rejoicing at the recovery of a wandering sheep. Do not make a mistake here. Do not suppose that our Lord loves more the one soul that has wandered than the ninety and nine who have been preserved by his grace from going astray. Oh no! he thinks ninety-nine times more of ninety-nine than of one, for his sheep are each one equally precious to him. We must not suppose that he looks upon any one soul of his redeemed with a tenderness ninety-nine times greater than he gives to another.

But you will see the meaning of the passage by an illustration from your own experience. You have a family, and you love all your children alike. But little Johnny is very ill; he has a fever, and is likely to die, so now you think more of him than of all the rest. He recovers, and you bring him downstairs in your arms, and just then he is the dearest child of the whole company. Not that he is really more valued than his brothers and sisters, but the fact that he has been so ill, and was likely to die, has brought him more before your mind, and caused you more anxiety, and therefore you have more joy in him because of his recovery.

The great deeps of Christ's love are the same to all his flock, but on the surface there is sometimes a holy storm of joy when any one of them has been newly restored after wandering.

Learn the occasion of this demonstrative joy. The wandering one has caused great sorrow. We were all grieved that our brother should become a gross backslider, that such an earnest Christian as he seemed to be should disgrace his profession. Our Lord is still more grieved than we are. When the erring one comes back, we feel a new joy in him. In proportion to the sorrow felt over the wanderer is the joy manifested when he is restored.

Moreover, great anxieties were aroused; we feared that he was not the Lord's, and that he would go back unto hell. We trembled for him. That black dread is all over now: the sheep is safe, and the doubtful one is saved and restored to the fold. In proportion to the weight of the anxiety is the intensity of the relief.

The Shepherd had exercised also great labor over the lost one. He went up among the mountains to find his sheep; but now his labor is fully rewarded, for he has found his lost sheep. He remembers no more his travel and toil for joy that the sheep is safe.

Besides, in this newly restored one, *there are marks of salvation that cause joy.* He has been torn with the briars, but he is resting now. See how he lies down in the tender grass! He was weary and worn, and almost dead with his wanderings, but now how happy he is in the presence of his Shepherd! How closely he keeps to his Shepherd's footsteps! All this goes to make the Shepherd glad!

Besides, the shepherd rejoices when he brings back the lost sheep because *he makes that rescue an occasion and opportunity for having a special gala day.* He wishes all his sheep to learn his delight in them all by seeing his delight in one. I know it is so in the church. I bless the Lord when he keeps the feet of his saints: I bless him every day for preserving grace; but when some grievous wanderer is restored, then we bless him more emphatically. Then we have music and dancing. The elder brother wonders what these overflowing joys can mean, but everybody else can see good reason for special cheeriness when the lost one is found. Shepherds and their flocks cannot have a holiday every day; but when a lost one has been recovered, they feel such mutual delight in each other, and such a common delight in the saving of the lost, that they seize upon the occasion for rejoicing. I want you all to recognize that if you love the church of Christ, you are bound to keep a feast day when fallen ones are raised up; and in order that you may hold that festival, you are bound to put out all your strength to bring in the lost one.

Now we come to the tug-of-war, that is, to look upon our divine Shepherd as he sets us a striking example.

We may view this text as *our personal missionary warrant.* Today we are called upon to think of missions; and as I think it vain to preach about missions in the big high-flying style, I have purposed to say something commonplace but practical. Brethren, we are all of us to be missionaries for Christ, and the text presents a warrant for each one to work earnestly as a soul winner.

What shall we do, then, to imitate our Lord? The answer is – Let us *go after one soul.* I cannot make a selection for you this morning, but I do implore all who are workers together with God to go after the ones. There is a kind of knack in speaking to individuals – everybody does not possess it, but every believer should labor to acquire it. Seek the souls of men one by one. It is far easier work for me to speak to you all than it would be to take each one apart by himself and speak to him personally of his soul; and yet such speaking to you one by one might be more successful than this message to you en masse. I implore you, as the Great Shepherd goes after one, do not think you will demean yourself by going after one poor man, or woman, or child; but do it now.

Listen again: *let that one be somebody that is quite out of the way.* Try and think of one who has grievously gone astray; it may be there is one such in your family, or you meet with one such in the course of business. Think carefully of that one soul, and reflect upon its sin and danger. You would like to pick out a hopeful case, in order that you might feel sure of success. Take another course this time: seek the one that is going astray and seems hopeless. Follow your Lord's example, and go after one who is the least likely to be found. Will you try this plan? If you do not, you will be leaving the way of your Lord.

"I have a class and a job," says one. Yes, I want you, for a little, to *leave the ninety and nine.* I pray that you may feel called to look after some one greatly depraved person, or some utterly neglected child. Keep up your ninety-and-nine class, if you possibly can, but, at all hazards, go after the one. Make an unusual effort; go out of your way; let ordinary service be placed second for the time being. It will be a healthy change for you and, perhaps, a great relief. Perhaps you will come back and do more good with the ninety and nine, after you have been away a little while with the straying one. You are getting a little moldy; and you are just a wee bit tired of the monotony of your work. Every Sunday it's the same girls, or the same boys, and the same form of lesson. Well, cut the whole concern for a little, and go after the one sheep that has gone astray. "You are giving us odd advice, Mr. Spurgeon." If it is not in my text, then do not follow it; but if it is in our dear Master's words, I trust you will carry it out bravely.

When you go after that one, *have all your wits about you.* Go and *seek;* and you cannot do that unless you are on the alert. Follow up the straying one. Did you say that you would wait until he called at your house? Is that your notion of seeking lost sheep? Is that the way of sportsmen in the autumn? Do they sit in the drawing room until the pheasants fly by the window? That would be poor sport.

> O come, let us go and find them,
>   In the paths of death they roam.

Go after them, for so the shepherd did. He braved the mountain's slippery side. I do not suppose the shepherd had any greater love for mountain tracks than you have, but up the rough tracks he climbed for the sheep's sake. Go after sinners into their poverty and wretchedness until you find them.

Here is one thing to cheer you. If you should win such a soul as that, *you will have more joy, a great deal, than in saving those for whom you regularly labor* – more joy over that lost one than over the ninety and nine hopeful ones. It will be such a support to your faith, such a stimulus for your joy, such a bright light to your labor to have won such a specially guilty one. I should not wonder but what you will talk about it for many a day, and it will be a source of strength to you when things are not quite as you would desire. Such converts are our crown of rejoicing. May I specially recommend that you make a trial of this extra sheep-seeking? If you do not succeed, you will have done no harm, for you will have copied your Lord and Master. But you will succeed, for he is with you, and his Spirit works by you.

I would remind you that, *even under the old law, you would be bound to do this thing.* Turn to the twenty-third chapter of Exodus, and read the fourth and fifth verses. *If thou meet thine enemy's ox or his donkey going astray, thou shalt surely bring it back to him again. If thou see the donkey of him that hateth thee lying under his burden, and wouldest forbear to help him, thou shalt surely help with him.* You are bound to do good even to your enemy. Will you not serve your best friend? If your enemy's ox or donkey needed to be taken back to him, you are bound to do it. How much more when the sheep belongs to him whom you love with all your heart! Prove your love for Jesus by laboring to take back to him his strays!

Turn to the twenty-second chapter of Deuteronomy, the first to the fourth verses, and there you will find another bit of the law. *Thou shalt not see thy brother's ox or his sheep go astray, and hide thyself from them: thou shalt in any case bring them again unto thy brother.* Oh, will you not bring in the stray sheep of your greater Brother, *the firstborn among many brethren* (Romans 8:29)? *And if thy brother be not nigh unto thee, or if thou know him not, then thou shalt bring it unto thine own house, and it shall be with thee until thy brother seek after it, and thou shalt restore it to him again.* If you cannot get a soul to Christ, at any rate get it to yourself. If you cannot lead it immediately to conversion, show it some hospitality within your own doors, by ministering such comfort as you can. Do what you can to cheer the poor heart until Christ comes after it. *Thou shalt not see thy brother's donkey or his ox fall down by the way, and hide thyself from them: thou shalt surely help him to lift them up again.* How easy it is to *hide ourselves*! That is the expression used by Moses: *Thou shalt not . . . hide thyself from them.*

When you know that people are very wicked, the usual plan is to wish them well, but keep out of their way. Caution makes you hide yourself from them. The whole street may swarm with harlots, but then you have gone to bed, and the door is shut. What has their sin to do with you? There are many drunken men around; but you do not drink to excess, so what has their drinking to do with you? That is what is meant by "hiding ourselves from them." How easily that can be done! Take an illustration that is worth telling. A vessel, the other day, was crossing the Atlantic, and it fell in with a disabled emigrant ship, the *Danmark*. Suppose the captain had kept on his course. He might have looked another way, and resolved not to be detained. He might have argued, "I am bound to do the best for my owners. It will hinder me greatly if I go puttering about after this vessel. I had better go by and not see it, or make haste to port and send out help." It could have been done, and nobody would have been the wiser, for the ship would have gone down soon. However, the captain of that vessel was a man of a nobler breed. He did not hide himself, nor turn the blind eye towards the vessel in distress. But what did the captain do? All honor to him, he came near, and took the ship in tow. This was not all. He found that she could not keep afloat, and he resolved to take those hundreds of emigrants on board his own ship. But he could not carry them and his cargo too. What then? The decision was greatly to his honor. Overboard goes the cargo!

God's blessing rest on the man! Into the sea went the freight, and the passengers were taken on board and carried to the nearest port. He could have easily hidden himself, could he not? So can you, you Christian people, as you call yourselves. Can you go through this world and always have a blind eye to the case of lost sinners? Can you come in and out of this tabernacle and never speak to the strangers who throng these aisles? Will you let them go to hell unwarned and uninstructed? Can you hide yourselves from them? How dare you call yourselves Christians! How will you answer for it at last? Brothers, sisters, let us shake off this inhuman indifference, and deny ourselves rest, ease, and credit so that we may save poor sinking souls. Overboard with cargo cheerfully, so that you may, in the power of the Holy Spirit, save souls from death.

Once more, this text is *the great missionary warrant for all the church of God*. We are to go, as the Savior did, *to seek and to save that which was lost*; and we are to do this, not on account of the numbers of the heathen, but for one of them. I grant you there is a great power in the argument of numbers – so many hundreds of millions in China, so many hundreds of millions in India. But if there were only one person left unsaved in any part of the world, it would be worthwhile for the entire Christian church to go after that one person; for he who is greater than the church, as the Bridegroom is greater than the bride, left heaven, alas, and left the sweet society of his own beloved, that he might go after the one that had gone astray. Do not care, therefore, about numbers; save the smallest tribes. Have an eye to the hamlets in England. I believe that the scattered cottages of our land are in a worse condition than the villages. Care for the ones. Your Lord did so, and here is your warrant for doing the same.

Next, notice that we ought never to be moved by the supposed superiority of a race. I have heard it said that it would be far better to try and convert the superior races than to consider the more degraded ones. Is it not better to bring in the educated Brahmins than the wild hill tribes? "What a fine sort of people these are, these philosophical Hindus! If we could win them, they would be worth converting!" That is not at all according to the mind of Christ. The shepherd sought a lost sheep, and when he had found it, it was no great spoil for him, for it was so worn-out as to be nothing but a destroyed sheep. Yet he went after that one poor animal. Let us feel that the degraded Africans, the dwarfs of the woods, the cannibals of New Guinea, and all such, are to be sought quite as much as more advanced races. They are men; that is enough.

Once more, the motive for missionary enterprise must never be the excellence of the character of the individuals. The shepherd did not go after the sheep because it never went astray, nor because it was docile, but because it *did go* astray, and was *not* docile. The sin of men is their claim upon the church of God. The more sin, the more reason for abounding grace. Oh, that the church would feel it to be her duty, if not to go to the most degraded ones first, yet not to leave them to the last! Where you seem least likely to succeed there go at once, for there you will find room for faith; and where there is room for faith, and faith fills the room, God will send a blessing.

Dear friends, as you cannot, all of you, go abroad to the heathen, though some of you ought to do so, I ask you to do what you can do. Contribute to the collection, which is for the support of mission work. Here is a small opportunity; and if you do not avail yourselves of it, you are not likely to do the greater thing to which I have invited you. The Lord bless you! Amen.

Chapter 11

The Parable of the Lost Sheep

What man of you, having an hundred sheep, if he lose one of them, doth not leave the ninety and nine in the wilderness, and go after that which is lost, until he find it? And when he hath found it, he layeth it on his shoulders, rejoicing. And when he cometh home, he calleth together his friends and neighbours, saying unto them, Rejoice with me; for I have found my sheep which was lost. I say unto you, that likewise joy shall be in heaven over one sinner that repenteth, more than over ninety and nine just persons, which need no repentance. (Luke 15:4-7)

Our Lord Jesus Christ, while he was here below, was continually in the pursuit of lost souls. He was seeking lost men and women, and it was for this reason that he went down among them, even among those who were most evidently lost, that he might find them. He took pains to put himself where he could come into communication with them, and he exhibited such kindliness towards them that in crowds they drew near to hear him. I dare say it was a strange-looking assembly, a disreputable rabble, that made the Lord Jesus its center. I am not astonished that the Pharisee, when he looked upon the congregation, sneered and said, "He collects around him the pariahs of our community, the wretches who collect taxes for the foreigner of God's free people; and the fallen women of the towns, and similar riffraff make up his audiences; and he, instead of repelling them, receives them, welcomes them, looks upon them as a class to whom he has a peculiar relationship. He even eats with them. Did he not go into the house of Zacchaeus, and the house of Levi, and partake of the feasts that these low people made for him?"

We cannot tell you all the Pharisees thought, as it might not be edifying to attempt it; but they thought as badly of the Lord as they possibly could, because of the company which surrounded him. And so, he condescends in this parable to defend himself; not that he cared much about what they might think, but that they might have no excuse for speaking so bitterly of him. He tells them that he was seeking the lost, and where should he be found but among those whom he was seeking? Should a physician shun the sick? Should a shepherd avoid the lost sheep? Was he not exactly in his right position when there *drew near unto him all the publicans and sinners for to hear him?*

Our divine Lord defended himself by what is called an *argumentum ad hominem,* an argument to the men themselves; for he said, *What man **of you**, having an hundred sheep, if he lose one of them, doth not ... go after that which is lost, until he find it?* (emphasis added). No argument directs itself more powerfully upon men than one that comes close to home in their own daily life, and the Savior put it so. They were silenced, if they were not convinced. It was a peculiarly strong argument, because in their case it was only a sheep that they would go after; but in his case, it was something infinitely more precious than all the flocks of sheep that ever fed on the Plain of Sharon or Mount Carmel, for it was the soul of man that he sought to save. The argument had in it not only the point of peculiar adaptation, but also a force at the back of it unusually powerful for driving it home upon every honest mind.

It may be opened out in this fashion – "If you men would each one of you go after a lost sheep, and follow in its tracks until you found it, how much more may I go after lost souls, and follow them in all their wanderings until I can rescue them?" The going after the sheep is a part of the parable that our Lord meant them to observe. The shepherd pursues a route that he would never think of pursuing if it were only for his own pleasure; his way is not selected for his own ends, but for the sake of the stray sheep. He takes a track up hill and down dale, far into a desert, or into some dark woods, simply because the sheep has gone that way, and he must follow it until he finds it.

Our Lord Jesus Christ, as a matter of taste and pleasure, would never have been found among the publicans and sinners, nor among any of our guilty race. If he had considered his own ease and comfort he would have consorted only with pure and holy angels, and the great Father above. But he was not thinking of himself; his heart was set upon the lost ones, and therefore he went where the lost sheep were, *for the Son of man is come to seek and to save that which was lost.* The more steadily you look at this parable, the more clearly you will see that our Lord's answer was complete. We need not this morning regard it exclusively as an answer to Pharisees, but we may look at it as an instruction to ourselves, for it is quite as complete in that direction. May the Holy Spirit instruct us as we meditate upon it.

In the first place, I call attention to this observation: the one subject of thought to the man who had lost his sheep. This sets forth to us the one thought of our Lord Jesus Christ, the Good Shepherd, when he sees a man lost to holiness and happiness by wandering into sin.

The shepherd, on looking over his little flock of one hundred, can only count ninety-nine. He counts them again, and he notices that a certain one has gone. It may be a white-faced sheep with a black mark on its foot; he knows all about it, for *the Lord knoweth them that are his.* The shepherd has a photograph of the wanderer in his mind's eye, and now he thinks but little of the ninety and nine who are feeding in the pastures of the wilderness, but his mind is agitated by the one lost sheep. This one idea possesses him: A sheep is lost! This agitates his mind more and more – A sheep is lost. It masters his every faculty. He cannot eat bread; he cannot return to his home; he cannot rest while one sheep is lost.

To a tender heart a lost sheep is a painful subject of thought. It is a sheep, and therefore utterly *defenseless* now that it has left its defender. If the wolf should spy it out, or the lion or the bear should come across its tracks, it would be torn in pieces in an instant. Thus, the shepherd asks his heart the question – "What will become of my sheep? Perhaps at this very moment a lion may be ready to spring upon it, and if so, it cannot help itself!" A sheep is not prepared for fight, and even for flight it has not the swiftness of its enemy. That makes its compassionate owner all the more sad as he thinks again, "A sheep is lost; it is in great danger of a cruel death."

A sheep is of all creatures the most *senseless*. If we have lost a dog, it may find its way home again, and possibly a horse might return to its master's stable; but a sheep will wander on and on, in endless mazes lost. It is too foolish a thing to think of returning to the place of safety. A lost sheep is lost indeed in countries where lands lie unenclosed and the plains are boundless. That fact still seems to ring in the man's soul – "A sheep is lost, and it will not return, for it is a foolish thing. Where may it not have gone by this time? Weary and worn, it may be fainting; it may be far away from green pastures, and ready to perish with hunger among the bare rocks or upon the arid sand." A sheep is *shiftless;* it knows nothing about providing for itself. The camel can scent water from afar, and a vulture can spot its food from an enormous distance; but the sheep can find nothing for itself.

Of all wretched creatures, a lost sheep is one of the worst. If anybody had stepped up to the shepherd just then and said, "Good sir, what ails you? You seem in great concern," he would have replied, "And well I may be, for a sheep is lost."

"It is only one, sir, and I see you have ninety-nine left."

"Do you call it nothing to lose one? You are no shepherd yourself, or you would not trifle so. Why, I seem to forget these ninety-nine that are all safe, and my mind only remembers that one that is lost."

What is it that makes the Great Shepherd lay so much to his heart the loss of one of his flock? What is it that makes him agitated as he reflects upon that supposition – *if he lose one of them*?

I think it is, first, because of *his property in it*. The parable does not so much speak of a hired shepherd, but of a shepherd proprietor. *What man of you, having an hundred sheep, if he lose one of them.* Jesus, in another place, speaks of the hireling, whose own the sheep are not, and therefore he flees when the wolf comes. It is the shepherd proprietor who lays down his life for the sheep. It is not a sheep alone, and a lost sheep, but it is one of his own lost sheep that this man cares for. This parable is not written about lost humanity in the bulk – it may be so used if you please – but in its first sense it is written about Christ's own sheep; as also is the second parable concerning the woman's own money; and the third, not concerning any prodigal youth, but the father's own son. Jesus has his own sheep, and some of them are lost: yes, they were all once in the same condition; for *all we like sheep have gone astray; we have turned every one to his own way.*

The parable refers to the unconverted, whom Jesus has redeemed with his most precious blood, and whom he has undertaken to seek and to save. These are those other sheep whom also he must bring in. *For thus saith the Lord God; Behold, I, even I, will both search my sheep, and seek them out. As a shepherd seeketh out his flock in the day that he is among his sheep that are scattered; so will I seek out my sheep, and will deliver them out of all places where they have been scattered in the cloudy and dark day* (Ezekiel 34:11-12). The sheep of Christ are his long before they know it – they are his even when they wander; and when they are brought into the fold by the effective working of his grace, they become manifestly what they were in covenant from of old.

The sheep are Christ's, first, because he chose them from before the foundations of the world – *Ye have not chosen me, but I have chosen you.* They are his, next, because the Father gave them to him. How he dwells upon that fact in his great prayer in John 17: *Thine they were, and thou gavest them me* (verse 6); *Father, I will that they also, whom thou hast given me, be with me where I am* (verse 24). We are the Lord's own flock, furthermore, by his purchase of us; he says, *I lay down my life for the sheep* (John 10:15). It is nearly nineteen centuries ago since he paid the ransom price, and bought us to be his own; and we shall be his, for that purchase-money was not paid in vain. And so the Savior looks upon his hands, and sees the marks of his purchase; he looks upon his side, and sees the token of the effective redemption of his own elect unto himself by the pouring out of his own heart's blood before the living God.

This thought, therefore, presses upon him: "One of my sheep is lost." It is a wonderful supposition, that which is contained in this parable – *if he lose one of them.* What! Lose one whom he loved before ever the earth was? It may wander for a time, but he will not have it lost forever; that he cannot bear. What! Lose one whom his Father gave him to be his own? Lose one whom he has bought with his own life? He will not endure the thought. That word – *if he lose one of them* – sets his soul on fire. It shall not be.

You know how much the Lord has valued each one of his chosen, laying down his life for their redemption. You know how dearly he loves every one of his people; it is no new passion with him, neither can it grow old. He has loved his own and must love them to the end. From eternity that love has endured already, and it must continue throughout the ages, for he changes not. Will he lose one of those so dearly loved? Never, never. He has eternal possession of them by an everlasting covenant relationship, wherein the Father has given them to him. This it is which in great measure stirs his soul so that he thinks of nothing but this fact – One of my sheep is lost.

Secondly, he has yet another reason for this all-absorbing thought, namely, *his great compassion* for his lost sheep. The wandering of a soul causes Jesus deep sorrow; he cannot bear the thought of its perishing. Such is the love and tenderness of his heart that he cannot bear that one of his own should be in jeopardy. He can take no rest as long as a soul for whom he shed his blood still abides under the dominion of Satan and under the power of sin; therefore, the Great Shepherd neither night nor day forgets his sheep: he must save his flock, and he is distressed until it be accomplished.

He has a deep sympathy with each stray heart. He knows the sorrow that sin brings, the deep pollution and the terrible wounding that comes of transgression, even at the time; and the sore heart and the broken spirit that will come of it before long; and so the sympathetic Savior grieves over each lost sheep, for he knows the misery that lies in the fact of being lost. If you have ever been in a house with a mother and father, and daughters and sons, when a little child has been lost, you will never forget the agitation of each member of the household. See the father as he goes to the police station, and calls at every likely house; for he must find his child or break his heart. See the deep oppression and bitter anguish of the mother; she is like one distracted until she has news of her darling. You now begin to understand what Jesus feels for one whom he loves, who is graven on the palms of his hands, whom he looked upon in the glass of his foreknowledge, when he was bleeding his life away upon the tree; he has no rest in his spirit until his beloved is found. He has compassion like God, and that transcends all the compassion of parents or of brothers – the compassion of an infinite heart brimming over with an ocean of love. This one thought moves the pity of the Lord – *if he lose one of them.*

Moreover, the man in the parable had a third relation to the sheep that made him possessed with the one thought of its being lost – *he was a shepherd to it.* It was his own sheep, and he had therefore for that very reason become its shepherd; and he says to himself, "If I lose one of them, my shepherd work will be done wrong." What dishonor it would be to a shepherd to lose one of his sheep! Either it must be for lack of power to keep it, or lack of will, or lack of watchfulness; but none of these can pertain to the chief Shepherd. Our Lord Jesus Christ will never have it said of him that he has lost one of his people, for he glories in having preserved them all. *While I was with them in the world, I kept them in thy name: those that thou gavest me I have kept, and none of them is lost, but the son of perdition; that the scripture might be fulfilled.*

The devil shall never say that Jesus permitted one whom his Father gave him to perish. His work of love cannot in any degree become a failure. His death in vain? No, not in jot or tittle. I can imagine, if it were possible, that the Son of God could live in vain, but to die in vain? It shall never be. The purpose that he meant to achieve by his passion and death he shall achieve, for he is the Eternal, the Infinite, and the Omnipotent, and who shall stop his hand or baffle his purpose? He will not have it. *If he lose one of them,* says the passage, imagine the consequence. What scorn would come from Satan! What derision would he pour upon the Shepherd! How hell would ring with the news, "He has lost one of them." Suppose it to be the feeblest one; then would they cry, "He could keep the strong, who could keep themselves." Suppose it to be the strongest one; then would they cry, "He could not even keep one of the mightiest of them, but of necessity let him perish." This is good argument, for Moses pleaded with God, "What will the Egyptians say?" *It is not the will of your Father which is in heaven, that one of these little ones should perish;* neither is it for the glory of Christ that one of his own sheep should be eternally lost.

You see the reason for the Lord's heart being filled with one burning thought. First, the sheep is his own; next, he is full of compassion; and then again, it is his office to shepherd the flock.

All this is while the sheep is not thinking about the shepherd, or caring for him in the least degree. Some of you are not thinking at all about the Lord Jesus. You have no wish nor will to seek after him! What folly! Oh, the pity of it, that the great heart above should be yearning over you today, and should fail to rest because you are in peril, and you, who will be the greater loser, for you will lose your own soul, are sporting with sin, and making yourself merry with destruction. Ah, me! How far you have wandered! How hopeless would your case be if there were not an almighty Shepherd to think upon you.

Now we come to the second point, and observe the one object of search. This sheep lies on the shepherd's heart, and he must at once set out to look for it. He leaves the ninety and nine in the wilderness, and goes after that which is lost until he finds it.

Observe here that it is *a definite search.* The shepherd goes after the sheep, and after nothing else; and he has the one particular sheep in his mind's eye. I should have imagined, from the way in which I have seen this text handled, that Christ, the Shepherd, went down into the wilderness to catch anybody's sheep he could find. Many were running about, and he did not own any one of them more than another, but was content to pick up the one that he could first lay hold upon, or rather, that which first came running after him. Not so is the case depicted in the parable. It is his own sheep that he is seeking, and he goes distinctly after that one. It is his sheep that was lost– a well-known sheep; well-known not only to himself, but also to his friends and neighbors – for he speaks to them as if it were perfectly understood which sheep it was that he went to save. Jesus knows all about his redeemed, and he goes definitely after such and such a soul.

When I am preaching in the name of the Lord, I delight to think that I am sent to individuals with the message of mercy. I am not going to draw the bow at random at all; but when the divine hands are put on mine to draw the bow, the Lord takes such aim that no arrow misses its mark. Into the very center of the heart the Word finds its way; for Jesus goes not forth by chance in his dealings with men. He subdues the will and conquers the heart, making his people willing in the day of his power. He calls individuals and they come. He says, *Mary,* and the response is: *Rabboni* (John 20:16). I say, the man in the parable sought out a distinct individual, and rested not until he found it; and so does the Lord Jesus in the movements of his love go forth with no uncertainty. He does not grope about to catch whom he may, as if he played at blindman's bluff with salvation; but he seeks and saves the one out of his own sheep that he has his eye upon in its wanderings. Jesus knows what he means to do, and he will perform it to the glory of the Father.

Note that this is *an all-absorbing search.* He is thinking of nothing but his own lost sheep. The ninety and nine are left in safety, but they *are* left. When we read that he leaves them in the wilderness, we are apt to think of some barren place; but that is not intended. It simply means the open pasture, the grassland, the prairie. He leaves them well provided for, leaves them because he can leave them.

For the time being he is carried away with the one thought that he must seek and save the lost one, and therefore he leaves the ninety and nine in their pasture. "Shepherd, the way is very rocky!" He does not seem to know what the way is; his heart is with his lost sheep. "Shepherd, it is a heavy climb up yonder mountainside." He does not note his toil; his excitement lends him the feet of the wild goat; he stands securely where at other times his foot would slip. He looks around for his sheep and seems to see neither crag nor chasm. "Shepherd, it is a terrible path by which you must descend into yonder gloomy valley." It is not terrible to him; his only terror is lest his sheep should perish. He is taken up with that one fear, and nothing else. He leaps into danger, and escapes it by the one strong impulse that bears him on. It is grand to think of the Lord Jesus Christ with his heart set immovably upon the rescue of a soul that at this moment is lost to him.

It is *an active search* too; for observe, he goes after that which is lost until he finds it, and he does this with *a personal search.* He does not say to one of his subordinates, "Here, hasten after that sheep that was lost, and bring it home." No, *he* follows it himself. And if ever there is a soul brought from sin to grace, it is not by us poor ministers working alone, but it is by the Master himself, who goes after his own sheep. It is glorious to think of him still personally tracking sinners who, though they fly from him with a desperateness of folly, are nevertheless still pursued by him – pursued by the Son of God, by the Eternal Lover of men – pursued by him until he finds them.

For notice *the perseverance of the search: until he find it.* He does not stop until he has done the deed. You and I ought to seek after a soul, for how long? Why, until we find it; for such is the model set before us by the Master. The parable says nothing about his not finding it; no hint of failure is given; we dream not that there may be a sheep belonging to him that he will never find. Oh brethren, there are a great many whom you and I would never find; but when Jesus is after his own lost sheep, depend upon it that such is his skill, so clearly does he see, and so effectively does he intervene, that he will surely bring them in. A defeated Christ I cannot conceive of. It is a personal search, and a persevering search, and *a successful search,* until he finds it. Let us praise and bless his name for this.

Observe that when the shepherd does find it, there is a little touch in the parable not often noticed – he does not appear to put it back into the fold again. I mean, we do not find it so written, as a fact to be noted. I suppose he did so place it ultimately, but for the time being he keeps it with himself rather than with its fellows. The next scene is the shepherd at home, saying, *Rejoice with me; for I have found my sheep which was lost.* It looks as if Jesus did not save a soul so much for the church as for himself, and though the saved are in the flock, the greatest joy of all is that the sheep is with the Shepherd. This shows you how thoroughly Christ lays himself out that he may save his people. There is nothing in Christ that does not tend towards the salvation of his redeemed. There are no pullbacks with him, no half-consecrated influences that make him linger. In the pursuit of certain objects we lay out a portion of our power; but Jesus lays out all his powers upon the seeking and saving of souls.

The whole Christ seeks after each sinner; and when the Lord finds it, he gives himself to that one soul as if he had but that one soul to bless. How my heart admires the concentration of all the deity and manhood of Christ in his search after each sheep of his flock.

Now, we must pass on very briefly to notice a third point. We have had one subject of thought and one object of search; now we have one burden of love. When the seeking is ended, then the saving appears – *When he hath found it, he layeth it on his shoulders, rejoicing.* Splendid action this is! How beautifully the parable sets forth the whole of salvation. Some of the old writers delight to put it thus: in his incarnation he came after the lost sheep; in his life he continued to seek it; in his death he laid it upon his shoulders; in his resurrection he bore it on its way, and in his ascension he brought it home rejoicing. Our Lord's career is a course of soul winning, a life laid out for his people; and in it you may trace the whole process of salvation.

But now, see, the shepherd finds the sheep, and *he layeth it on his shoulders*. It is *an uplifting action,* raising the fallen one from the earth on which he has strayed. It is as though he took the sheep just as it was, without a word of rebuke, without delay or hesitancy, and lifted it out of the swamp or the briers into a place of safety. Do you not remember when the Lord lifted you up from the horrible pit? when he sent from above, and delivered you, and became your strength? I shall never forget that day. What a wonderful lift it was for me when the Great Shepherd lifted me into newness of life. The Lord said of Israel, *I bare you on eagles' wings* (Exodus 19:4); but it is a dearer emblem still to be borne upon the shoulders of the incarnate Lord.

This laying on the shoulders was *an appropriating act.* He seemed to say, "You are my sheep, and therefore I lay you on my shoulders." He did not make his claim in so many words, but by a rapid action he declared it; for a man does not bear away a sheep to which he has no right. This was not a sheep stealer, but a shepherd proprietor. He holds fast the sheep by all four of its legs, so that it cannot stir, and then he lays it on his own shoulders, for it is all his own now. He seems to say, "I am a long way from home, and I am in a weary desert; but I have found my sheep, and these hands shall hold it." Here are our Lord's own words: *I give unto [my sheep] eternal life; and they shall never perish, neither shall any man pluck them out of my hand.* Hands of such power as those of Jesus will hold fast the found one. Shoulders of such power as those of Jesus will safely bear the found one home. It is all well with that sheep, for it is positively and experimentally the Good Shepherd's own, just as it always had been his in the eternal purpose of the Father. Do you remember when Jesus said unto you, *Thou art mine* (Isaiah 43:1)? Then I know you also appropriated him, and began to sing,

> So I my best Beloved's am,
> And he is mine.

More condescending still is another view of this act: It was *a deed of service* to the sheep. The sheep is uppermost, the weight of the sheep is upon the shepherd. The sheep rides, the shepherd is the burden bearer. The sheep rests, the shepherd labors. *I am among you as he that serveth* (Luke 22:27), said our Lord long ago. *Being found in fashion as a man, he humbled himself, and became obedient unto death, even the death of the cross.* On that cross he bore the burden of our sin, and what is more, the burden of our very selves. Blessed be his name, *the Lord hath laid on him the iniquity of us all* (Isaiah 53:6), and he has laid us on him, too, and he bears us. Remember that choice Scripture: *In his love and in his pity he redeemed them; and he bare them, and carried them all the days of old* (Isaiah 63:9). Soul-melting thought, the Son of God became subservient to the sons of man! The Maker of heaven and earth bowed his shoulders to bear the weight of sinners.

It was a *rest-giving* act, very likely *needful* to the sheep that could go no farther, and was faint and weary. It was a full rest to the poor creature if it could have understood it, to feel itself upon its shepherd's shoulders, irresistibly carried back to safety. What a rest it is to you and to me to know that we are borne along by the eternal power and deity of the Lord Jesus Christ! *The beloved of the Lord shall dwell in safety by him; . . . and he shall dwell between his shoulders* (Deuteronomy 33:12). The Christ bears us up today: we have no need for strength, and our weakness is no impediment, for he bears us. Has not the Lord said, *I have made, and I will bear; even I will carry, and will deliver you* (Isaiah 46:4)? We shall not even stumble, much less fall to ruin; the shepherd's feet shall travel all the road in safety. No portion of the way back should cause us fear, for he is able to bear us even to his home above.

What a sweet word is that in Deuteronomy: *The Lord thy God bare thee, as a man doth bear his son, in all the way that ye went, until ye came into this place* (Deuteronomy 1:31). Blessed rest of faith, to give yourself up entirely to those hands and shoulders to keep and carry you even to the end! Let us bless and praise the Lord. The shepherd is consecrated to his burden: he bears nothing on his shoulders but his sheep; and the Lord Jesus seems to bear no burden but that of his people. He lays out his omnipotence to save his chosen; having redeemed them first with the price of blood, he redeems them still with all his power. *And they shall be mine, saith the Lord of hosts, in that day when I make up my jewels* (Malachi 3:17). Oh, the glorious grace of our unfailing Savior, who consecrates himself to our salvation, and concentrates upon that object all that he has and is!

We close by noticing one more matter, that is, *the one source of joy.* This man who had lost his sheep is filled with joy, but his sheep is the sole source of it. His sheep has so taken up all his thoughts, and so commanded all his faculties, that as he found all his care centered upon it, so he now finds all his joy flowing from it.

I invite you to notice the first mention of joy we get here: *When he hath found it, he layeth it on his shoulders, rejoicing.* "That is a great load for you, shepherd!" Joyfully he answers, "I am glad to have it on my shoulders." The mother does not say when she has found her lost child, "This is a heavy load." No, she presses it to her bosom. She does not mind how heavy it is; it is a dear burden to her. She rejoices to bear it once again. *He layeth it on his shoulders, **rejoicing*** (emphasis added). Remember that text: *Who for the joy that was set before him endured the cross, despising the shame* (Hebrews 12:2).

A great sorrow was on Christ when our load was laid on him; but a greater joy flashed into his mind when he thought that we were thus recovered from our lost estate. He said to himself, "I have taken them up upon my shoulders, and none can hurt them now, neither can they wander to destruction. I am bearing their sin, and they shall never come into condemnation. The penalty of their guilt has been laid on me so that it may never be laid on them. I am an effective and efficient Substitute for them. I am bearing, that they may never bear, my Father's righteous wrath." His love for them made it a joy to feel every lash of the scourge of justice; his love for them made it a delight that the nails should pierce his hands and feet, and that his heart should be broken with the absence of his Father, God. Even *Eloi, Eloi, lama sabachthani,* when the deeps of its woe have been sounded, will be found to have pearls of joy in its caverns. No shout of triumph can equal that cry of grief, because our Lord delights to bear even the forsaking of his Father for the sin of his chosen whom he had loved from before the foundation of the world.

Oh, you cannot understand it except in a very feeble measure! Let us try to find an earthly miniature likeness. A son is taken ill far away from home. He is laid sick with a fever, and a telegram is sent home. His mother says she must go and nurse him; she is wretched until she can set out on the journey. It is a dreary place where her boy lies, but for the moment it is the dearest spot on earth to her. She delights to leave the comforts of her home to stay among strangers for the love of her boy. She feels an intense joy in sacrificing herself; she refuses to withdraw from the bedside, she will not leave her charge; she watches day and night, and only from utter exhaustion does she fall asleep. You could not have kept her in England, she would have been too wretched. It was a great, deep, solemn pleasure for her to be where she could minister to her own beloved.

Soul, remember you have given Jesus great joy in his saving you. He was forever with the Father, eternally happy, infinitely glorious, as God over all; but yet he needed to come to this place out of boundless love to take upon himself our nature, and to suffer in our place to bring us back to holiness and God. *He layeth it on his shoulders, rejoicing.* That day the shepherd knew but one joy. He had found his sheep, and the very pressure of it upon his shoulders made his heart light, for he knew by that sign that the object of his care was safe beyond all question.

Now he goes home with it, and this joy of his was then so great that it filled his soul to overflowing. The parable speaks nothing as to his joy in getting home again, nor a word concerning the joy of being saluted by his friends and neighbors. No, the joy of having found his sheep eclipsed all other gladness of heart, and dimmed the light of home and friendship. He turns around to friends and neighbors and implores them to help him bear the weight of his happiness. He cries, *Rejoice with me; for I have found my sheep which was lost.* One sinner had repented, and all heaven must make a holiday concerning it.

Oh, brethren, there is enough joy in the heart of Christ over his saved ones to flood all heaven with delight. The streets of paradise run knee-deep with the heavenly waters of the Savior's joy. They flow out of the very soul of Christ, and angels and glorified spirits bathe in the mighty stream. Let us do the same. We are friends if we are not neighbors. He calls us today to come and bring our hearts, like empty vessels, that he may fill them with his own joy, that our joy may be full. Those of us who are saved must enter into the joy of our Lord.

When I was trying to think over this text, I rejoiced with my Lord in the bringing in of each one of his sheep, for each one makes heaven full of joy. But oh, to see all the redeemed brought in! Jesus would have no joy if he should lose one: it would seem to spoil it all. If the purpose of mercy were frustrated in any one instance, it would be a dreary defeat for the great Savior. But his purpose shall be carried out in every instance. *He shall see of the travail of his soul, and shall be satisfied* (Isaiah 53:11). He shall not fail nor be discouraged. He shall carry out the will of the Father. He shall have the full reward of his passion. Let us joy and rejoice with him this morning!

But the text tells us there was more joy over that one lost sheep than over the ninety and nine that went not astray. Who are these just persons that need no repentance? Well, you should never explain a parable so as to make it run on four legs if it was only meant to go on two. There may not be such persons at all, and yet the parable may be strictly accurate. If all of us had been such persons, and had never needed repentance, we would not have given as much joy to the heart of Christ as one sinner does when he repents. But suppose it to mean you and me who have long ago repented – who have, in a certain sense, now no need of repentance, because we are justified men and women – we do not give so much joy to the heart of God, for the time being, as a sinner does when he first returns unto God. It is not that it is a good thing to go astray, or a bad thing to be kept from it.

You understand how that is. There are seven children in a family, and six of them are all well; but one dear child is taken seriously ill, and is brought near to the gates of death. It has recovered, its life is spared, and do you wonder that for the time being it gives more joy to the household than all the healthy ones? There is a great deal more expressed delight about it than over all those that have not been ill at all. This does not show it is a good thing to be ill. No, nothing of the kind; we are only speaking of *the joy* that comes of recovery from sickness. Take another case. You have a son who has been long away in a far country, and another son at home. You love them both equally, but when the absent son comes home, he is for a season most upon your thoughts. Is it not natural that it should be so? Those at home give us joy constantly from day to day, but when the stream of joy has been dammed back by his absence, it pours down in a flood upon his return. Then we have "high days and holy days" and "bonfire nights."

There are special circumstances of repentance and conversion that produce joy over a restored wanderer. There was a preceding sorrow, and this sets off the joy by contrast. The shepherd was so touched with compassion for the lost sheep that now his sorrow is inevitably turned into joy. He suffered a dreadful suspense, and that is a killing thing; it is like an acid eating into the soul. That suspense that makes one ask, Where is the sheep? Where can it be? is a piercing of the heart. All those weary hours of searching, and seeking, and following are painfully wearing to the heart. You feel as if you would almost sooner know that you never would find it than be in that doubtful state of mind. That suspense when it is ended naturally brings with it a sweet liberty of joy.

Moreover, you know that the joy over repentant ones is so unselfish that you who have been kept by the grace of God for many years do not grieve that there should be more joy over a repenting sinner than over you. No; you say to yourself, "There is good cause. I am myself among those who are glad." You remember that good men made great rejoicing over you when you first came to Jesus; and you heartily unite with them in welcoming newcomers. You will not act like the elder brother and say you will not share the joy of your Father. Not a bit of it; but you will enter heartily into the music and dancing, and count it your heaven to see souls saved from hell. I feel a sudden flush and flood of delight when I meet with a poor creature who once lay at hell's dark door, but is now brought to the gates of heaven. Do not you?

The one thing I want to leave with you is how our gracious Lord seems to give himself up to his own redeemed. How entirely and perfectly every thought of his heart, every action of his power, goes toward the needy, guilty, lost soul. He spends his all to bring back his banished ones. Poor souls who believe in him have his whole strength engaged on their behalf. Blessed be his name! Now let all our hearts go forth in love towards him who gave all his heart to work our redemption. Let us love him. We cannot love him as he loved us as to measure, but let us do so in like manner. Let us love him with all our heart and soul. Let us feel as if we saw nothing, knew nothing, loved nothing except Jesus crucified. As we filled all *his* heart, let him fill all *our* hearts!

Oh poor sinner, here today, will you not yield to the Good Shepherd? Will you not stand still as he draws near? Will you not submit to his mighty grace? Know that your rescue from sin and death must be of him, and of him alone. Breathe a prayer to him – "Come, Lord, I wait for your salvation! Save me, for I trust in you." If you thus pray, then you have the mark upon you of Christ's sheep, for he says, *My sheep hear my voice, and I know them, and they follow me.* Come to him, for he comes to you. Look to him, for he looks to you.

Chapter 12

Our Great Shepherd Finding the Sheep

Until he find it? And when he hath found it . . .
And when he cometh home. (Luke 15:4-6)

The love of Jesus, the Great Shepherd, is very *practical* and active. There is a sheep lost, and the Lord regrets it; but his love does not spend itself in regrets. He arises, and goes forth *to seek and to save that which was lost.* The love of Jesus Christ is love not in word only, but also in deed and in truth. The love of Jesus is *anticipatory.* He does not wait until the sheep is willing to return, or until it makes some attempt to come back; but no sooner is its lost estate known to the Shepherd than he starts off, that he may find that which was lost. The love of Jesus for the lost sheep is *preeminent.* He leaves the ninety and nine in their pasture; and for a while forgets them, so that all his heart, his eye, and his strength may be given to the one that has gone astray. O sweet love of Christ, so practical, so preeminent, so anticipatory! Let us ask for grace that we may imitate it, especially those of us who are called to be shepherds of men.

Among God's people most of the saints have a charge to watch over. However little the flock may be, even if it be restricted to our own family, or to the little class that gathers around us on the Sabbath, yet we are all our brother's keeper in some measure. Let us learn the love of Christ, so that we may be wise in shepherdy. Let us not talk about our friends, and say we love them; but let us show it by earnest, personal, and speedy endeavors to do them good. Let us not wait until we see some goodness in them – until they seek after instruction. But

> Oh, come, let us go and find them,
>   In the paths of death they roam.

And long before they have a thought of coming home, let us be on their track, eager to grasp them, if by any means we may save some. Oh, to have in our hearts such love of souls that it engrosses us so that we forget earthly needs, and only remember this yet higher necessity! It is a good house, said Saint Bernard, in which Martha has to complain of Mary – where gracious pursuits put other work in the background. It is a choice crime that men should even grow lax about their lower business for a while, that they may devote their chief energy to the saving of the lost sheep.

Let that stand as an introduction. May we see the love of Jesus, as Bernard saw it, and we shall have had enough of a sermon.

In my text there are three periods to which I call your attention.

Christ, the Good Shepherd, first seeks the lost sheep *until he find it*. Just put a mark under those words. That is our first topic – *until he find it*. It is a long reach *until he find it*.

I like the expression. The Lord Jesus did not come down to earth to make an *attempt* to find men, but he came to *do* it, and he did it. He abided here, seeking the lost sheep until he found it; he never gave up until his work was done. At this hour, in his work of grace among his chosen, he does not make an attempt at their salvation, and suffer defeat; but he keeps at soul-seeking work until he finds it.

Look at the seeking shepherd: he is looking for the sheep. Notice his anxious countenance *until he find it*. We read that after he found it he rejoiced; but there is no rejoicing until he finds it. He is all excitement, quick of ear to catch the faintest sound, for it may be the bleating of his lost sheep. His eyes are like the eyes of eagles. He saw something stir in the large, coarse fern yonder, and he will be there in a bound or two; he is so eager. No; it was a mistake. It was not the sheep; perhaps it was some frightened fox. He climbs a heap of stones, and from the top of it he looks all around. I was about to say that he looks with ears and eyes together. He puts his whole soul into the organs of watchfulness, if perhaps he may discern the sheep. Is there a smile on his face? Ah, no! not *until he find it*. His whole soul is in his eyes and ears until he finds it.

This is a faint yet true picture of that Great Shepherd who came here to seek his flock. Just so have the Gospel writers drawn him in their pen-and-ink sketches of him – always watchful; spending night and day in prayers, and tears, and pleadings; never more to have a joy until he finds the lost one. Then, when he did find a single sheep, finding his meat and his drink in it, he becomes refreshed from the fact that he has so far accomplished his beloved work. The Great Shepherd is all energy, care, and concentration of thought concerning his sheep, *until he find it*.

There is no hesitating with Jesus. The sheep is lost, and the news is brought to the shepherd; he girds his loose robe around him and is on the way. He knows within a little while which way that stray sheep will go, and he is on its track at once, though he knows that he must mark that track with his blood. See the blessed shepherd pressing on; there is no pausing nor resting *until he find it*. He has made up his mind that no sheep of his shall be lost, and he travels over hill and dale after the wanderer until he finds it.

If you look into that shepherd's face, there is no trace of anger there. He does not say, "Oh, that I should be worried about this silly sheep thus going astray!" No thought is there but that of anxious love. It is all love, and nothing else but love, before he finds and until he finds it; and you may be sure that careful tenderness will be in full action after he has found it. He is looking with anxious eyes of love. *"As I live, saith the Lord God, . . . I have no pleasure in the death of him that dieth* (Ezekiel 18:3, 32), but that he should turn unto me and live." *Until he find it* there will be no thought of anxiety, but a fullness of pitying care for the lost sheep.

And, mark, there is no giving up. That sheep has wandered now for many hours. The sun has risen, and the sun has set, or, at least it is just going down; but as long as the shepherd can see, and the sheep is still alive, he will pursue it *until he find it*. He has been disappointed a great many times; and when he thought that he should have found it, he has missed it; but still, he will never give it up. He is impelled onward by irresistible love, and he must continue his weary search until he finds it. It was precisely so with our Lord Jesus Christ. When he came after you and after me, we ran from him, but he pursued us; we hid from him, but he discovered us; he had almost grasped us, but for as long as we eluded him, he still pursued with love unwearied until he found us.

Oh, if he had given up after the first ten years – if he had ceased to care for some of us after fifty different occasions in which we had choked conscience and quenched the Spirit, then we would have been lost. But he would not be turned away. If he determines to save, he continues to pursue the rambling sheep until he finds it. He cannot, he must not, he will not cease from the work of seeking and finding until he finds it. I wish that the time had come with some here that it would be said, "The Savior did pursue such and such a one until he found him – found him in the tabernacle, and ended all his wanderings there – found him standing in yonder gallery, and ended all his wanderings at the foot of the cross." God grant that it may be so! But whether it be so with you or not, be sure of this – that the Lord Jesus has in hundreds and thousands of cases pursued sinners with unflagging mercy, leaping to them over hills of sin, and following them until he has found them. We are now his forever and ever, for he who has found us will never lose us. Blessed be his name!

Learn this lesson before I move on. If ever you are seeking the conversion of any man, follow him until you find him. Do not be discouraged. Put up with a great many rebuffs and rebukes; you will have him nevertheless. He is surest to succeed who cannot be put off from his aim. From some it will be necessary to receive a great deal that is most discouraging. Receive it, and say nothing about it; only whisper to yourself, "I might well have put the Great Shepherd off from caring for me, and yet was not so turned aside. If he persevered with me even to the death, I may well persevere as long as I live in seeking and finding a soul." I have heard of wives who have pleaded with God for their husbands for twenty years, and yet have seen them converted after all.

There are instances in this place in which inexhaustible love has followed up ungodly relatives until they have at last been saved by sovereign grace. Persevere with loving pleadings! until you bury your unsaved ones, do not consider them dead, and do not bury them spiritually until they are dead really. Some are easily baffled. They have written the death warrant of their friend by ceasing to pray for him, and yet that death warrant will never be written in the records of heaven, for their friend will be brought to the Savior's feet.

Until he find it. Go out, you undershepherds for Christ. Wear this motto on your right hand: "Until I find it." Live or die, or work or suffer, whether the time be short or long, or the way be smooth or rough, let each one of you be bound to seek a soul *until he find it.* You will find it then, even as Christ found you. There I leave that first point.

And now we come to the second – *And when he hath found it.* When he has found it, what does he do then? Well, first, *he takes a firm hold. He layeth it on his shoulders, rejoicing.* So when he has found it, the first thing is to get a tight grip on it. See him: he has gotten up close to the sheep. The poor thing is weary, and yet may have strength enough to get away; therefore, the shepherd takes good care that he shall not. He grasps his legs and holds him tight. That is what the Lord Jesus does when at last he gets a man broken down under a sense of sin, weary and worn-out as to further resistance of divine mercy. Our Lord gets such a grip on the rebel that he will never get away anymore. I remember when he laid hold of me. He has never lost his grasp even to this day. But oh, it was a grasp! Nothing ever gripped my fickle mind like the hand of Christ. When the divine hand, which fixed the foundations of the earth, had fixed itself on me, my wanderings were ended once and for all.

The next thing after the firm hold was *the gracious lift.* He lifted this poor sheep up and put it on his shoulders, and there it was with all its weight, carried by powerful shoulders. That is what the Savior does for poor weary sinners. He carries the weight of their sin, no, the weight of themselves. He takes us just as we are, and instead of driving us back by his law, he carries us home by his love. Instead of urging us to go home, he becomes the great burden bearer of his redeemed, and bears them on his shoulders. And now you have before you one of the loveliest portraits that imagination can ever sketch – that great crowned Shepherd of the sheep, King of Kings and Lord of Lords, bearing on his shoulders, as a burden he delights to carry, the sheep that had gone astray. Oh, I pray God that you may lie on those broad shoulders if you have never been so favored. The shoulders of omnipotence bearing up our weakness – the mighty Savior bearing us and all our sin and all our care, and our whole being upon the shoulders of his strength – this is a sight for angels.

And as he thus carries the weight, observe that *the distance is removed.* We read in the next verse: *When he cometh home,* but there is nothing said about the road; for somehow our Master has the knack of being at home at once. The sinner may weary himself by twenty years of sin, but in five minutes that may all be gone. It may have taken you fifty years to make yourself such a hell-deserving sinner as you are, but it will not take Jesus fifty ticks of the clock to wash you and make you whiter than snow, and to get you back into the great Father's house. Truth be told, the Shepherd's redeeming work is already done.

> How dreadful was the hour,
> > When God our wanderings laid,
> And did at once his vengeance pour
> > Upon our Shepherd's head!
>
> How glorious was the grace,
> > When Christ sustained the stroke!
> His life and blood the Shepherd pays,
> > A ransom for the flock.

By that redeeming process he brought us near to God.

There is no weary journey back for shepherd or sheep. He grasps the sheep; he puts it on his shoulders, and they are both back at the fold.

But the particular point I want you to notice is when the Great Shepherd gets this burden on his back. We read: *When he hath found it, he layeth it on his shoulders* – with great anxiety? Look to see whether it is so. It is nothing of the sort. But is it not, "He layeth it on his shoulders with great weariness"? No. See! See! *He layeth it on his shoulders, rejoicing – rejoicing*! He does not remember all the weariness that he has had to suffer. He does not think of the folly of his sheep in having lost good pasture, in having involved itself in so much danger, and in costing him so much labor. Not a word is mentioned of it. *He layeth it on his shoulders, rejoicing.* He says to himself, "I am glad to carry this burden, happy to carry my lost sheep home."

And oh! I do love to picture to myself at this moment the joy in the heart of the blessed Christ. *For the joy that was set before him [he] endured the cross, despising the shame.* And now, whenever he gets a lost sheep to carry back, he rejoices. His heart leaps within him. All anxiety is gone. Fullness of delight is upon him. *He layeth it on his shoulders, rejoicing.* I wonder whether the sheep could see that the shepherd rejoiced. I do not suppose that it could, but it could feel it. There are two ways, you know, of handling a sheep, and the sheep very soon knows which one expresses pleasure on its owner's part; at any rate, I am sure that a dog knows well enough what your movements mean. If you speak angrily to a sheep, and throw it upon your shoulder with indignation, that is one thing; but if you have not a word to say, except it be, "Poor thing, I am glad I have found you," and you cast it on your shoulders rejoicing, why, sheep as it is, it knows the difference.

At any rate, I know that Christ has a way of saving us: oh, so gently, so lovingly, so gleefully, that he makes us happy in being saved. There is a way of turning a penny into stone or into gold according to the way in which you give it to a poor man. You can fling it at him as if he were a dog, and he will be about as grateful to you as a dog, or not so much. But there is a way in which you can say, "I am sorry for your needs. This is all I can give you now. Take it, and do what you can with it." Given with a brotherly look, it will be gratefully received and made the most of. There is much in the manner as well as in the matter of a gift. The mannerism of Christ is grandly gracious: he saves us rejoicingly. It is a matter of thanksgiving to him when he gets hold of his lost sheep, and gets it on his shoulders. It makes me glad to think that it is so.

We are not saved by a grudging Christ, who seems as if he were weary of us, and must save us out of hand, to get rid of us. He does not act with us as some rude surgeon might do who says, "I will attend to you directly, but I have plenty else to do, and you free patients are a trouble." Nor does he roughly set the bone. No; Jesus comes, and, as with a lady's dainty hand, he molds the dislocated joint; and when he sets it, there is bliss even about the method of the setting. We look into his face, and we see that he puts his most tender sympathy into each movement. You know the different ways that workmen have. Some kinds of work a man is soon sick of. The principle of division of labor is a very admirable one for the production of results upon a large scale; but it is a miserable business for the workman to have to do the same thing over and over again, all day long, as if he were a robot.

Get a man at work on a statue – an artist whose whole soul is in his chisel, who knows that there is a bright spirit within that block of marble, and who means to chip off all that hides the lovely image from his sight. See how he works! No man does a thing well who does it sorrowfully. The best work that can be done is done by the happy, joyful workman; and so it is with Christ. He does not save souls as of necessity – as though he would rather do something else if he might; but his very heart is in it, he rejoices to do it, and therefore he does it thoroughly, and he communicates his joy to us in the doing of it.

Now, learn a lesson before I go away to the third point. *When he hath found it.* Suppose that any of you should very soon meet with a poor troubled sinner, anxious to come to Christ. When you have found him, let me recommend to you that you imitate the Master's example: get a tight grip on him. Do not let him slip. Get a hold of him, and then, if he is in trouble, take all that trouble upon yourself. Try to see whether you cannot get him upon your shoulders. Imitate your Master in that way. Try to bear all his burden for him, as Christ bore yours. Conduct him to the Christ who is the true burden bearer; and all the while be very happy about it. I do not think we ought to go and talk to young converts in a dreadfully solemn tone, as though it would be something horrible to find a Savior. They will never come again, you may depend upon it. They will give you a wide berth. But just go, and in a joyful spirit say, "I am so glad to find you caring about your soul."

The best thing that can happen to a soul seeker is to meet with a troubled conscience; show that you think so. "But," say you, "I have not the time." Always have time, even in the middle of the night, to see a poor conscience-stricken sinner. But perhaps you are very weary, or not well. If I were weary, I would not be weary any longer when I came across a lost sheep; and if I were ill, I would get well on purpose to see after a sin-sick sinner. Talk in that way, with sweet and pleasant encouragement, for this is the way to help your brother sinner to the Savior.

My time has gone, but just a few words more on this last point.

When he cometh home. When he cometh home, he calleth together his friends and neighbours, saying unto them, Rejoice with me; for I have found my sheep which was lost.

Some hurried observations. First, *heaven is a home. When he cometh home;* and the next verse makes a comparison with heaven. Heaven is a home. Do you not like to think of it from that aspect? It is the home of Jesus; and if it is the home of Jesus, can any other home be equal to it? *When he cometh home.*

Note, next, that *lost ones are known in heaven.* I give you that thought more from the Greek than from the English here. *When he cometh home, he calleth together his friends and neighbours, saying unto them, Rejoice with me; for I have found my sheep* – the lost one. That is how it should read. It is as if the friends knew that one had been lost, and the loss had been lamented; and the shepherd says, "I have found my sheep; you know which one – the lost one." Up there they know which are Christ's sheep and which are lost. Heaven is nearer to earth than some of us dream. How long does it take to get there?

> One gentle sigh the spirit breaks:
> We scarce can say, "He's gone,"
> Before the ransomed spirit takes
> Its mansion near the throne.

And there are more communications between earth and heaven than some folks dream; for here it is clear that when the shepherd came home, he said to them, "I have found the sheep," the lost one. So they knew all about it. It is evident, again, that they all knew that the shepherd had gone after the sheep, for he says, *I have found my sheep which was lost.* They all knew that he had gone on a search, and therefore they could all understand his joy when he came back with the sheep. I believe that they know in heaven when Christ is seeking after anyone. It must be a great satisfaction to some up there who die with an unconverted son, or an unconverted girl, to know, after a little while, that son or daughter is converted to Christ. I am persuaded they know it. They cannot help knowing it, because they are Christ's friends and neighbors, and, according to the parable, he tells them, and he says to them, *Rejoice with me;* and if he says, *Rejoice with me,* why, of course, he tells them why.

If I had been converted after my mother's death, I can imagine that when Jesus said to all of them, "*Rejoice with me; for I have found my sheep,* the lost one," my mother would say, "My Lord, I can rejoice more than any of them, for that was my boy, and he is saved at last." Your mother in glory will be twice glorified , John, if you give your heart to Christ; and I pray that you will. Your father, now before the throne, will think that paradise has grown more paradisiacal than ever if he hears it whispered down the golden streets that the wanderer has come home.

Notice, next, very briefly, that *Jesus Christ loves other people to rejoice with him,* so that, when he finds a sinner, he has so much love in his heart that his joy runs over, and he cries to others, "Come friends, come neighbors, come and help me to be glad, for I have saved another soul." Let us catch the blessed infection. If you have just heard of somebody being saved, be glad about it. Though you do not know the person, yet be glad about it, because Jesus is glad.

Notice, next, that *repentance is regarded as "coming home."* This sheep was not in heaven. No, but as soon as it had been brought into the fold it is described as having repented, and Jesus and the angels begin to rejoice over it. If a man truly repents, and Christ saves him, it is clear that he never will be lost. A certain old proverb forbids us to count our chickens until they are hatched, and I do not think that angels would do so in the case of immortal souls. If they believed that repenting sinners might afterwards be lost, they would not ring the marriage bells just yet, but they would wait a while to see how things went on. If they can still perish, then there is not one convert that the angels dare rejoice over; for if any child of God might fall away and perish, why not every one of us? If anyone falls from grace, I fear that I shall.

O my brother, do you not fear the same for yourself? "No," say you, "I don't think so." Well then, you are a proud fellow, and you are the most likely one to desert your Lord. If ever a sheep of Christ's shall fall away, I shall. I see more of my own tendencies to wander, and more of my own temptations to offend than I do of yours. I would not have the angels rejoice over a man because he repents, if repentance be only a sign of human improvement, and not a token of heavenly love. I would say, "Stop, you angels; for this man may go back and perish after all, if, according to the modern gospel, Christ loves today and hates tomorrow, and a child of God may still be a child of the devil." I do not believe a word of such doctrine. I believe that where the Lord begins the good work of grace, he will carry it on and perfect it; and when the Lord has once given to a man to know him, he will see that he is preserved in that knowledge forever. There is a text that clenches it: *I give unto [my sheep] eternal life; and they shall never perish, neither shall any man pluck them out of my hand.* Now, if they have eternal life, it cannot come to an end; for eternal life *is* eternal, evidently; and if they have eternal life, the Shepherd and his friends may justifiably sing when one single possessor of that eternal life is brought to life and salvation. In the repentant man a work is done that never can be undone; and he is put where he never can be lost. Yes,

> I to the end shall endure,
>> As sure as the earnest is given;
> More happy, but not more secure,
>> Are the glorified spirits in heaven.

Sing away, angels! There is something to sing about now; and we will join with you in blessing and praising the unchanging God forever and forever. Amen.

Chapter 13

Sown among Thorns

And some fell among thorns; and the thorns
sprung up, and choked them. (Matthew 13:7)

He also that received seed among the thorns is he
that heareth the word; and the care of this world,
and the deceitfulness of riches, choke the word,
and he becometh unfruitful. (Matthew 8:22)

W hen that which comes of his sowing is unfruitful, the sower's
work is wasted; he has spent his strength for nothing. Without
fruit, the sower's work would even seem to be insane; for he takes good
wheat, throws it away, and loses it in the ground. Preaching is the idlest
of occupations if the Word be not adapted to enter the heart and produce good results. O my friends, if you are not converted, I waste time
and energy in standing here! Men might well think it madness that
one whole day in the week should be given up to hearing speeches; and
madness, indeed, it would be if nothing came of it to the conscience
and the heart. If you do not bring forth fruit unto holiness, and the
end is not everlasting life, then I would be better employed in breaking
stones on the roadside than in preaching to you.

Fruit bearing made the difference appear in the various soils upon
which the sower scattered seed. You would not so certainly have known

the quality if you had not seen the failure or success of the seed. We do not know your hearts until we see your bearing towards the gospel. If it produces in you holiness and love for God and man, then we know that there is good soil in you; but if you are merely promising people, but not performing people, then we know that the ground of your heart is hard, or stony, or thorny. The Word of the Lord tests the heart and mind of the children of men, and in this it is as the fire that distinguishes between metal and dross.

O my dear friends, you undergo a test today! Perhaps you will be judging the preacher, but something greater than the preacher will be judging you, for the Word itself shall judge you. You sit here as a jury upon yourselves; your own condition will be brought clearly out by the way in which you receive or refuse the gospel of God. If you bring forth fruit to the praise of God's grace, good; but if not, however you may seem to hear with attention, and may retain what you hear in your memories, if no saving effect is produced upon your souls, then we shall know that the soil of your heart has not been prepared for the Lord, but remains in its native barrenness.

What fruit have you borne up to this time from all your hearing? May I risk to put the question to each one of you very pointedly? Some of you have been hearers from your childhood – are you anything better? What long lists of sermons you must have heard by now! Count over your Sundays; how many they have been! Think of the good men now in heaven, to whom you once listened! Remember the tears that were drawn from you by their discourses! If you are not saved yet, will you ever be saved? If you are not holy yet, will you ever be holy? Why has the Lord spent so much on one who makes no return? To what purpose is this waste? Surely you will have much to answer for in that great day when the servants of God shall give in their accounts, and shall have no joy when they come to mention you. How will you excuse yourselves before God for having caused them so much disappointment?

At this time, I will only deal with one class of you. I will not speak to those of you who hear the Word and retain none of it because of the hardness of your hearts; such are the wayside hearers. Neither will I address myself to those who receive the truth with sudden enthusiasm, and just as readily leave it when trial happens to them; such are the rocky-ground hearers. But I will deal with those of you who hear the Word attentively, and, in a sense, receive it into your hearts and understandings, so that the seed grows in you, though its fruit never comes to perfection. You are religious persons, and to all appearance you are under the influence of godliness. You exhibit plenty of leaf, but there is no wheat in the head, no substance in your Christianity. I cannot speak with any degree of physical vigor to you, by reason of the infirmity under which I struggle; but what I do say to you is steeped in earnest desire that the Lord may bless it to you. An eloquent congregation will make any preacher eloquent; help me then this morning. If you will give me your ear, you will make up for my deficiency of tongue; especially if you give to God your hearts, he will bless his truth, however feebly I may utter it.

First, I desire to talk to you a little about *the seed* that you have received; secondly, about *the thorns;* and thirdly, about *the result.*

First, a little about the seed. Remember, first, that *it was the same seed in every case.* Yonder it has brought forth thirtyfold; it was the same seed that was lost upon you. In a still better case, the seed has brought forth a hundredfold; it was precisely the same wheat with which your field has been sown. The sower went to his master's granary for all his seed; how is it that in your case it is all lost? If there were two gospels, we might expect two results without fault in the soil that failed. But with many of you to whom I speak there has been only one gospel throughout the whole of your lives. You have been attending this house of prayer, where we have never changed our seed, but have gone on sowing the one eternal truth of God. Many have brought forth fruit a hundredfold from the seed that has been scattered over a broad area from this platform. They heard no more than you have heard, but how much better they treated it than you have done! I want you to consider this. How covered with briars and thorns must your mind be that the gospel that converted your sister or friend never touched you! Though you may be nominally a believer in the Word of God, it has never so affected you as to make you gracious and holy. You are still a hearer only. How is this? The fault is not in the seed, for it is the same seed that has been so useful to others.

You have heard the gospel with *pleasure.* "Heard it!" you say, "I heard it when a little child." Your mother brought you to the house of God in her arms. You have heard it, and still hear it, though it is rather like an old song to you; but is this to be all? I am very grateful that you do hear the gospel, for I hope that one of these days God may cause it to grow in you, and yield fruit. But still a grave responsibility is upon you. Think how favored you have been! How will you answer for this privilege if it is neglected and rendered useless by that neglect? Dear friends, if we lived in the heart of Africa, and we died without believing in a Christ of whom we had not heard, we could not be blamed for that; but here we are in the heart of London, where the gospel is preached in all our streets, and our blood will be on our own heads if we perish. Do you mean to go down to hell? Are you so desperate that you will go there wearing the garb of Christians? If you do persist in ruining your souls, my eyes shall follow you with tears, and when I cannot warn you any longer, I will weep in secret places because of your perversity.

Those described in my text were not only hearers, but in a measure *they also accepted the good Word.* The seed fell not only on this ground, but also into it, so that it began to grow. Of you it is true that you do not refuse the gospel, or raise disputes concerning it. I am glad that you have no difficulties about the inspiration of Scripture, or the deity of our Lord, or the fact of his atonement. You do not confuse yourself with "modern thought," but you profess your belief in the old, old gospel. So far so good; but what shall I make of the strange fact that your acceptance of the truth has no effect upon you? It is a very lamentable case, is it not, that a man should believe the gospel to be true, and yet should live as if it were a lie? If it be the truth, why do you not yield obedience to it? The man knows that there is an atonement for sin, but he has never confessed his sin and accepted the great sacrifice.

As for those great truths, which circle around the cross like a crown of stars, he has seen their beauty and enjoyed their brilliance, but he has never allowed their light to enter his heart, and find a reflection in his moral character. This is evil, only evil. If you believe the truth, what do you believe more than the devil? No, you are behind him, for he believes, *and trembles,* and you have not gone so far as the trembling. It should be so, that every great truth that is believed should influence the mind, sway the thoughts, and mold the life; this is the natural fruit of great spiritual truth. The doctrine of grace, when it takes possession of the mind and governs the heart, produces the purest results; but if it be held in unrighteousness, it is a curse rather than a blessing to have mere head knowledge. Is it not a dreadful thing to believe God's revelation without receiving God's Spirit? This is to accept a well, but never to drink of the water; to accept wheat in the barn, and yet die of hunger. God have mercy upon the possessors of a dead faith!

The seed sown among thorns *lived, and continued to grow.* And in many men's minds the gospel of divine truth is growing to a certain extent: they understand it better, can defend it more valiantly, and speak of it more fluently. Moreover, it does influence them in some form and degree, for gross sins are forsaken. They are decent imitations of believers; you can see the shape of an ear: the stalk has struggled up through the thorns until you can see its head, and are led to expect wheat. But go to that apparent wheat ear, and feel it: there are the sheaths, but there is nothing in them; you have all the makings of an ear of wheat, but it will yield no grain.

I would speak to those before me who, perhaps, have been baptized, and are members of the church; I want to ask them a question or two. Do you not think that there is a great deal of empty profession nowadays? Do you not think that many have a name to live and are dead? "Yes," say you, "I know a neighbor whom I judge to be in that condition." May not another neighbor judge the same of you? Would it not be well to raise the question about yourself? Have you really believed in the Lord Jesus? Are you truly converted from sin and self? Turn that sharp eye of yours homeward for a while. Examine your own actions, and judge your condition by them. Put yourself into the fire.

O my God, what if I should be a preacher to others, and should be myself a castaway! Will not every deacon and elder, and every individual church member speak to himself after the same fashion? You will go to your Sunday school class this afternoon; will you be teaching the children what you do not know? You mean to go to a meeting this evening, and talk to others about conversion; will you be exhorting them to that which you have never yourself experienced? Will it be so? You do not need fine preaching, but you do need probing in the conscience. A thorough examination will do the healthy no harm, and it may bless the sick. "Lord, let me know the worst of my case," is one of my frequent prayers, and I suggest it to you.

So much then about the seed. It was good seed, it was sown, it was received by the soil, it grew and promised well, but yet in the end it was unfruitful. No doubt multitudes who receive Christianity become regular attenders at our place of worship, and are honest in their moral character; but Christ is not all in all to them; he holds a very secondary place in their affections. Their wheat is overshadowed by a thicket of thorns, and is so choked that it comes to nothing. Their religion is buried beneath their worldliness. Sad will their end be. God in mercy save us from such a doom!

But now, secondly, I would speak a little about the thorns. They are by Matthew described as *the care of this world, and the deceitfulness of riches* (Matthew 13:22). Luke adds, *and pleasures of this life* (Luke 8:14); and Mark still further mentions *the lusts of other things* (Mark 4:19). I suppose that the sower did not see any thorns when he threw the handful of wheat; they had all been cut down level with the surface. He probably hoped that it was all good ground, and therefore he sowed it, little suspecting that the thorns were in possession.

Note well that *thorns are natural to the soil*. Since the fall, these are the firstborn children of the ground. Any evil that hinders religion is not at all an extraordinary thing – it is what we ought to expect among fallen men. Grace is exotic, thorns are indigenous. Sin is very much at home in the human heart, and, like an ill weed, it grows swiftly. If you wish to go to heaven, I might take a little time to show you the way, and I would need to stir you up to diligence; but if you must needs go to hell – well, "easy is the way to destruction" – it is only a little matter of neglect. *How shall we escape, if we neglect so great salvation?*

Evil things are easy things, for they are natural to our fallen nature. Great things are rare flowers that need cultivation. If any of you are being injured by the cares of the world and the deceitfulness of riches, I am not astonished; it is natural that it should be so. Therefore, be on your guard against these mischiefs. I pray you say to yourself, "Come, there is something in this man's talk. He is very slow and dull, but still there is something in what he says. I may, after all, be tolerating those thorns in my heart that will kill the good seed, for I am of similar passions and infirmities with other men." I implore you to look to yourselves, that you be not deceived to the end.

The thorns were already established in the soil. They were not only the natural inhabitants of the soil, but they were also rooted and fixed in it. Our sins within us claim the freehold of our faculties, and they will not give it up if they can help it. They will not give way to the Holy Spirit, or to the new life, or to the influences of divine grace, without a desperate struggle. The roots of sin run through and through our nature, grasp it with wonderful force, and keep up their grasp with marvelous tenacity.

O my dear friend, whoever you may be, you are a fallen creature! If you were the pope himself, or the president of the United States, or the queen of England, it would be true of you that you were born in sin, and shaped in iniquity, and your unconverted heart is deceitful above all things, and desperately wicked. The established church of the town of Mansoul has the devil for its archbishop. Sin has grasped our nature as a boa constrictor surrounds its victim; and when it has maintained its hold for twenty, forty, or sixty years, I hope you are not so foolish as to think that holy things will easily get the mastery. Our evil nature is radically conservative, and it will endeavor to crush out every attempt at a revolution by which the grace of God should reign through righteousness. Therefore, watch and pray, lest temptation choke that which is good in you. Watch earnestly, for grace is a tender plant in a foreign soil, in an uncongenial climate; while sin is in its own element, and is strongly rooted in the soil.

Do you know why so many professing Christians are like the thorny ground? It is because processes have been omitted that would have gone far to alter the condition of things. It was the husbandman's business to uproot the thorns, or burn them on the spot. Years ago, when people were converted, there used to be such a thing as conviction of sin. The great subsoil plow of soul anguish was used to tear deeply into the soul. Fire also burned in the mind with exceeding heat: as men saw sin and felt its dreadful results, the love of it was burned out of them. But now we are bombarded with braggings about rapid salvations.

As for myself, I believe in instantaneous conversions, and I am glad to see them; but I am still more glad when I see a thorough work of grace, a deep sense of sin, and an effective wounding by the law. We shall never get rid of thorns with plows that scratch the surface. Those fields grow the best wheat that are best plowed. Converts are likely to endure when the thorns cannot spring up because they have been plowed up. Dear friend, are you undergoing today a very severe conviction of sin? Thank God for it. Are you in awful trouble and anguish? Do not think that a calamity has happened to you. May God himself continue to plow you, and then sow you, and make sure work in you for years to come! So you see those thorns were natives, and old established natives, and it would have been well had they been cut up.

The thorns were bound to grow. There is an awful vitality in evil. First the thorns sent up a few tiny shoots. These shoots branched out, and more and more came to keep them company, until the wheat stood as a lonely thing in a thicket of briars, and was more and more surpassed and shadowed by them. The thorns aspired to the mastery, and they soon obtained it; and that having been done, they set to work to destroy the wheat. They blocked it up, crowded it out, and some of the thorn-shoots twisted around it, and held the wheat by the neck until it was choked.

The thorns sucked away all the nutrients from the wheat, and it was starved; for there is only a certain quantity of nourishment in the soil, and if the thorns have it, the wheat must go without it. There is only a certain amount of thought and energy in a man; and if the world gets it, Christ cannot have it. If our thoughts run upon care and pleasure, they cannot be eager about true religion; is that not clear? That is the way in which those thorns served the wheat; they starved it by devouring its food, and they choked it by keeping off the air and sun; and the poor thing became shriveled and weak, and quite unable to produce the grain that the sower expected of it.

So it is with many professing Christians. They are at first worldly, but not so very worldly. They are fairly religious, though by no means too zealous. They seek the pleasures of the world, but by no means quite so much as others we could name. But very soon the thorns grow, and it becomes doubtful which will win – sin or grace, the world or Christ. Two masters there cannot be; and in this case it is specially impossible, since neither of the contending powers will tolerate a rival. Sin has sprung from a royal, though evil, stock, and if it be in the heart, it will struggle for the throne. So it came to pass that the tares, being tolerated, choked the good seed.

Let me describe these thorns a little. Putting together Matthew, Mark, and Luke, we find that there were four sorts of thorns. The first is called *the care of this world*. This assuredly comes to the poor: they are apt to grow anxious and mistrustful about worldly things. *What shall we eat? or, What shall we drink? or, Wherewithal shall we be clothed?* (Matthew 6:31). This trinity of sad questions considerably afflicts many. But anxiety comes to rich people also. Care dwells with wealth as well as with poverty. "How shall I get more? How shall I lay it up? How shall I still increase it?" and so on. It is "the care of the age" that we are most warned against. Each age has its own special fret. It is not a care for God – that is not the care of any age; but the care of the age is some vanity or another, and as a standing thing it is the ambition to keep up with your fellows, to be respectable, and to keep up appearances. This is the care that eats as does a poison in the case of many.

Grim care turns many a black hair white, and furrows many a brow. If you let care grow in your soul, it will choke up your religion; you cannot care for God and for wealth too. "We must have care," says one. There is a care that is proper, and there is an anxiety that is improper. That is proper care which you can cast upon God – *Casting all your care upon him; for he careth for you* (1 Peter 5:7). That is an improper care which you dare not take to God, but have to bear yourself. Take heed of anxiety; it will eat the heart out of your religion.

There were others who felt *the deceitfulness of riches.* Our Lord does not just say *riches,* but *the deceitfulness of riches.* The two things grow together: riches are forever deceitful. They deceive people in the getting of them, for they judge matters very unfairly when a prospect of gain is before them. The jingle of the charming shilling, or of "the almighty dollar" makes a world of difference to the ear when it is hearing a case. Men cannot afford to lose by integrity, and so they take the doubtful way, and either sail near the wind, or speculate until it amounts to gambling. They would not endure the idea of such conduct, were it not that the hope of gain deceives them. Our line of conduct ought never to be ruled by gain or loss. Do right if the heavens fall. Do no wrong, even though a kingdom should be its reward.

Men turn to Adam Smith's *The Wealth of Nations,* a wonderful book, and there they find certain laws that I believe to be as fixed and unalterable as the law of gravity. Led on by the deceitfulness of riches, men make these laws into an excuse for grinding the faces of the poor. They might as well take people to the top of a rock, fling them down, dash them to pieces, and then cry out, "This is the natural result of the law of gravity." Of course, the law of gravity operates remorselessly, and so will the law of supply and demand; but we must not use either of these laws as a cover for cruelty to the poor and needy, and yet many do so through *the deceitfulness of riches*.

Riches are very deceitful when they are gained, for they breed in men many sins that they do not themselves suspect. One man is purse-proud, but he thinks he is humble. He is a self-made man, and worships him that made him. Is it not natural that a man should worship his maker? In his heart he thinks, "I am somebody. I came up to London with half a crown in my pocket, and now I could buy a whole street!" People ought to respect a man of that kind, ought they not, even though he may have made his money by very strange practices? It little matters how you make money nowadays; only get it, and you will have plenty of admirers, and the deceitfulness of riches will enable you to admire yourself.

With pride comes a desire for wealthy society and vain company; and thus again religion receives severe injury. There is apt to grow up in the mind an idolatry of this world and its treasures. "I don't love money," says one. "You know it is not money that is the root of all evil, but the love of it." Just so; but are you sure that you do not love it? Your thoughts run a good deal after it. You hug it rather closely, and you find it hard to part with it. I will not accuse you, but I would have you awaken to the fact that riches worm themselves into a man's heart before he is well aware of it.

You may perceive the deceitfulness of riches if you note the excuses that men make for getting so much and withholding it from the cause of God. "They intend to do a great deal of good with it." Did you hear the devil laugh? I am not speaking of many dear brethren in this place who are doing a great deal of good with their means, but I am speaking of those who are simply living to accumulate wealth and say that they will one day do a great deal of good with it. They say so. Will it ever be more than saying? I fear that in this thing many rich men deceive themselves. They go on accumulating the means, but never using them: making bricks, but never building. All they will get will be a corner in *The Illustrated London News* to say that they died worth so much.

O sirs, how can you be content thus to have your good things choked? Wherever this deceitfulness of riches is allowed the upper hand, it chokes the good seed. A man cannot be eager to get, and eager to keep, and eager to increase, and eager to become a millionaire, and at the same time be a true servant of the Lord Jesus. As the body grows rich, the soul grows poor.

Luke tells us of another kind of weed, namely, the *pleasures of this life*. I am sure that these thorns play a dreadful part nowadays. I have nothing to say against recreation in its proper place. Certain forms of recreation are needful and useful, but it is a wretched thing when amusement becomes a vocation. Amusement should be used to do us good like a medicine; it must never be used as the food of the man. From early morning until late at night some spend their time in a round of frivolities, or else their very work is simply carried on to furnish them funds for their pleasures. This is vicious. Many have had all holy thoughts and gracious resolutions stamped out by perpetual trifling. Pleasure so called is the murderer of thought. This is the age of excessive amusement: everybody craves for it, like a baby for its rattle. In the more sober years of our fathers, men had something better to live for than silly sports. The thorns are choking the age.

Mark adds, *and the lusts of other things.* I will not list all those other things; but all things except the things of Christ and of the Father are *other things*. If anybody spends his life on any object, however good, short of the glory of God, then the good seed is choked by the inferior object. One person is very scientific, and he will do well if his science is used for holy purposes; but it can be used to choke the seed. One man is a great expert in the arts, and he does well if the arts are used as a mule for Christ to ride upon; but if art is used to ride upon Christ, then it is ill enough.

I met with a clergyman many years ago who was going a long distance to find a new beetle. He was a great entomologist, and I did not blame him for it, for to a thoughtful man entomology may yield many profitable lessons. But if he neglected his preaching to catch insects, then I do not wonder that a parishioner should wish that the beetles would nibble his old sermons, for they were very stale. I call it choking the seed when any inferior pursuit becomes the master of our minds, and the cause of God and truth takes a secondary place. The seed is choked in our souls whenever Christ is not our all in all. You see my drift. Be it what it may – gain, glory, study, pleasure – all these may be briers that will choke the seed.

Mr. Jay was never more pleased than when at Bristol he had a note sent up to him that read as follows: "A young man, who is prospering in business, begs the prayers of God's people that prosperity may not be a snare to him." Take care that you look thus upon your prosperity. My dear friend, Dr. Taylor, of New York, speaks of some Christians nowadays as having a "butterfly Christianity." When time, and strength, and thought, and talent are all spent upon mere amusement, what else are men and women but mere butterflies? "Society" is just a mass of idle people keeping each other in composure.

O dear friends, surely we did not come into this world to play away our days! I do not think we came into this world either to slave ourselves to death, or to rust away in laziness. We have come here as a man enters the porch so that he may afterwards enter the house. This life is the doorway to the palace of heaven. Pass through it in such a style that you may enter before the King with holy joy. If you give your minds and thoughts to these passing things, be they what they may, you will ruin your souls, for the good seed cannot grow.

So I close in the last place by noticing the result. The seed was *unfruitful*.

These briers and thorns could not pull the seed up, or throw it away; it remained where it was, but they choked it. So it may be that your business, your cares, and your pleasures have not torn up your religion by the roots – it is there still, such as it is. But these things suffocate your better feelings. A man that is choked is not good for much. If a thief gets into his house, and he desires to defend his property, what can he do while he is choked? He must wait until he gets his breath again. What an amount of choked religion we have around us! It may be alive. I do not know whether it is or not, but it looks very black in the face. God save you from having your religion choked!

I have already told you it was drained of all its sustenance. Look at many Christians; I call them Christians, for they call themselves so. A boy in the streets, selling mince pies, kept crying, "Hot mince pies!" A person bought one of them, and found it quite cold. "Boy," said he, "why did you call these pies hot?"

"That's the name they go by, sir," said the boy. So there are plenty of people that are called Christians, but they are not Christians – that's the name they go by, but all the substance is drained out of them by other matters. You see the shape of a Christian, the make of a Christian, and some of the talk of a Christian, but the fruit of a Christian is not there. That is the result of the choking by the thorns of care, riches, pleasure, and worldliness in general.

What life there was in the wheat was very sickly. Let me remind certain persons that their spiritual life is growing weak at this time. Morning prayer this morning, how long did it take? Do not grow red in the face. I will say no more about it. You are not coming out tonight, are you? Half a Sunday is enough worship for you. Would you not like to live in some country place where you did not need to go out to a place of worship even once? Bible reading, how much do you do of that? Family prayer, is that a delight to you? Why, numbers of so-called Christians have given up family religion altogether. How about week-day services? You are not often at a prayer meeting. No, the distance is too great! Thursday-night service? "Well, well, you see I might come, but there happens to be a lawn tennis party that night." Will you come in the winter? "Yes, I would, but then a friend drops in, and we have an evening of bagatelle." How many there are in this condition! I am not going to judge them; but I remember that a distinguished minister used to say, "When weekday services are forsaken, farewell to the life of godliness." Such people never seem to bathe in their religion, but they give themselves a wetting with the end of the towel; thus they try to look decent, but they are not inwardly cleansed.

As to confessing Christ before men, many fail altogether. If you were pushed into a corner, and were asked if you were a Christian, you would say, "Well, I do go to a place of worship," but you are by no means anxious to acknowledge the soft indictment. Our Salvation Army friends are not ashamed of their religion; why should you be? Our Quaker friends used to wear broad brims, but they are very properly giving up their peculiar garb. I hope it is not to be to you an indication that you may conceal your religion, and be as much as possible like the world. Do you hope to be soldiers, and yet never wear your military clothing? This is one of the marks of feeble religion.

When it comes to defending the gospel, where do you see it in this age? I hoped that many would be found among Baptists who would care for the truth; but now I come to the conclusion that it is with many, as with the showman, when asked which was Wellington, and which was Bonaparte: "Whichever you please, my little dears. Pay your money, and take your choice!" Free will or free grace, human merit or Christ's atonement, it does not matter now. New theology or old theology, human speculation or divine revelation – who cares? What do they care whether God's truth stands or the devil's lies? I am weary of these nonsensical ones! The thorns have choked the seed in the pulpits and in the churches as well as in private individuals. Oh, that God would return! Oh, that his Spirit would raise up among us men who believe indeed, and prove the power of their belief!

The fruit of much modern piety is nothing. I sat down one day with three or four old Christian men. We had no sooner met than we began to speak of the providential dealings of God with his people. We related instances of answers to prayer, and we spoke of the sovereign grace of God, and his faithfulness to his saints. When we had gone a little forward in the conversation, one remarked how he had enjoyed the talk. "Alas!" said he, "nobody talks about God now. His providence and his readiness to hear prayer are seldom mentioned now; the talk is all about the markets, and the weather, and home rule, and Mr. Gladstone, and disestablishment; but little about the Lord Jesus Christ." That witness was true.

In old times the Lord's people spoke often one to another, and the Lord stood at the window and listened. *The Lord hearkened, and heard it.* He liked their talk so well, that he said he would print it – *A book of remembrance was written before him for them that feared the Lord, and that thought upon his name* (Malachi 3:16). Where do you get experiential Christian talk now? The thorns choke holy communion upon the best things. Fervent prayer! Mighty prayer! Where do you meet with it? Thank God, we have some brethren here whose prayers could unlock the windows of heaven, or shut them up; but it is not so with many. Go to the prayer meetings of most of the churches.

What poor things! Of course I find in country places that many drop the prayer meeting during hay-time and harvest. In London they do not drop the prayer meetings in summer, because they are too small to need dropping. They take up the fragment of a prayer meeting and mend with it the worn-out lecture, so that it becomes neither lecture nor prayer meeting. How can we expect a blessing when we are too lazy to ask for it? Is it not evidence of a dying religion when, to cover their carelessness about meeting for prayer, we even hear ministers doubting the value of prayer meetings, and calling them "religious expedients"?

Where do you meet with intense enjoyment of the things of God? The spiritual life is low when there is little delight in holy service. Oh, for the old Methodist fire! Oh, to feel our hearts dance at the sound of Jesus' name! Oh, to flame up like beacon fires, and blaze towards heaven with holy ecstasy! It is a sorrowful day when religion goes abroad without wearing her ornaments of joy. When an army has left its flag behind, it has evidently given up all hope of victory.

If there is a weakening in spiritual life, we cannot expect to see deeds of holy consecration. Oh, for men and women who bring their alabaster boxes to Jesus! I am glad when I hear this kind of lamentation: "My dear sir, I have not done for the Lord what I ought to have done. I have been a believer now for many years, but I have not given to his cause what I ought to have given; tell me what I can do." There are hopeful signs in such inquiries, and therefore they are well; but it would be better to begin early, and avoid such regrets.

I would put it to you, my dear friend, have you been fruitful? Have you been fruitful with your wealth? Have you been fruitful with your talent? Have you been fruitful with your time? What are you doing for Jesus now? Salvation is not by doings, you are saved by grace; but if you are so saved, prove it by your devoted lives. Consecrate yourself anew this day wholly to your Master's service. You are not your own, but are bought with a price; and if you would not be like these thorn-choked seeds, live while you live, with all-consuming zeal.

"Well," says one, "but there are the thorns." I know there are. They were here when our blessed Lord came among us, and they made him a cruel crown. Are you going to grow more of them? May I urge you to give up cultivating thorns? They are useless; they come to no good.

Whatever the pursuit is, short of the glory of God, it is a thorn, and there is no use in it. It will in the end be painful to you as it was to your Lord. A thorn will tear your flesh, alas, tear your heart. Especially when you come to die will these thorns be in your pillow. Even if you die in the Lord, it will grieve your heart to think you did not live more for Jesus. If you live for these things, you will regret the day, for they are like thorns, painful in the getting, painful in the keeping, and painful in the extraction. You who have had a thorn in your hand know what I mean. Worldly cares come with pain, they stay with pain, and they go with pain.

Still, there is a use for thorns. What is that use? First, if you have thorns around you today, make a child's use of them. What does a child do? If he gets a thorn in his finger, he looks at it, and cries. How it smarts! Then he runs off to his mother. That is one of the sweet uses of his adversity – it admits him to his mother at once. She might say, "What are you coming in for? Run back outside." But he cries, "Please, mother, I've got a thorn in my anger." This is quite enough argument to secure him the best attention of the queen of the house. See how tenderly she takes out the little dagger! Let your cares drive you to God. I shall not mind if you have many of them if each one leads you to prayer. If every fret makes you lean more on the beloved, it will be a benefit. Thus make good use of the thorns.

Another service to which thorns may be put is to make a hedge of them, to keep the goats of worldly pleasure from eating the young shoots of your graces. Let the sorrows of life keep off temptations that otherwise might do you serious mischief.

May we meet in heaven! Oh, may we all meet in heaven! What a congregation I have addressed this morning! I feel overawed as I look at you. From the ends of the earth have many of you come. The Lord bless you! Strangers are here in vast numbers, for most of our regular church attenders are at the seaside. I may never see you again on earth. May we all meet in heaven, where thorns will never grow! May we be gathered by the angels in that day when the Lord shall say, *Gather the wheat into my barn* (Matthew 13:30). Amen. So let it be.

Chapter 14

The Seed upon Stony Ground

*And some fell on stony ground, where it had not much
earth; and immediately it sprang up, because it hath no
depth of earth: but when the sun was up, it was scorched;
and because it had no root, it withered away.* (Mark 4:5-6)

The gospel seed, according to the parable, falls upon all kinds of
soil. Some of its precious grains drop upon the hard pathway, some
upon the rock, some among the thorns, and only a portion, perhaps a
smaller proportion than one in four, falls upon good ground, in which
it finds a congenial, abiding place. The preacher, therefore, will not meet
with unmixed success in all directions. He may look for a full recompense from his work as a whole, but he must not fondly suppose that
everywhere the good Word will become effective; for in many it will be
a savor of death unto death, and not of life unto life. Even when Jesus
preached, only a few received him, and of Paul's ministry it is recorded
that *some believed the things which were spoken, and some believed not*
(Acts 28:24). It is for the beginner in holy service to go forward with
reasonable expectations, lest he should before long weary of the work
and leave it because of his bitter disappointments.

Observe, with care, that the sower in the parable is not blamed for
having scattered his seed upon soil that proved to be unproductive. Not
a word of rebuke is recorded against him on that account, from which

it is fair to infer that he did no more and no less than his duty, and that the minister of Christ is to scatter the seed of the gospel over a broad area among all mankind. It is God's work to direct the saving word into the chosen hearts that he has prepared to receive it; but as for us, we are to preach the gospel to every creature, and going out into the streets and lanes of the city, as many as we find we are to bid to come to the supper. Many are called but few are chosen. It was never intended that the external call should be as narrow as the election; yet there are some ministers whose preaching consists far more of an analysis of soils than of a sowing of seed. Leaving the analyzing of the soil to God, I take my commission from his hands and desire to fulfill it.

Stony-ground hearer, there is a handful of seed for you. You who are hard like the trodden road, there is a handful for you. Even among the thorns, which are plentiful enough in this age, shall the good seed fall like a heavenly shower; and if God shall graciously direct it to his own chosen, and they, like the good ground, shall receive it, it will be his doing; it will never be accomplished by any skill of mine. It is mine to sow beside all waters, and his to give the increase. The best shot that was ever made with bow and arrow was taken at random, and Ahab the king was pierced between the joints of his harness; so also, while drawing my bow to preach the gospel to every creature, my faith feels confident that the Lord will direct the arrow and accomplish his purposes of grace.

I feel that I have very solemn work on hand. I always have pleasure in preaching upon encouraging topics, but this morning my themes are for sifting and testing. We have to deal with certain apparently good people, and to show that they are not what they seem. We have to put wheat from the barn floor into the sieve, and it may be there will be much chaff to be blown away. This is an operation not pleasant to the flesh, and one that needs much of the Spirit of God so that we may perform it correctly, lest the weak ones be sorely troubled, which is far enough from our desire. Solemn discourse should have a solemn heart to utter it, and solemn hearts to hear it. May God grant it may be so at this time, that the message may be greatly profitable to every one of us, whether professors of the gospel or not.

First, we shall *read the history of stony-ground hearers;* secondly, we shall *mark the radical defect of their character;* and thirdly, we shall try to *learn a lesson* from the whole.

First, we have here a brief biography of certain professors of religion. Let us read it carefully. It is said of them, first, that *they heard the Word. These are they likewise which are sown on stony ground; who, when they have heard the word, immediately receive it with gladness* (Mark 4:16). They enjoyed the great privilege of hearing God's Word. They heard the real gospel; they did not pay attention to ritualistic falsehoods or philosophic speculations: it was *the* Word that they heard. The sower did not sow tares, but he sowed good wheat. How happy are those who sit under a downright gospel ministry! May God be pleased to multiply such ministries everywhere, and the lovers of them! How can we expect salvation to come to us if we do not hear the soul-saving gospel? If we are listening merely to opinions and notions and philosophies and superstitions, and not to the very Word of God, we cannot expect to find salvation. The Holy Spirit does not save men by means of lies, but if we hear the truth as it is in Jesus, we may hope that he will make it effective to our conversion.

Remember, next, that hearing is not enough. *Hearers only* will not enter heaven; there must be a doing of the Word as well as a hearing of it. These people were good hearers, grand hearers, for they went further than hearing – *they received the Word;* not in the divine power or supernatural effect of it, but they nevertheless received it; that is to say, they never fussed about it, they agreed to it as they heard it, and they recognized it as God's truth. Receiving it, it produced an effect upon them. They were, in a measure, impressed by it. If the sermon spoke of the wrath of God on account of sin, they were alarmed; if it told them of the love of God in Christ Jesus, they were encouraged. They did not always hear with dry eyes; they were not always like the seats they sat upon, unmoved and unemotional; but they received the Word. It stirred their affections and their emotions, they felt its moving effects, and were thus led to many changes of life.

They went home and swept the chambers that had been full of filthiness. They cleansed, at any rate, the outside of their cups and platters, and took care that the sepulcher, if not cleansed of the dead men's bones, should be decently whitewashed, so as to shock no passerby. They were improved and reformed externally by what they heard, and so far, they received it.

And there is this said about them, in the third place, that they *received it immediately.* In them it aroused no questions, doubts, or conflicts. The preacher said, "This the Word of God," and they were content to believe him, though they knew not why. While other minds were asking for the authority of the message, and then, having recognized the authority, were battling hard with a thousand difficulties, these persons saved themselves a world of trouble by never thinking at all. It was their father's religion and their mother's religion; therefore, they believed it, they swallowed the pill with their eyes shut, caring nothing about whether it was God's truth or Satan's lie. Anything like spiritual nibbling at the doctrine they did not attempt, but they endorsed wholesale whatever they were taught.

Priests themselves could not desire more artificial material. These hearers had no hard stragglings to get at the Savior, no sense of sin to hold them back, no horrors of conscience to make them afraid, no alarms lest they should not be the Lord's own people after all, no testings and siftings to see whether they possessed real repentance and acceptable faith. They sprang into religion as a man may leap into a bath, head over heels at once. They said, "Surely this is the right thing, and we will have it"; and in accordance with a certain nature they did have it: not with any depth of consideration or weight of judgment, but immediately they received the Word.

It is added, that *they received it with gladness.* The immediate effect of receiving the Word was to make them very happy; and there are not a few who suppose that to be made very happy is a sure sign of being converted. Believe me, it is a very dubious sign indeed. No doubt, one grand effect of the reception of the gospel into the heart is to bring joy and peace through believing, but there are many kinds of joy, and many sorts of peace; and there is a joy that is not the fruit of grace, but the growth of nature, and a peace that comes from delusion, and not from the Spirit of God.

We must take care that we do not conclude that we are safe because we are "so happy." The rich man who went to hell was happy when he ate sumptuously every day; the farmer, who said he would pull down his barns and build greater ones, was happy when he surveyed his stock; and so was the Prodigal Son happy while he was spending his living riotously. But theirs was a very different kind of joy from that which is the fruit of the Spirit. The characters in our text looked at the happy side of religion exclusively. "There," said the stony-ground hearer, "there is my mother; what a happy Christian she is. I have seen her in deep trial borne up by the Spirit of God; I have observed her when we have had deaths in the house, and have seen how peaceful and quiet she has been. I will lay hold on Christ, for then I shall be as happy as she is." These stony-ground hearers thought what a happy thing it must be to be forgiven; and so, indeed, it is, but they dwelt upon that alone.

To be pardoned, to be a child of God, to be accepted in the beloved – what precious things these must be! And what a delightful thing to be numbered with God's saints, to go to the Communion table, and to be thought much of in the church! Are not all these ways of pleasantness? And to go to heaven at last, to die triumphantly, to be taken up to dwell where Jesus is amidst the glory – what joyful things! Who doubts it? But these people dwelt only upon this view of the matter, and did not recollect that between this and heaven there are temptations to be combated and to be overcome, trials to be endured, stern trials, too, through which we can only be brought by divine help. Right arms must be cut off, and right eyes must be plucked out; there are costs to be counted, and reckonings to be made as to whether the future will repay for the labors of the present.

Youthful hopefuls vow that they will have the brave country of Canaan, but they do not recollect the roughness of the road there. Like Pliable, they set out for the Celestial City, but they have not reckoned upon the Slough of Despond, and therefore after the first mouthful of mud they are ready to turn back, and let those have the brave country who care for it. As for them, if they can keep whole bones in their body, they will be well content to let the future go as it may.

These people, then, immediately received the Word with joy. How hopeful all this must have looked to the sower! Do you not see how easily ministers may be deceived? When you have only to preach, and men are willing to hear; only to preach and men are willing to receive – to receive the gospel at once, without causing you any difficulty in arguing with them; when they receive it with gladness, and you have not the trouble to cheer them up, and to meet their doubts and anxieties with a thousand promises selected out of the Word of God, is not this splendid work that will richly repay the sower? Alas, we must not reckon our fruit by our buds! All is not gold that glitters, and it is not every egg that will be hatched.

We read yet further that these characters *made rapid progress* – they sprang up because they had no depth of earth; because of their shallow soil they were very rapid in their external growth. These people heard the gospel one day, received it, and felt sure that they were saved. At once they were full of joy and exhilaration, and hurried to make a profession. They did not require time to sit down and see whether they could bear out that profession, or seek grace so that they might not run before they were called; but away they went, just as if a spark had been dropped into so much powder. They made a profession, and the next week they were teaching in the Sunday school. They were so sure they were on the right road, that they were very irritated with other pilgrims who did not travel so rapidly.

When they heard of Christians being anxious as to their condition, they said, "What nonsense! What reason is there for it?" If they saw a deep-taught Christian tremblingly examining himself, they said, "Oh, you must not look at all at yourself; never consider what is going on within." They had received a one-sided gospel only, and that quite contented them; but as to anything like the work of the Spirit of God in the soul, and the holy jealousy that is one of the best fruits of vital godliness, these they quite dispensed with. They were going to drag the church behind them, and drive the world before them; and very soon they would distance even the ministry that had been the means, as they said, of their conversion. They grew from hyssops on the wall to cedars of Lebanon in about a week. They were the men, and wisdom would die with them. Grand work to have to deal with these men, is not it? We shall see by and by, and shall have to learn that not every stem that puts forth leaves is a fruit-bearing branch.

In due time, according to the parable, *came the trial.* The seed was up, and soon the sun was up too, and began to scorch it. None will get to heaven without being tried on the road. Ask concerning those who stand in their white robes before the throne of God, who are those, and from where did they come? And the answer will be, *These are they which came out of great tribulation, and have washed their robes, and made them white in the blood of the Lamb.* There is not a fragment of gold in all God's temple but what has passed through the fire. Untested faith is no faith; untested grace is no grace. God will test his people and discern between the precious and the wretched.

According to the Savior's explanation of the text, the trial came in the form of persecution. Ah! how many there are who have received the Word with gladness, who, if there were a stake in Smithfield, would very soon drop the profession of Christianity, for it would be too hot for them; or if there were a prison ready for them in which they must lie until the moss grew on their eyelids, they would soon forsake the truth and turn aside to error. We need not be much afraid of the revival of such tests, but there are other forms of persecution that mere pro-fessing Christians are equally unable to bear. A sneer in society; a remark against Christianity from a person whom you are accustomed to respecting; a look from someone who is above you in wealth, as he despises you for professing to be a follower of Christ; unkind remarks from a father, opposition from a husband, the desertion of some young companion with whom you hoped your life would be linked; such mat-ters – nothing like the stake or the prison – are yet quite sufficient to overcome flimsy professing Christians so that they are offended and turn their backs upon the religion that they once so quickly embraced.

In many instances, to follow principle would involve a great loss in business; they could not afford to incur such a loss. If Christ could be had at a cheaper rate, they would have him, but to lose all the treasures in Egypt! No, they could not do that, and so they renounce again that Christ whom they once called their all in all.

With others it has not been such a trial as that, but it has been providential affliction. I painfully remember a man and his wife, who were members of this church for some time, and it was certainly true, as they affirmed, that from the very hour they made a profession of religion they began to be in trouble; and therefore they renounced the consolation because of the affliction, for they drew the conclusion that surely they could not be the people of God, or else God would not have so tested them – a conclusion that is the reverse of the teachings of Scripture. Many will have Christ if he will pat them on the cheek, but not if he flogs them with the rod. They will follow the Lord while he is on the giving hand, but they cannot believe in a God who takes away. They can bless him while he enriches them, but they know nothing of that Job-like faith that exclaims, *The Lord gave, and the Lord hath taken away; blessed be the name of the Lord.*

Or perhaps it may be that when they first made a profession of religion they did not know much about the temptations of life. But now they have moved from home, and they have come by a situation where there are young men who tell them of haunts of pleasurable sin; or they have left the circle of godly people in which they once moved, and are cast among ungodly ones, and alas, their mouths are watering for the sweets of the world. The snake of sinful pleasure has cast a spell over them, and now Christ may be left for Belial, true religion for worldliness, and following God for the indulgence of the flesh. Ah, how often is this the case!

Or perhaps another shining of the sun has come upon them. They thought they believed the gospel, but they have fallen among debaters; they are surrounded by a skeptical circle, where they have heard arguments they never heard before, and never having weighed anything, or considered the reasons why they believed in God and in Christ, they are quite staggered. They have no depth of earth, no roothold of the truth by conviction and solemn judgment of it; and so as soon as they meet with an atheist or a deist, or a skeptic of any form, they are like thistledown before the wind. Having no ballast in their vessel, the first breeze oversets them and they are lost. What a grand thing it is to be established in the faith, rooted, grounded, and settled.

I remember reading of one who said, "When I read the arguments brought by infidels against the gospel, I laugh them to scorn, because they are nothing like so deep, cunning, or hard to answer as the arguments that my own heart has brought against the Lord in years gone by, which having answered and overcome, I feel myself more than a match for the puny oppositions of ungodly men." It is a grand thing not to be moved in these skeptical times, but to know the Lord by secret interaction with him, to know his truth by inner consciousness, and by a devout reading of his Word with eyes opened from above. Alas, many hearers and receivers of the Word have been destroyed by complaining infidels; they knew nothing thoroughly, and so were readily deceived.

It is said of the stony-ground people that *immediately they were offended.* They were just as soon out of love with the gospel as they had been in love with it. Immediately they were offended. They did not at first stop to inquire why they should be Christians, and now they do not stop to argue why they should renounce their profession. They took their religion hot from the oven, and dropped it before it was cool enough to feed on. Somebody said, "Believe, believe, believe!" and they were excited; and now another speaker says, "Do not believe; do not believe!" and they are excited the other way. They went in with a crowd of others all of a sudden during a revival; and now they are going out with the crowd during a season of lukewarmness. The minister took them in at the front door, and now he has to let them out at the back door. They have disappointed him, they have brought scandal upon the church and double responsibility upon themselves, and now they are just as earnest to give up religion as they were to profess it.

They are unhappy souls, volatile in everything, frivolous about the seriousness of eternity, ready to be right if rightly led, and as ready to be wrong if wrongly driven. Having no mind of their own, they are mollusk-like creatures – without a backbone, mere jellyfish; and nothing solid or consistent can be found in them. Their sand-built houses are no sooner up than they are washed down by the tide; they have no rocky foundations, no strong grips of truth, no principles; their motive powers are submission to persuasion, admiration of eloquence, and desire of praise. Unhappy! Unhappy! Unhappy! God grant that we may not belong to such a class.

I shall show their radical defect. Their radical defect, in the first place, lay in *an unbroken heart.* The parable does not refer to ground with stones in it, such as we commonly call stony ground, for that will grow corn well enough; but it refers to soil where there was a hard rock underneath, and only a very thin covering of earth. A hard pan of iron rock was at the bottom, and it was barely hidden by a little mold created by the lichen and moss, enough to catch the seed and make it germinate, but not enough to feed its roots for any length of time. In these people their hearts have never been broken. *Is not my word like as a fire? saith the Lord; and like a hammer?* (Jeremiah 23:29). They do not know, for it never hammered them. They got their joy and peace without a blow.

What is to be done with a piece of ground that has the rock so close to the surface? Nothing can be done with it by man. The only thing that can be done is for God to come in, and when God in his infinite mercy changes the rock into good soil, then the wheat will grow, but not until then. *A new heart also will I give you, and a new spirit will I put within you: and I will take away the stony heart out of your flesh, and I will give you an heart of flesh.* There must be a work of the Holy Spirit by which the natural rock of nature shall be turned into the good soil of grace, or else all the sowing in the world will never produce a harvest. These people skipped over that, and in fact they did not like to hear of it. They liked preachers who always preached simple faith in the work of Jesus, but never mentioned the work of the Holy Spirit – lopsided preachers, messengers whose legs are not equal, who deliver half God's message and no more; and under such teaching they found peace without soul trouble, and comfort without the new birth.

As for repentance, that old-fashioned grace, they despised it. Weeping before God on account of sin, terror under a sense of God's wrath, or fear lest the sentence of his law should be executed, they never knew. They passed into the land of hope without going around by the weeping cross, and every day I grow more and more suspicious of a man's religion if he has not gone around by that road. A man who was healed before he was wounded, clothed before he was stripped, filled before he was empty, and made alive before he was slain has good reason to suspect whether sovereign grace has ever laid its hand upon him.

These people with the unbroken heart had cheerful hopes and joyful confidences, but they all came to an end, as they will do in your case and mine if we are strangers to repentance. Let it ever be remembered that, true as it is that whosoever believes in Jesus Christ shall be saved, it is equally true that *ye must be born again* (John 3:7); *except ye be converted, and become as little children, ye shall not enter the kingdom of heaven* (Matthew 18:3); *that which is born of the flesh is flesh; and that which is born of the Spirit is spirit* (John 3:6); and *flesh and blood cannot inherit the kingdom of God* (1 Corinthians 15:50). It is only the birth of the spirit, the spiritual nature, that can enter into spiritual matters and become a possessor of truly spiritual joys. An unbroken heart is a fatal defect.

This led to a second fault, namely, *lack of depth*. The stony-ground hearer was all surface; everything about him was superficial. With the rock never having been broken, there was no depth of earth to plow. So, in many men who profess to be converted, there has been no real estimate of sin. "Yes, we are sinners," they say. "Oh yes, yes, of course we are all sinners." But to feel what it is to be a sinner is quite another thing. To be crushed down to the earth under a sense of having violated the three-times holy law of God, this sense many have never felt. And Jesus Christ – yes, he is a Savior, and they will say they take him for a Savior; but what it is to be saved, what it was he suffered, why he needed to suffer, what was the tremendous guilt that compelled such a sacrifice, they have never considered; in fact, they have never thought at all, and they do not mean to think. Bees descend into the flowers and suck out the honey, but butterflies alight on the lilies for a moment and fly away again – true emblems of flippant pretenders to grace.

Many persons who profess to be Christians seem to have no acquaintance with the plague of their own hearts. They believe that there is something amiss within, but they do not know that their heart is *deceitful above all things, and desperately wicked* (Jeremiah 17:9); consequently, though they admit they need divine grace, they do not know how much they need it. They would subscribe to the truth, *Without me ye can do nothing,* but they do not know it experimentally. They are strangers to those failures and inward disappointments that lead a man to feel his nothingness. It is surface work; nothing is deep about them. When they became professors of the religion of Christ, they never weighed the truth, or searched the Scriptures to see whether things are indeed so. They were Calvinists because the preacher was Calvinistic; they would have been Arminians quite as readily if the preacher had been Arminian. In fact, they would have been anything they were taught to be; they never judged, weighed, and considered for themselves. In embracing the truth as it is in Jesus, they never calculated the difficulties of a religious life. It did not strike them that they would have to fight with sin without and sin within; they never looked at that mighty trinity – the world, the flesh, and the devil – with which they would have to wage a lifelong combat. They took the sweets, and thought not of the bitter herbs. They were volatile, and are volatile still. They cannot think, neither can you persuade them to attempt it. This is a fault indeed.

And then there was a third defect: *The secret part of their religion was failure.* The seed on the stony ground did not fail in the sprouting, nor in the blade that appeared above; but it had no root. If you were to follow some professing Christians home, you would find no secret prayer. Let that word go through this congregation, if there are any of you living in the neglect of secret prayer. No secret prayer, no secret reading of the Word of God, no chewing of it to get the essence and the juice out of it, no vital contact with Christ in private, no communion of the soul in secret with the living God! This is a deadly sign! They were at the public meeting; they were fussy enough upon committees; they could be first and foremost if there were any singing to be done, or if there were any preaching required; but oh, the secret prayer, the secret living with God, the soul-searching, the testing of the mind to see whether they were right or wrong – they had given this all up. Taking it for granted that they must be right because they have a sort of faith, they look upon every question as to their safety as so much unbelief and the work of Satan, and so they wrap themselves up in their delusions. They think they must be the people of God because they profess themselves to be such, but they have never looked for the fruit that must be borne by every branch of the true Vine.

And so, fourthly, there was another thing that I do not think you will find in Mark, but you will see it in one of the other Gospel writers – *they lacked moisture.* Now, a plant must have moisture. Dew, rain, or some sort of watering must come to it. On that little soil with a hard rock at the bottom there was plenty of heat when the sun shone, and so the little moisture it had made the seed sprout at once, but it had no further moisture, and therefore became parched. So certain hearers get a little moisture, as it were, by contact with an earnest preacher; they come under that Word that drops as the dew and distills as the rain, but they have not the vitalizing Holy Spirit at their root to be the perpetual source of life. They have their lamps, but they have no oil in their vessels to keep them trimmed. They lack the moisture of the Holy Spirit. He it is that comes to his own people secretly, at the roots of their life, so that from him they suck up the life of God, and so they live; but the mere stony-ground convert has not the Holy Spirit.

And oh, permit me to say most solemnly to everyone here, if we have no more than nature gave us under its best conceivable circumstances, we have no more than the Pharisees, and that landed them in hell. We must have the Spirit of God, and from first to last the religion of our hearts must be worked by the Spirit, and sustained by the Spirit, and if it be not, the sooner we are rid of such a religion the better, for it will only deceive us. I feel the necessity of preaching such a message as this because I perceive church members going aside into open sin, and others turning aside to one or another of the new delusions of the present age, and there seems to be a new one every month. Some foolish people stand with their mouths open ready for any novelty to fly down their throats. They are as dry straw, only wanting some impostor to apply the spark to them, and yet they call themselves Christians. There are so many nowadays who do not know what they believe, and so become the prey of Roman Catholics, ritualists, atheists, or some other deceivers. There is a little plant in the garden, and a thief comes along and takes away root and all. He will not do so with a well-rooted oak, I warrant you; and if we were well rooted like the oak, we would believe what we do believe, and know what we do know, and would have principle to keep us steady.

The old Nonconformists might have been dragged to prison or to the stake without difficulty; but to get them to yield their nonconformity, or put aside their principles, was not possible; alas for the degenerate sons of such sturdy fathers. If what you believe be not true, fling it away; but if it be true, let your faces be like flints and your natures like iron against all the temptations of this wicked, ever-changing age, which flies this way and that, but always away from its God. Oh, when shall it be that those who know the Lord shall stand fast, and having done all, shall still stand!

Thirdly, I must close by trying to teach the lesson of the text. That lesson is fourfold. It says to each one of us, *Be deeply in earnest.* Do not play at religion. Do not think of a religious profession as a garb that you can put on and take off. Pray God to make sure work in your soul, sure work for eternity. You have to die, you have to face the judgment seat; have a religion that will bear those ordeals. Pray to have such a work of the Spirit in your soul that neither death nor judgment can alarm you. Cry to God that repentance may be cut deep into you, making lasting marks in you, that your faith may be no sham faith, but a giving up of your soul entirely into the hands of Christ; that your love for Christ may be no rhapsody, but a matter of real heart affection; that your religious walk may not be for other people to see, but be a walk before God; that all your actions may be the result of principle, and that you may not be swayed by company, but rather may sway company, and may have a vital force within yourself of God's implanting, that will bear you on in the straight road, whichever way others may take. I say again, be awfully in earnest about everything that concerns religion, and pray God to forgive you if in any measure you have been flippant concerning it.

Secondly, *watch the effect of your own daily trials.* See how they affect you. If a boat is ready to sink in the River Thames, it ought never to be trusted at sea. If your religion already begins to fail you, what will it do by and by? You were laughed at, and you were half inclined to give it all up; what would you do if you were more sternly persecuted? You have already been willing to go back, your heart has faltered; what will you do if fiercer temptations attack you? You have already been terribly put to it by the arguments of a fool; what would you do if some of the deep thinkers were to argue with you? *If thou hast run with the footmen, and they have wearied thee, then how canst thou contend with horses? and if in the land of peace, wherein thou hast trustedst, they wearied thee, then how wilt thou do in the swelling of Jordan?* (Jeremiah 12:5). I do not object to your growing slowly if you grow surely. If my house takes a long time in building, I would rather give the builder his time than tell him to run it up in a week or two, and make it so frail that the first wind would blow it away like cardboard. You have to live in this house eternally; pray God to build it surely. As to building fast, that little matters.

O you that can hardly go a step towards heaven without question and dispute, I do not so much tremble concerning you, as about some who never have any question or doubt, because they have never any thought at all, but pass it all by with a heedless carelessness, taking things for granted. See, then, how you stand in your present trials. You have grown richer; do you love the Lord as much as you did? You transact more business; can you still keep the world out of your heart? You have received more praise lately; can you still cling to Christ as you used to do when you had but few friends? You have been in good health lately; have you lived as near to God as when you were ill? Or you have come down in the world and are numbered with the poor;

do you love the Lord as much as you did when he enriched you? You have lately heard the remarks of a cunning hater of the gospel; were you able to feel that, though you could not answer him in words, yet your heart answered him, and threw off his falsehood as the roof throws off the rain? If not, look to it. If your vessel is ready to go down in smooth water, what will she do in a storm? If you cannot keep the water out of her now, what will you do when the hurricane overtakes her? It will be all over with you then, I fear.

Another lesson is: *Constantly examine yourself.* A great many persons get into the bankruptcy court, but as far as I recollect there was never one that came there through too much attendance to his business. I never heard of a farmer losing his crop through being too diligent in husbandry; and of all the souls that are lost, not one has perished through being too much in earnest as to self-examination. Dear brethren, choose a faithful, testing ministry. Do not look after a smooth-tongued preacher who will always cry, *Comfort ye, comfort ye my people* (Isaiah 40:1). You lack comfort, and should have it, but you lack searching as well, and you must have it. Do pray that you may be faithfully dealt with, that there may be no glossing over matters, no covering of wounds, but that there may be honest dealings between you and the minister, and between you and your God. God grant that we may be willing to be searched, for when we are unwilling to be searched, we may reckon it quite certain that there is something amiss with us. When we cry, "I am afraid I am a hypocrite," there is very little fear of it; but presumption is fatal.

Now, lastly, let all this show us *how necessary it is that we cast all the stress and burden of our salvation entirely upon the Lord Jesus Christ,* because whenever a man does that, there is honest and good ground in his soul, and the seed has sprung up right. Whenever a man can truly say, "I rest alone in Jesus;

> Nothing in my hand I bring:
> Simply to thy cross I cling,"

that is the great secret of a true hope. Jesus lived and died for us, and if we do entirely and alone depend upon him, it is well with our souls.

It is well to live continually at the foot of the cross, looking up to Jesus, finding all our hope in him, and none in ourselves. Beloved, it is the work of the Spirit of God to bring us there and keep us there. If we search ourselves in the light of the cross, we shall be willing to judge ourselves that we be not judged; in the presence of those dear wounds from where drips the atoning blood, we shall cry, *Try my reins* [mind] *and my heart* (Psalm 26:2). But if any man says, "I believe in Jesus; therefore, I will not search. I trust in Jesus; therefore, I will live as I like," then that man's religion is vain; he has profaned the cross by his reckless reasoning, and let him take heed how God shall judge him, for of all judgments surely that will be the heaviest that shall come upon the man who dared to take the doctrine of the cross as a reason for careless living, and made the mercy and the cleansing power of the Redeemer himself an apology for walking heedlessly before God, and continuing in vain presumption. God grant us grace to receive the seed into good ground, for Jesus' sake.

Chapter 15

The Parable of the Sower

And when much people were gathered together, and were
come to him out of every city, he spake by a parable: a
sower went out to sow his seed: and as he sowed, some fell
by the way side; and it was trodden down, and the fowls
of the air devoured it. And some fell upon a rock; and
as soon as it was sprung up, it withered away, because it
lacked moisture. And some fell among thorns; and the
thorns sprang up with it, and choked it. And other fell
on good ground, and sprang up, and bare fruit an hun-
dredfold. And when he had said these things, he cried,
He that hath ears to hear, let him hear. (Luke 8:4-8)

In our country, when a sower goes forth with his seed, he enters into an enclosed field, and begins at once with due order and precision to scatter the seed from his basket along every ridge and furrow. But in the East, the wheat-growing country, close by a small town is one vast unenclosed plain. True, it is divided into different properties, but there are no hedges, no divisions, except the ancient landmark, or perhaps on rare occasions a simple ridge of stones to divide one man's field from another. Through these wide-open common lands there are footpaths, the most frequented being called the highways. You must not imagine these highways to be in the slightest degree like our macadamized roads, but simply frequented paths that are trodden tolerably hard. Here and there are byways, along which travelers who wish to avoid the public road may journey with a little more safety when the main road is infested with robbers; and the hasty pedestrian can take a shortcut for himself across the plain, and so open a fresh road for others who are journeying in the same direction.

When the sower goes out in the morning to sow his seed, he finds, perhaps, a little spot of ground scratched over with the primitive Eastern plow. He begins to scatter his seed there, of course most plentifully, but there runs a path right through the very center of his field, and unless he is willing to leave a broad headland, he must throw a handful on the pathway. And yonder, there is a rock cropping out just in the midst of the plowed land, and the seed falls on that. And there too, fostered by the negligent husbandry of the East, there is a corner full of the roots of nettles and thistles, and the sower sows his seed there too; the corn and the nettles come up together, and as we know by the parable, the thorns being the strongest spring up and choke the seed, so that it brings forth *no fruit to perfection* (Luke 8:14). The recollection that the Bible was written in the East, and that its metaphors and allusions are fully to be explained to us only by Eastern travelers, would very often help us to understand a passage far better than the common English reader can possibly do.

Now the preacher of the gospel is like the sower. He does not make his seed; the seed is given to him by his Master. It would not be possible for a man to make the smallest seed that ever germinated upon the earth, much less that celestial seed of eternal life. The minister goes to his Master in secret, and asks him to teach him his truth, and thus he fills his basket with the good seed of the kingdom. What the minister has to do is to go forth in his Master's name and scatter precious truth. If he knew where the best soil was to be found, perhaps he might limit himself to that which had been prepared by the plow of conviction. But not knowing men's hearts, it is his business to preach the gospel to every creature – to throw a handful on that hard heart yonder, and another handful on that overgrown heart, which is full of cares and riches and pleasures of this world. He has to leave the fate of the seed in the care of the Master who gave it to him, for well he understands that he is not responsible for the harvest, he is only responsible for the care, the fidelity, and the integrity with which he scatters the seed right and left with both his hands.

What if not a single ear should ever make glad the sheaves? If there would never be seen a single green blade springing up among the furrows, the man would be accepted and rewarded by his Master, if he had but sown the right seed, and sown it with careful hand. Alas! Alas! if it were not for this fact – that we are not responsible for our success – with what despairing agony must we remember that too often we labor in vain, and spend our strength for nothing. The cry of Isaiah of old must be our cry still: *Who hath believed our report? and to whom is the arm of the Lord revealed?* (Isaiah 53:1). But one seed in four finds hopeful soil. The three portions out of the four scattered on evil places produce no good effect, for they are lost, and shall never be seen again, except when they shall rise up in judgment against our ungracious hearers to condemn them.

Here let me remark, that the measure of our duty is not limited by the character of our hearers, but by the command of God. We are bound to preach the gospel, whether men will hear, or whether they will refrain. Let men's hearts be what they may, I am not loosed from my obligation to sow the seed on the rock as well as in the furrow, on the highway as well as in the plowed field.

My plan this morning will be very simply to address myself to the four classes of hearers that are to be found in my congregation. We have, first of all, those who are represented by the *wayside,* the *mere* hearers; then those represented by the *stony-ground hearers,* those in whom there is a momentary impression produced, but so momentary, however, that it never comes to any lasting good; then those on whom *a large and good impression is produced,* but the cares of this life, and the deceitfulness of riches, and the pleasures of this world choke the seed; and, lastly, that small class – God be pleased to multiply it exceedingly – that small class of *good-ground hearers,* in whom the Word brings forth fruit, in some thirty, in some sixty, and in some a hundredfold.

First of all, then, I am to address myself to those hearts that are like the wayside – *Some fell by the way side; and it was trodden down, and the fowls of the air devoured it.* There are many of you who did not come here this morning to get a blessing. You did not intend to worship God, or to be affected by anything that you might hear. You are like the highway that was never intended to be a wheat field. If a single grain of truth should fall into your heart and grow, it would be a miracle, as great a wonder as for the wheat to grow upon the hardly trodden wayside. You are the wayside hearer. If the corn, however, shall be cleverly scattered, some of it will fall upon you and rest for a while upon your thoughts. The "true you" will not understand it, but nevertheless, if it be placed before you in an interesting style, it will lodge for a little season. Until some more congenial entertainment shall attract you, you will talk of the words that you heard from the minister of truth. But even this meager benefit is brief, for in a very little season you will forget what manner of man you are.

Would to God I could hope that my words would abide with you, but we cannot hope for it, for the soil of your heart is so well beaten by continual traffic that there is no hope of the seed finding a lasting and living roothold down its roots. There is too much traffic in your soul to let the good seed remain uncrushed. The foot of Satan is always passing over your heart, with his herd of blasphemies, lusts, lies, and vanities. Then the chariots of pride roll along it, and the feet of greedy wealth tread it until it is as hard as a stone. Alas! for the good seed, it finds not a moment's respite; crowds pass and return; in fact, your soul is an exchange, across which continually pass the busy feet of the merchants that make merchandise with the souls of men. You are buying and selling, but you little think that you are selling the truth, and that you are buying your soul's destruction; you are busy here and there around this body, the husk of your manhood, but you are negligent of that internal, precious thing, your soul. You have no time, you say, to think of religion. No, the road of your heart is such a crowded thoroughfare that there is no room for this wheat to spring up. If it did begin to germinate, some rough foot would crush the green blade before it could come to anything like perfection.

There have been times with you when the seed has lain long enough to begin to germinate, but just then there was some place of amusement open, and you entered there, and as with an iron heel, the spark of life that was in the seed was crushed out; it had fallen in the wrong place; there was too much traffic there for it to possibly grow. During the plague of London, when men were carried to their long home by multitudes, the grass grew in the streets; but wheat could not grow in Cornhill, however excellent might be the seed that you would sow there. Ransack the world, and you cannot purchase wheat that would flourish where such traffic continually rolls along. Your heart is just like that crowded thoroughfare; for there are so many thoughts, and cares, and sins, and so many proud, vain, evil, and rebellious thoughts against God continually trafficking through it, that the truth is like seed cast on the highway; it cannot grow, it is crushed down; and if it does remain for a moment, the birds of the air come and steal it away.

Alas, but it is a very sad thought that if you should scatter seed on the highway, it is not only the foot of a bad man that would prevent its growing, but also the foot even of a saint would help to destroy its life. Alas! men's hearts may be hardened, not merely by sin, but also by the very preaching of the gospel. There is such a thing as being gospel hardened; it is possible to sit under sermons until your heart becomes dead, and callous, and careless. Like the blacksmith's dog that lies and sleeps while the sparks are flying around his nostrils, so you will lie and sleep under the hammer of the law while the sparks of damnation are flying around you, never startled, never astonished. You have heard all that before; we tell you but a three-times-told tale when we warn you of the wrath to come.

The men that work in the huge boilers in the Southwark factories, when they are first put inside to hold the hammer, their ears are stunned and they cannot hear a sound; but by degrees, I am told, they get so used to that hideous noise that they could sleep in the midst of the engine while men were battering it and beating it, although the reverbera-tions are like the loudest thunder. So has it become with you. Minister after minister has trodden along the highway of your soul, until it has become so hard that unless God himself shall be pleased to crack it in pieces with an earthquake, or with a heart-quake, there will never be room for the seed of heaven to lodge there. Your soul has become like a hard, well-beaten path that has much traffic on it.

We have observed this hard roadside; let us now describe what becomes of the good Word, when it falls upon his heart. It does not grow. It would have grown if it had fallen on right soil, but it is in the wrong place, and it remains as dry as when it fell from the sower's hand. Its life lies asleep, the life germ in the gospel hides itself, and it lies upon the surface of the heart, but never enters into it. Like the snow, which sometimes falls upon our streets and does not lie there for an instant, but drops upon the wet pavement and is dissolved and gone, so it is with this man. The Word has not time to stimulate the souls of such casual hearers of it. It lies there for an instant, but it never begins to strike its root, or to take the slightest effect.

But, we say, why do men come to hear if the Word is never made useful to them, and never enters the heart? That has often puzzled me. There are some in our audience who would not be absent on the Sunday for all the world, and who seem to be quite delighted to come up with us to worship, but yet the tear never trickles down their cheek, their soul never seems mounting up to heaven on the wings of praise, nor do they truly join in our confessions of sin. When do they ever think about the wrath to come, or the future state of their souls? Their heart is iron; the minister might as well preach to a heap of stones as preach to them. What brings these senseless sinners here? Shall we talk to brows of brass and hearts of steel? Surely we are as hopeful of converting lions and leopards as these untamed, unmoved hearts.

Oh feelings! you have fled to brutal beasts, and men have lost their reason. I suppose these men often come because it is respectable, and again, because it even helps to make them hard. If they stepped away, conscience would prick them, and there would be a little life in them; but they go so that they may be able to flatter themselves with the notion that they are doing right after all. They are not irreligious, not they; they are not careless about God's house and his servant; they come so that they may get hardened, and may be more and more dulled in their state of sin and insensibility.

Oh! my friends, your case is one that might make an angel weep; to have the sun of the gospel shining on your faces, and yet to have blind eyes that never see the light. The music of heaven sounds sweetly, but your ears are deaf, and the faintest accent never reaches your poor spirit. The minister is to you as one who plays upon a goodly instrument, but he plays before a statue that has no ears to hear. You can catch the turn of a phrase, and you can find out the meaning of a metaphor, but the hidden meaning, the divine life, is all lost upon you. You are sitting down at the marriage feast, but you eat not of the delicacies, you drink not of those wines; you hear the bells of heaven sounding joy over ransomed spirits, but you yourself live unransomed, without God, and without Christ. You are standing at the gate of the narrow way, at the very gate, but yet you do not enter it; you are close to the house of mercy, and the door is on the jar; you stand, and sometimes look within, but never take the final and decisive step. Let us do what we may to urge you, let us plead with you and pray for you and weep over you; you still remain just as hardened, as careless, and as thoughtless as ever you were. Oh! may God have mercy on you, and bring you out of this evil state, that you may yet be saved. O Holy Spirit, break up this hard highway, and cause it yet to bring forth abundantly.

We have not, however, completed the picture. The passage tells us that the birds of the air devoured it. Is there a man here this morning who is one of these wayside hearers? Perhaps he did not mean to come in, but he saw a great crowd standing in the Strand, and he thought he would even turn in and spend the hour, and he will hear something, perhaps, that he will not readily forget. But when he shall get outside and go home, some old companion will propose to him that they should go on some excursion this afternoon. He agrees, and that poor seed that fell on such an unpromising spot will be devoured by the birds of the air. There are plenty of evil ones ready always to eat up this good seed. There is the devil himself, that prince of the air, ready at any time to snatch away a good thought, or quench a holy resolution.

And then, the devil is not alone – he has legions of helpers. He may set a man's own wife, a man's own children, he may set that shop of yours upon you, and it may eat up the good seed. There may be a customer waiting at the door, and though you have no wish to serve him today, yet you may be afraid of losing him, and you may do it, and then the good seed is gone, and all its good effect is carried away. Oh, sorrow upon sorrow, that heavenly seed should become devil's meat; that God's wheat should feed the devil's birds.

Let me turn personally to you again this morning. O my friends, if you have heard the gospel from your youth, what wagonloads of sermons have been wasted on you! In your younger days, you heard old Dr. So-and-so, and how that dear old man was accustomed to praying for his hearers until his eyes seemed red with tears! Do you recollect those many Sundays when you said to yourself, "Let me go to my chamber and fall on my knees and pray"? But you did not; the birds of the air ate up the seed, and you went on to sin just as you had sinned. Since then, by some strange impulse, you are very rarely absent from God's house, but now the sparks of the gospel fall into your soul as if they dropped into an ocean, in which they are quenched forever. The law may be thundered at you; you do not sneer at it, but it never affects you. Jesus Christ may be lifted up; his dear wounds may be exhibited; the streaming blood may flow before your very eyes, and you may be bidden with all earnestness to look to him and live; but it has now become a matter of perfect indifference to you.

You have not said so much in words: "If I am to be lost, I shall be lost, and if I am to be saved, I shall be saved." You have not *said* so much, but you have come to *think* so much, and now we may do what we will with you, and what we will for you, your flinty spirits we cannot penetrate, and into your hard heart we cannot thrust a holy thought. What shall I do for you? Shall I stand here and rain tears upon this hard highway? Alas! my tears will not break it; it is far too hard for that. Shall I bring the gospel-plow upon it? Alas! it will break the steel, but the plowshare will not enter. What shall we do? O God, you know how to dash the flint in pieces. You can melt the stony, long-traveled heart with the precious blood of Jesus. Do it now, we beg you, to the praise and glory of your grace, that the good seed may yet live and produce that heavenly harvest, after which the soul of your servant yearns, without which he cannot live, but with which he can rejoice with joy unspeakable and full of glory.

I shall now turn to the second class of hearers. *And some fell upon a rock; and as soon as it was sprung up, it withered away, because it lacked moisture.* You can easily picture to yourselves that piece of rock cropping out in the midst of the field. By some disruption of nature, it has been heaped upwards into the midst of the plain, and of course the seed falls there as it does everywhere else. We have hearers who cause us more pleasure and yet more subsequent pain than many of you would believe. None but those who love the souls of men can tell what hopes, what joys, and what bitter dashings of our expectations to the ground these stony places have caused us. We have a class of hearers whose hearts inwardly are very hard, but outwardly they are apparently the softest and most affected of men. While other men see nothing in the sermon, these men weep. It is but an ordinary discourse to most of our hearers, but these men are moved to tears. Whether you preach the terrors of the law or the love of Calvary, they are alike stirred in their souls, and the liveliest impressions are apparently produced.

I have some such here this morning. They have resolved, re-resolved, and yet have procrastinated. They are not the sturdy enemies of God who clothe themselves in steel, but they seem to bare their breasts, and lay them open, and say to the minister, "Cut here; here is a naked breast for you. Here aim your arrows. They shall find a ready lodging place." Gladdened in heart, we shoot our arrows there, and they appear to penetrate; but, alas, there is a secret armor worn underneath the flesh that blunts every dart, and though it abides awhile, it falls away, and no work is done. We read of this character under this language – *Some fell upon stony places, where they had not much earth: and forthwith they sprung up, because they had no deepness of earth* (Matthew 13:5). Or as another passage explains it: *And these are they likewise which are sown on stony ground; who, when they have heard the word, immediately receive it with gladness; and have no root in themselves, and so endure but for a time: afterward, when affliction or persecution ariseth for the word's sake, immediately they are offended* (Mark 4:16-17).

Oh! have we not tens of thousands of our hearers who receive the Word with joy? They have no deep convictions, it is true, no terrible alarms, but they leap into Christ all of a sudden, and profess an instantaneous faith in him, and that faith too has all the appearance of being genuine. When we look at it, the seed has really sprouted. There is a kind of life in it, there is the real green blade. We thank God, and bow our knees, and clap our hands – there is a sinner brought back, we say; there is a soul born to God, there is an heir of heaven. But our joy is premature – they sprang up all of a sudden, and received the Word with joy, because they had no depth of earth; and from that very cause that hastened their reception of the seed, they also, by and by when the sun is risen with its fervent heat, withered away. These men we see every day in the week. They often come to join the church; they tell us a story of how they heard us preach on such and such an occasion, and oh, the Word was so blessed to them that they never felt so happy in their lives! "Oh sir, I thought I must leap from my seat when I heard about a precious Christ, and I believed on him there and then; I am sure I did."

We ask them whether they ever felt their need of a Savior. They say yes, but they mean no. We question them as to whether they were ever convinced of sin. Well, they think they were, but they don't know; but one thing they know: they feel a great pleasure in religion. We put it to them: "Do you think you will hold on?" Oh, they are confident they shall. They could not go back to their old acquaintance, they are quite sure of it. They hate the things they once loved, they are sure they do. Everything has become new to them. And all this is all of a sudden. We inquire when the good work began. We find it began when it ended; that is to say, there was no previous work, no plowing of the soil, but all of a sudden they sprang from death to life and out of condemnation into grace, as a man standing on the edge of a river might leap into the flood.

Still we are very thankful for these men. We cannot deny that there seems to be every appearance of grace. Perhaps we receive them into the church, but in a week or two they are not so regular as they used to be at a place of worship. We gently reprove them, and they say, well, they meet with such opposition in religion that they are content to yield a little. Another week and we lose them altogether. The reason is that they have been laughed at, exposed to a little opposition, and they have gone back. They are the Mr. Pliables; they will go to heaven with Christian, for heaven is a brave country. So, they walk arm in arm, chatting so sweetly together about the world to come. But by and bye there is a bog – the Slough of Despond – and in goes poor Christian, and Mr. Pliable falls in too. "Oh!" says he, "I did not bargain for this; I did not bargain to have my mouth filled with dirt. If I can at once get out, and get back, you may have the brave country all to yourself for me."

So, the poor man flounders out as best he can, and lands on the same side as his own house; and back he goes, so glad to think he has escaped from the melancholy necessity of being a Christian. And what do you think are the feelings of the minister? He feels that he had reckoned too early upon his success. He is like the husbandman who sees his field all green and flourishing, and at night a frost nips every shoot, and the poor farmer mourns because his hoped-for gains are gone. So does the minister; he goes to his chamber, and casts himself on his face before God, and cries, "Oh, I have been deceived; this man has returned like the dog to his vomit, and like the sow that was washed, to her wallowing in the mire."

You will remember that ancient picture of Orpheus, who had such skill upon the lyre, that the ancients said he made the very oaks and stones dance around him. It is a poetical fiction, and yet it has sometimes happened to the minister, that not only have the godly rejoiced, but also the very oaks and stones have danced from their places; but alas! they have been oaks and stones still. Hushed is the lyre, and the oak returns to its rooting place, and the stone casts itself once more heavily to the earth. The sinner, who, like Saul, was among the prophets, goes back to plan mischief against the Lord Most High. He who sang yesterday, and prayed the day before in the public assembly, goes to the tavern to curse; he rolls through the streets on the Sabbath night that follows his reception into the visible church on earth. I had one man who caused me many bitter tears.

In a certain village he was the ringleader of all that was bad. He was a tall, fine, big fellow, and a man that could drink more largely than perhaps any man for miles around him. He was the terror of the neighborhood – a man who would curse and swear, and never knew a thought of fear. He stepped in one day to hear the Word of God, and he wept. The whole church was astonished. There was old So-and-so weeping, and it was rumored around that Tom felt impressed; he began regularly to attend the chapel, and was clearly an altered man. The tavern lost an excellent customer; he was not seen in the skittle alley, nor was he detected in the drunken rows that were so common in the neighborhood. At last he ventured to come forward at the prayer meeting; he talked about what he had experienced, what he had felt and known. I heard him pray; it was rough, rugged language, but there was such impassioned earnestness. I set him down as being a bright jewel in the Redeemer's crown. He held out six, no, nine months he persevered in our midst. If there was rough work to be done, he would do it; if there was a Sunday school to be maintained six or seven miles away, he would walk there. At any risk, he would be out to help in the Lord's work; if he could but be of service to the most ordinary member of the church of Christ, he rejoiced greatly.

So, he went on; but at last, the laughter to which he was exposed, the jeers and scoffs of his old companions – though at first he bore them like a man – became too much for him. He began to think he had been a little too fanatical, a little too earnest. He slinked up to the place of worship instead of coming boldly in. He gradually forsook weeknight services, and forsook the Sabbath day at last; and though often warned, and often rebuked, he returned to his old habits, and though never again such a monster in sin as he had been before, yet any thoughts of God or godliness that he had ever known seemed to die away. He could again take the blasphemer's oath; once more could he act wickedly with the profane. And he – of whom we had often boasted and said in our meetings together, "Oh! how much is God to be glorified by this! what can grace not do!" – to the confusion of us all, was to be seen sometimes drunk in our streets, and then it was thrown in our teeth: "This is one of your Christians, is it? One of your converts gone back again, and become as bad as he was before?"

If it is bad to be like the wayside hearer, I cannot think it is much better to be like the rock. And yet this second class of hearers certainly gives us more joy than the first. There is a sort of people who always come around a new minister; and I have often thought it is an act of God's kindness in Providence that he always sends some of these people at first, while the minister is young, and has but few to stand by him – a class of people who are easily moved, and if he preached earnestly they feel it, and they love him, and they gather around him. But time, which proves all things, proves them. They seemed to be made of good and true metal, but they are put in the fire, they are tested, they are proved, and they are consumed in the furnace.

I see as I look here some one or two of that kind. I do not know most of you, but I do see some of whom I must say, "You are the very persons described here." I have looked at you when I have been preaching, and often have I thought, "There, that man one of these days will come out from the world, I am sure he will." I have thanked God for him. Ah! but these seven years have we preached to you and you are the same as you were. Well, there may be seven years more, who can tell? And are those to be seven years of wasted efforts? Are those to be seven years of warnings rejected and of invitations refused? Can it be so, and must you be carried to your tomb at last, and shall I stand over the mouth of that open sepulcher, and think, "Here lies a blasted hope, a flower that withered in its bud, a man in whom grace seemed to struggle, but in whom it never reigned, who gave some hopeful spasms of life, and then they all subsided into the coldness and languor of eternal death"? God save you! Oh! may he deal with you effectively, and may you, even you, yet be brought in, that Jesus may have all the glory.

I shall have very brief time to expound upon the third class, and may the Spirit of God assist me to deal faithfully with you. *And some fell among thorns; and the thorns sprang up with it, and choked it.* Now this was good soil. The two first characters were bad; the wayside was not the proper place, the rock was not a congenial situation for the growth of any plant, but this is good soil, for it grows thorns. A soil that will grow thistles will surely grow wheat. Wherever the thistle will spring up and flourish, there would wheat flourish too. This was very rich, fat, and fertile soil; it was no marvel, therefore, that the husbandman dealt largely there, and threw handful after handful upon that corner of the field. See how happy he is when in a month or two's time he visits the spot. The seed has sprung up. True, there's a suspicious little plant down there of about the same size as the wheat. "Oh!" he thinks, "that's not much, the wheat will outgrow that; when it comes up it will choke these few thistles that have unfortunately mixed with it."

Alas, Mr. Husbandman, you do not understand the force of evil, or you would not thus dream! He comes again, and the seed has grown, there is even the wheat in the head, but the thistles, the thorns, and the briars have become intertwined with one another, and the poor wheat can hardly get a ray of sunshine. It is so festooned with brambles every which way, that what with the drippings from the brambles and the absence of sunlight, it looks to have a yellow and grayish hue. Still it lives; it perseveres in growing, and it does seem as if it would bring forth a little fruit, but it never comes to anything. With it the reaper never fills his arm. There is the sign of fruit, but there is no reality in it; it brings forth no fruit unto perfection.

Now we have this class very largely among us. We have the gentlemen and ladies who come up to hear the Word, and they understand what they hear too. They are not ignorant and unenlightened men and women who cast away what they have heard. We are not throwing pearls before swine when we preach to them, but they recollect and treasure up the words of truth; they take them home; they think them over; they come, they come, they come again. They even go the length of making a profession of religion. The wheat seems to bud, and bloom and blossom; it will soon come to perfection. Be in no hurry, for these men and women have a great deal to look after. They have the cares of a large concern; their establishment employs so many hundred hands; do not be deceived about their godliness – they have no time for it. They will tell you that they must live; that they cannot neglect this world; that they must anyhow look out for the present, and as for the future, they think they will be able to take care of that by and by. They continue to attend, and that poor little dwindled blade keeps on growing. And now that they have gotten rich, they can come up to the place of worship in their carriage, and they have all that a heart can wish for now.

Ah! now the seed will grow, will it not? No, no. They have no cares now. The shop is given up, they live in the country, and they do not have to ask, "Where shall the money come from to meet the next bill?" or "How shall we be able to provide for our increasing family?" No, now they have too much instead of too little, for they have their *riches*. "Well, but," says one, "they might spend their riches for God; they might be talents that they could put out at interest." Oh no, it is not that; their riches are deceitful. Now they have to entertain much company, now they must be respectable, now they must think about becoming members of parliament, now they must have all the deceitfulness that riches can possibly confer. Yes, but they begin to spend their riches, so they have surely gotten over that difficulty. They give largely to the cause of Christ, they are generous in the cause of charity, and the like; now that little blade will grow, will it not?

No, for now behold the thorns of pleasure. Their liberality to others involves liberality to themselves. They take pleasure in what they have, and quite right they should too; but at the same time these pleasures become so tall and so big that they choke the wheat, and the good grains of gospel truth cannot grow because they have this pleasure, that musical party, that dance, and that party; so they cannot attend to the things of God because the pleasures of this world choke the seed. I know several fearful specimens of this class. It would not be fair to tell the story if it should be known again, but I might tell of scores of stories like this.

I know one who stands high in court circles who has often confessed to me that he wishes he were poor, for he thinks that then he might enter the kingdom of heaven. He holds a high position, but he has said it – and said it too with marks upon his countenance that showed that he meant what he said – "Ah! sir, these politics, these politics, I wish I were rid of them, for they are eating the life out of my heart; I cannot serve God as I would. I only wish I could retire to some sequestered place to seek my Savior." I know of one, too, overloaded perhaps with riches, always kind and noble with them too; that man has said to me – when we have walked together and I have read his very thoughts – "Ah! sir, it is an awful thing to be rich, for one cannot find it easy to keep to the Savior with all this earth around me."

Ah! my dear friends, I will not ask for you that God may lay you on a bed of sickness, that he may strip you of all your wealth, that he may bring you to poverty, that he may take away your comforts. I will not ask that; but oh, if he were to do it, and you were to save your soul, it would be the greatest bargain you could ever make. If the king could remove his crown to be saved; if those mightiest among the mighty who now make this complaint, that the thorns choke the seed, could give up all their riches and be banished from all their pleasures; if all their luxury should be turned into poverty; and if they that get on sumptuously every day could take the place of Lazarus on the dunghill, and have dogs to lick their sores, it would be a happy change for them if their souls might be but saved.

Mind you, I do not believe but what a man may be honorable and rich, and have much pleasure in the mercies of God, and then go to heaven hereafter; but it will be hard work with him. *It is easier for a camel to go through the eye of a needle, than for a rich man to enter into the kingdom of God* (Matthew 19:24). Some of those camels do go through the needle's eye; God does make some rich men enter the kingdom of heaven, but hard is their struggle, and desperate is the strife they always have against their proud flesh, to keep it under and subdue it. Steady, young man, steady! Do not hurry to get up there. It is a place where your head will turn. Do not ask God to make you popular; they that have popularity hate it, and would desire to be rid of it. Do not ask that he would make you famous and rich; they that are famous and rich often look within, and wish that they could go back to the quietude they once enjoyed. Cry with Agur – *Give me neither poverty nor riches* (Proverbs 30:8). God give me to tread the middle ground, and may I ever have in my heart that good seed, which shall bring forth fruit a hundredfold to his own glory.

I now close with the last character, namely, the good ground. Of the good soil as you will observe, we have but one in four. Ah! would to God there were one in four of us here with well-prepared hearts to receive the Word. The ground was good; not that it was good by nature, but it had been made good by grace. God had plowed it; he had stirred it up with the plow of conviction, and there it lay in ridge and furrow as it should be. And when the gospel was preached, the heart received it, for the man said, "That's just the Christ I need. Mercy! It's just what a needy sinner requires. A refuge! God help me to fly to it, for a refuge I sorely need." The preaching of the gospel was the thing to give comfort to this disturbed and plowed soil. Down fell the seed; it sprung up. In some cases it produced a fervency of love, a largeness of heart, and a devotedness of purpose, like seed that produced a hundredfold.

The man became a mighty servant for God, he spent himself and was spent. He took his place in the vanguard of Christ's army, stood in the hottest of the battle, and did deeds of daring that few could accomplish – the seed produced a hundredfold. It fell in another heart of similar character; the man could not do the most, but still he did much. He gave himself, just as he was, up to God, and in his business he had a word to say for the business of the world to come. In his daily walk, he quietly adorned the doctrine of God his Savior – he brought forth sixtyfold. Then it fell on another, whose abilities and talents were but small; he could not be a star, but he would be a glowworm; he could not do as the greatest, but he was content to do something, even though it was the least. The seed had brought forth in him tenfold, perhaps twentyfold.

How many do I have of such in this vast congregation today? I came here with my soul all on fire to preach to you, but a sudden darkness and heaviness of soul has possessed me, and while I have been addressing you, I have preached in my own spirit against wind and tide. But may I hope that notwithstanding the awkwardness with which I throw the seed, it may light on some good spot, some happy soil? Is there one who prays within himself, "O Lord, save me; God be merciful to me a sinner"? The seed has fallen in the right spot. Soul, your prayer shall be heard; God never sets a man longing for mercy without intending to give it.

And does another whisper, "Oh! that I might be saved!" Soul, believe on the Lord Jesus Christ, and you, even you, shall be saved. Have you been the chief of sinners? Trust Christ, and your enormous sins shall vanish as the millstone sinks beneath the flood. Is there no man here that will now trust the Savior? Can it be possible that the Spirit is entirely absent? that he is not moving in one soul? not producing life in one spirit? We will pray that now he may descend, that scattered badly as the seed may be, the protecting God may watch over it, and foster and nourish it, until it shall come to an eternal harvest.

What a solemn thought it is to think of these great Sunday gatherings these many years, coming and going, coming and going, and so many yet unsaved! I suppose it is my lot to address more than one or two million every year of precious immortal spirits, and how many out of these millions hear with deaf ears, are not moved in their souls, but continue as they were, dead in trespasses and sins! The thought sometimes staggers me – shall these congregations pass before my eyes in eternity, and if I have been unfaithful, shall I be spit upon by every mouth of every man whom I have deceived? Shall every eye of the millions I have addressed flash fiery damnations on me throughout eternity? They must, *they must,* if I have not sought your welfare, and if I have not preached to you the gospel of our Lord and Savior Jesus Christ. I implore you, I beg you, if your blood must fall somewhere, at least take heed to what I say now, or permit me to hope that you will accept me as having tried to be faithful to you, lest your blood be found on my garments. But why should that blood be scattered anywhere? Is there not hope? Is there not salvation? Is there not, while life lasts, still an open door of escape?

Flee, flee, my friend, flee! I beg you to flee, I implore you by the living God, by time, by eternity, by heaven, by hell, to flee, flee to Jesus, before death overtakes you. He is after you – that skeleton rider on his pale horse – and before damnation reaches you, flee, flee to him whose opened arms are ready to receive you now. Trust Jesus and you are saved. *He that believeth [on the Lord Jesus] and is baptized shall be saved; but he that believeth not shall be damned* (Mark 16:16). Am I fanatical or enthusiastic in begging, in begging you to think of these things? "Fanatic" at the day of judgment will only mean a man who was in earnest. An "Enthusiast" will only mean one who meant what he said. Oh, believe on the Lord Jesus Christ, lest now, even while you are here, God's wrath should burn, and his swift justice overtake you.

> Come, guilty souls, and flee away,
>   To Christ, and heal your wounds;
> This is the welcome gospel-day,
>   Wherein free grace abounds.

Chapter 16

Satan's Punctuality, Power, and Purpose

*Then cometh the devil, and taketh away the word out of their
hearts, lest they should believe and be saved.* (Luke 8:12)

I t is a great comfort that such multitudes are willing to hear the Word
of God. Even though many should turn out to be as the rock, the
wayside, or the thorny ground, still it is a cheerful circumstance that
the seed can be sown over so large an acreage. Yet the thoughts excited
by the sight of a vast congregation are not all pleasurable; the question most naturally arises – What will come of all this preaching and
hearing? Will the heavenly seed produce a harvest or fall on barren
soil? The thoughtful Christian, in considering this question, takes into
consideration the condition of the persons addressed, and remembers
that many are unprepared for the gospel. So far from being like a field
furrowed to receive the seed, they are like a trodden pathway. They hear
the gospel, and so far we are hopeful of them, but they have no idea of
allowing it to enter their inmost souls.

The ground of their hearts is too much occupied already; other feet
will tread there and speedily obliterate the sower's footprints, and as for
the good seed, it may lie where it falls, but entrance into the inner man it
can have none. Nor is this all, for the anxious observer remembers that

there is yet another difficulty: the archenemy of God and man is opposed to the salvation of souls, and therefore he is present with destructive power wherever the seed of the Word is being sown. It is of this we shall now speak – the activity of Satan during the preaching of the gospel. He is out of sight, but we may not allow him to be out of mind: he does all the more mischief if men sleep. Let us watchfully turn our eyes towards him, and prove that we are not ignorant of his schemes to deceive.

Our divine Lord in the words before us reminded his hearers of the devil's punctuality – **then** *cometh the devil* (emphasis added); of his power – *and taketh away the word out of their hearts;* and of his purpose, which is the prevention of saving faith – *lest they should believe and be saved.* At this time, when special services are being held, it may be well to bring these points clearly forward so that all may be warned against the wicked one, and so by the grace of God his plans may be frustrated.

First observe the Evil One's punctuality. No sooner does the seed fall than the birds devour it. Our text says *then;* that is, there and then, *cometh the devil.* Mark renders it: *Satan cometh immediately* (Mark 4:15). Whoever else may loiter, Satan never does. No sooner does a camel fall dead in the wilderness than the vultures appear. Not a bird was visible, nor did it seem possible that there could be one within a radius of many miles, yet speedily there are specks in the sky, and soon the devourers are gorging themselves with flesh. Even thus do the spirits of evil smell their prey from afar, and hasten to their destroying work. The lapse of time might give opportunity for thought, and thought might lead to repentance, and therefore the Enemy hurries to prevent the hearer from considering the truth he has heard. When the gospel has somewhat affected the hearers, so that in some slight degree it is in their hearts, *then* swifter than the flight of the eagle is the haste of the devil to take the Word out of their hearts. A little delay might put the case beyond satanic power, thus the promptitude of demonic activity. O that we were half as quick and active in the service of our Lord, one-half as prompt to seize every opportunity for blessing the souls of men!

No doubt Satan acts at times directly upon the thoughts of men. He personally suggested to Judas the selling of his Master, and many another black insinuations has he cast into men's minds. Like the foul vulture that constantly feasted itself upon the innards of Prometheus, so does the devil tear away the good thoughts that would be the life of a man's soul. Insatiably malicious, he cannot endure that a single divine truth should bless the heart. Fearful blasphemies, lewd imaginations, gross unbeliefs, or vain frivolities the devil casts into the mind like infernal bombshells to destroy any newborn thought that looks toward Christ and salvation. At one time he fascinates the mind, and immediately he terrifies it; his one aim being to distract the man's thoughts from the gospel, and prevent its lodgment in the conscience and heart.

Since Satan cannot be everywhere present at one time, he frequently does his evil work by his servants, sending the inferior spirits to act as birds in devouring the seed, and these again employ various agents. With great cunning are the common incidents of life used in the evil business, so that even by things indifferent in themselves the purposes of the adversary are brought about. The preacher has some specialty in his manner, utterance, or appearance, and this becomes the bird that devours the seed. The hearer is so taken up with a trifling oddity in the minister that he forgets the truth that was spoken. An anecdote was related, an illustration employed, or a word used that awakened a memory in the hearer's breast, and away went the Word out of his heart to make room for mere vanity.

Or if the sermon was preserved to its close, it then encountered a fresh peril. A lost umbrella, an extra pressure in the aisle, a foolish jest over-heard in the crowd, or the absurd dress of an unknown person, any one of them may then answer the devil's purpose and snatch away the Word. Little does it signify whether the seed is devoured by black crows or white doves, by great birds or little sparrows. If it does not abide in the heart, it cannot bring forth fruit, and thus the devil arranges that somehow he will take away the seed at once. If he never visits a place of worship at any other time, he will be sure to be there when a revival has begun – *then cometh the devil*. He lets many a pulpit alone, but when an earnest man begins preaching, *Satan cometh **immediately*** (emphasis added).

Secondly, we will now for a moment notice his power. *And taketh away the word out of their hearts*. It is not said that he tries to do it, but that he actually does so. He sees, he comes, and he conquers. The Word is there, and the devil takes it away as easily as a bird removes a seed from the wayside.

Alas, what a sway has the Evil One over the human mind, and how ineffective is the preacher's work unless a divine power is put forth with it. Perhaps from the striking manner in which it was stated, a little of the truth abides in the memory, but the Enemy takes it quite out of the heart, and so the main part, the all-important part, of our work is undone. *We* may be foolish enough to aim at the head only, but he who is crafty beyond all craft deals with the heart. Who will, may win the intellect; if Satan can keep the affections, he is quite content. To the man's heart the good seed is lost, the birds have devoured it; it has become to him a nothingness, having no power over him, no life in him. Not a trace is left, any more than there would be a mark remaining of seed cast on the wayside after the birds had taken it away: so effective is the work of the prince of the power of the air. When Satan thinks it worth his while to come, and come immediately, he means business, and he takes care that his errand shall not fail.

His power is partly derived from his natural wisdom. Fallen as he now is, he was once an angel of light, and his superlative faculties, though perverted, defiled, and dimmed by the blemished influence of sin, are still vastly superior to those of the human beings upon whom he tries his skillful plans. He is more than a match for preacher and hearer united if the Holy Spirit is not there to baffle him. He has also acquired fresh cunning by long practice in his accursed business. He knows the human heart better than anyone, except its Maker; for thousands of years he has studied the anatomy of our nature, and is occupied with our weaker points. We are all young and inexperienced compared with this ancient tempter, all narrow in our views and limited in our experience compared with this serpent, who is more subtle than all the beasts of the field. What wonder that he takes away the Word that is sown in hard hearts.

Moreover, he derives his chief power from the man's condition of soul. It is easy for birds to pick up seed that lies exposed on a trodden path. If the soil had been good and the seed had entered it, he would have had far greater difficulty; he might even have been foiled. But a hard heart does the devil's work for him in great measure; he need not use violence or craftiness; there lies the unreceived Word upon the surface of the soul, and he takes it away. The power of the Evil One largely springs from our own evil. Let us pray the Lord to renew the heart so that the testimony of Jesus may be accepted heartily, and may never be taken away. Great is the need for such prayer. Our adversary is no imaginary being; his existence is real, his presence constant, his power immense, his activity inexhaustible. Lord, match him, and overmatch him. Drive away this foulest of birds, break up the soil of the soul, and let your truth truly live and graciously grow within us.

Our short sermon closes with the third point, which is the devil's purpose. He is a sound theologian, and knows that salvation is by believing in the Lord Jesus, and therefore he fears above all things lest men should *believe and be saved.* The substance of the gospel lies in those few words, *believe and be saved,* and in proportion as Satan hates that gospel, we ought to prize it. He is not so much afraid of dead, empty works as he is of faith.

Lest they should believe and be saved. Satan takes away the Word out of their hearts. Here also is wisdom – wisdom hidden within the Enemy's cunning. If the gospel remains in contact with the heart, its tendency is to produce faith. The seed abiding in the soil springs up and brings forth fruit, and so will the gospel display its living power if it dwells within the man, and therefore the devil hastens to take it away. The Word of God is the sword of the Spirit, and the devil does not like to see it lie near the sinner for fear it should wound him. He dreads the influence of truth upon the conscience, and if he cannot prevent a man's hearing it, he labors to prevent his meditating upon it. *Faith cometh by hearing, and hearing by the word of God* (Romans 10:17). To obliterate that which has been heard is the satanic method of preventing faith. Here again is a practical word for the ear of caution – let us keep the gospel as much as possible near the mind of the unconverted, and let us sow and sow again, if by chance some grain may take root.

Countrymen were accustomed, in planting certain seeds, to put in "one for the worm, and one for the crow, and then a third which would surely grow," and we must do the same. In the book of Jeremiah the Lord describes his own action thus – *I have spoken unto you, rising early and speaking; but ye hearkened not unto me. . . . I have called unto them, but they have not answered* (Jeremiah 35:14, 17). Surely, if the Lord himself has thus continued to speak to an unanswering race, we need not murmur if much of our preaching should appear to be in vain. There is life in the seed of the gospel, and it will grow if it can be gotten into the soil of the heart; let us therefore have faith in it, and never dream of obtaining a crop except by the old-fashioned way of sowing good seed. The devil evidently hates the Word, so let us then keep to it, and sow it everywhere.

Friend, you have often heard the gospel; have you heard it in vain? Then the devil has had more to do with you than you have dreamed. Is the thought a pleasant one? The presence of the devil is defiling and degrading, and he has been hovering over you as the birds over the high road, and lighting upon you to steal away the Word. Think of this. Fellowship with the Father and with his Son Jesus Christ you are missing by your unbelief, and instead of that, you are having fellowship with Satan. Is this not horrible? Instead of the Holy Spirit dwelling in you as he dwells in all believers, the Prince of Darkness is making you his resort, coming and going at his pleasure into your mind. You remember Jacob's dream of a ladder, and angels ascending and descending from himself to heaven. Your life experience may be set forth by another ladder that descends into the dark abyss, and up and down its rounds, foul spirits come and go *to yourself*! Does not this startle you? The Lord grant that it may. Do you desire a change? May the Holy Spirit turn your heart into good ground, and then shall the seed of divine grace grow in you, and produce faith in the Lord Jesus.

Chapter 17

The Mustard Seed

A Message for the Sunday School Teacher

Then said he, Unto what is the kingdom of God like? and whereunto shall I resemble it? It is like a grain of mustard seed, which a man took, and cast into his garden; and it grew, and waxed a great tree; and the fowls of the air lodged in the branches of it. (Luke 13:18-19)

I shall not attempt to fully explain this great little parable. A full exposition may be left for another occasion. The parable may be understood to relate to our Lord himself, who is the living seed. You know also how his church is the tree that springs from him, and how greatly it grows and spreads its branches until it covers the earth. From the one man Christ Jesus, despised and rejected of men, slain and buried, and so hidden away from among men – from him, I say, there arises a multitude that no man can number. These spread themselves, like some tree that grows by the rivers of waters, and they yielded both gracious shelter and spiritual food. I called it a great little parable, and so it is: it has a world of teaching within the smallest scope. The parable is itself like a grain of mustard seed, but its meanings are as a great tree.

But at this time of the year, Sunday school teachers come together specially to pray for a blessing on their work; and pastors are invited to say a word to cheer them in their self-denying service. This request I would cheerfully fulfill, and therefore my discourse will not be a full explanation of the parable, but an adaptation of it to the cheering of those who are engaged in the admirable work of teaching the young the fear of the Lord. There is never a service more important; to over-look it would be a grave fault. We rejoice to encourage our friends in their labor of love.

In this parable light is thrown upon the work of those who teach the gospel. First, *notice a very simple work: a grain of mustard seed, which a man took, and cast into his garden.* Secondly, *observe what came of it: it grew, and waxed a great tree; and the fowls of the air lodged in the branches of it.*

First, notice a very simple work. The work of teaching the gospel is as the casting of a grain of mustard seed into the garden.

Note, first, *what the nameless man did. It is like a grain of mustard seed, which a man took.* He *took* it; that is to say, he picked it out from the bulk. It was only one grain, and a grain of a very insignificant seed, but he did not let it lie on the shelf; he took it in his hand to put it to its proper use. A grain of mustard seed is too small a thing for public exhibition; the man who takes it in his hand is almost the only one who spies it out. It was only a grain of mustard seed, but the man set it before his own mind as a distinct object to be dealt with. He was not sowing mustard over broad acres, but he was sowing *a grain of mustard seed* in his garden. It is well for the teacher to know what he is going to teach; to have that truth distinctly in his mind's eye, as the man had the grain of mustard seed between his fingers. Depend upon it, that unless a truth is clearly seen and distinctly recognized by the teacher, little will come of it to those taught. It may be a very simple truth, but if a man takes it, understands it, grasps it, and loves it, he will do something with it. Beloved, first and foremost let us ourselves take the gospel, and let us believe it, let us appreciate it, let us prize it beyond all things; for truth lives as it is loved, and no hand is so fit for its sowing as the hand that grasps it well.

Further, in this little parable we notice that this man *had a garden. Like a grain of mustard seed, which a man took, and cast into his garden.*

Some Christian people have no garden – no personal sphere of service. They belong to the whole clan of Christians, and they long to see the entire band go out to cultivate the whole world; but they do not come to personal particulars. It is delightful to be warmed up by missionary speeches, and to feel a zeal for the salvation of all the nations; but, after all, the net result of a general theoretic earnestness for all the world does not amount to much. As we would have no horticulture if men had no gardens, so we shall have no missionary work done unless each person has a mission. It is the duty of every believer in Christ, like the first man, Adam, to have a garden to dress and to till.

Children are in the Sunday schools by the millions. Thank God for that! But have *you* a class of your own? All the church at work for Christ! Glorious theory! Are *you* up and doing for your Lord? It will be a grand time when every believer has his allotment, and is sowing it with the seed of truth. The wilderness and the solitary place will blossom as the rose when each Christian cultivates his own plot of roses. Where should this unnamed man sow his mustard seed but in his own garden? It was near him, and dear to him, and there he went. Teach your own children, speak to your neighbors, seek the conversion of those whom God has especially entrusted to you.

Having a garden, and having this seed, *the man sowed it*. And simple as this is, it is the hinge of the instruction. You have a number of seeds in a pillbox. There they are; look at them! Take that box down this day for twelve months, and the seeds will be just the same. Lay them by in that dry box for seven years, and nothing will happen. Truth is not to be kept to ourselves, it is to be published and advocated. There is an old proverb: "Truth is mighty, and will prevail." The proverb is true in a sense, but it needs to be taken with a grain of salt. If you put truth away, and leave it without a voice, it won't prevail; it will not even strive. When have great truths prevailed? Why, when brave men have persisted in declaring them. Daring spirits have taken up a cause which has been, at the first, unpopular, and they have spoken about it so earnestly, and so often, that at length the cause has commanded attention. They have pressed on and on until the cause has triumphed altogether. Truth has been mighty, and has prevailed, but yet not without the men who gave it life and tongue. Not even the gospel itself, if it be not taught, will prevail. If revealed truth be laid on one side and kept in silence, it will not grow. Observe how, through the Dark Ages, the gospel lay asleep in old books in the libraries of monasteries, until Luther and his fellow reformers fetched it out and sowed it in the minds of men.

This man simply cast it into his garden. He did not wrap it around with a gold leaf, or otherwise adorn it; but he put it into the ground. The naked seed came into contact with the naked soil. O teachers, do not try to make the gospel look fine; do not overlay it with your fine words or elaborate explanations. The gospel seed is to be put into the young heart just as it is. Get the truth concerning the Lord Jesus into the children's minds. Make them know, not what you can say about the truth, but what the truth itself says. It is wicked to take the gospel and make a peg of it to hang our old clothes upon.

The gospel is not a boat to be laden with human thoughts, fine speculations, scraps of poetry, and pretty tales. No, no; the gospel is the thought of God. In and of itself it is the message that the soul needs. It is the gospel itself that will grow. Take a truth, specially that great doctrine that man is lost and that Christ is the only Savior, and see to it that you place it in the mind. Teach plainly the great truth that whosoever believes in him has everlasting life; and that the Lord Jesus bore our sins in his own body on the tree, and suffered for us, the just for the unjust. I say take these truths and set them forth to the mind, and see what will come of it. Sow the very truth – not your reflections on the truth, not your embellishments of the truth, but the truth itself. This is to be brought into contact with the mind; for the truth is the seed, and the human mind is the soil for it to grow in.

These remarks of mine are very plain and commonplace, and yet everything depends upon the simple operation described. Nearly everything has been tried in preaching lately, except the plain and clear statement of the glad tidings and of the atoning sacrifice. People have talked about what the church can do, and what the gospel can do; we have been informed as to the proofs of the gospel, or the doubts about it, and so forth; but when will they give us the gospel itself? Brethren, we must come to the point and teach the gospel, for this is the living and incorruptible seed that abides forever. It is an easy thing to deliver a talk upon mustard seed, to give the children a taste of the pungency of mustard, to tell them how mustard seed would grow, what kind of a tree it would produce, and how the birds would sing among its branches. But this is not sowing mustard seed. It is all very fine to talk about the influence of the gospel, the ethics of Christianity, the elevating power of the love of Christ, and so on; but what we want is the gospel itself, which exercises that influence.

Sow the seed: tell the children the doctrine of the cross, the fact that with the stripes of Jesus we are healed, and that by faith in him we are justified. What is needed is not talk about the gospel, but the gospel itself. We must continually bring the living Word of the living God into contact with the hearts of men. Oh, for the aid of the Holy Spirit in this! He will help us, for he delights to glorify Jesus.

That which is described in the parable was an insignificant business: the man took the tiny seed and put it into his garden. It is a very commonplace affair to sit down with a dozen children around you, and open your Bible and tell them the well-worn tale of how Jesus Christ came into the world to save sinners. No Pharisee is likely to stand and blow a trumpet when he is going to teach children; he is more likely to point to the children in the temple, and sneeringly say, *Hearest thou what these say?* (Matthew 21:16). It is a lowly business altogether; but yet to the mustard seed, and to the man with a garden, the sowing is the all-important matter. The mustard seed will never grow unless it is put into the soil; the owner of the garden will never have a crop of mustard unless he sows the seed.

Dear Sunday school teacher, do not become weary of your humble work, for none can measure its importance. Tell the boys and girls of the Son of God, who lived and loved and died so that the ungodly might be saved. Urge them to immediate faith in the mighty Savior, that they may be saved at once. Tell of the new birth, and how the souls of men are renewed by the Holy Spirit, without whose divine working none can enter the kingdom of heaven. Cast in mustard seed, and nothing else but mustard seed, if you want to grow mustard. Teach the gospel of grace, and nothing but the gospel of grace, if you wish to see grace growing in the hearts of your young people.

Secondly, let us consider *what it was that the man sowed.* We have seen that he sowed, but what did he sow? It was one single seed, and that seed a very small one, and so very, very small that the Jews were accustomed to saying, "As small as mustard seed." Thus the Savior speaks of it as the smallest among seeds, which it may not have been absolutely, but which it was according to common speech; and our Lord was not teaching botany, but was speaking a popular parable. Yes, the gospel seems a very simple thing: Believe and live! Look to Jesus dying in the sinner's stead! Look to Jesus crucified, even as Israel looked to the brazen serpent lifted up upon a pole. It is simplicity itself. In fact, the gospel is so plain a matter that our superior people are weary of it, and they look out for something more difficult to comprehend. People nowadays are like the servant who liked to hear the Scriptures "properly confounded," or like the other who said, "You should hear our minister dispense with the truth."

Sowing seed is work too ordinary for the moderns: they demand new methods. But, beloved, we must not run after vain inventions. Our one business is to sow the Word of God in the minds of children. It is yours and mine to teach everybody the simple truth, that Jesus Christ came into the world to save sinners, and *that whosoever believeth in him should not perish, but have everlasting life.* We know nothing else among men or among children. This one seed, apparently so little, so insignificant, we continue to sow. They sneeringly say, "What can be the moral result of preaching such a gospel? Surely it would be better to talk about morals, social economics, and the sciences."

Ah, friends! If you can do any good in those ways, we will not hinder you; but our belief is that a hundred times more can be done with the gospel; *for it is the power of God unto salvation to every one that believeth* (Romans 1:16). The gospel is not the enemy of any good thing; say, rather, that it is the force by which good things are to be carried out. Whatsoever things are pure and honest and of good repute, are all nurtured by that spirit that is begotten by the simple gospel of Christ. Yet conversions do not come by essays upon morals, but by the teaching of salvation by Christ. The cleansing and raising of our race will not be accomplished by politics or science, but by the Word of the Lord, *which liveth and abideth for ever.* To bring the greatest blessings upon our rising youth, we must labor to implant in their minds faith in the Lord Jesus. Oh, for divine power in this work!

But the seed, though very small, was a *living thing*. There is a great difference between a mustard seed and a piece of wax of the same size. Life slumbers in that seed. What life is, we cannot tell. Even if you take a microscope, you cannot spy it out. It is a mystery, but it is essential to a seed. The gospel has a something in it not readily discoverable by the philosophical inquirer, if, indeed, he can perceive it at all. Take a general truth of Socrates or of Plato, and inquire whether a nation or a tribe has ever been transformed by it from barbarism to culture. A general truth of a philosopher may have measurably influenced a man in some right direction, but who has ever heard of a man's whole character being transformed by any observation of Confucius or Socrates? I confess I never have. Human teachings are barren. But within the gospel, with all its commonplaceness and simplicity, there is a divine life, and that life makes all the difference. The human can never rival the divine, for it lacks the life fire. It is better to preach five words of God's Word than five million words of man's wisdom. Men's words may seem to be the wiser and the more attractive, but there is no heavenly life in them. Within God's Word, however simple it may be, there dwells an omnipotence like that of God, from whose lips it came.

Truth be told, a seed is *a very comprehensive thing*. Within the mustard seed, what is to be found? Why, there is all in it that ever comes out of it. It must be so. Every branch, and every leaf, and every flower, and every seed that is to be, is, in its essence, all within the seed; it needs to be developed, but it is all there. And so, within the simple gospel, how much lies in it that is rich? Look at it! Within that truth lie regeneration, repentance, faith, holiness, zeal, consecration, and perfection. Heaven hides itself away within the gospel.

Like a young bird in its nest, glory dwells in grace. We may not at first see all its results, nor, indeed, shall we see them at all, until we sow the seed and it grows; but still it is all there. Do you believe it, young teacher? Have you realized what you have in your hold when you grasp the gospel of the grace of God? It is the most wonderful thing beneath the skies. Do you believe in the gospel that you have to teach? Do you discern that within its apparently narrow lines the Eternal, the Infinite, the Perfect, and the Divine are all enclosed? As in the babe of Bethlehem there was the eternal God, so within the simple teaching of "Believe and live" there are all the elements of eternal blessedness for men, and boundless glory for God. It is a very comprehensive thing, that little seed, that gospel of God.

And for this reason it is so wonderful: *It is a divine creation.* Summon your chemists, bring them together with all their vessels and their fires. Select a jury of the greatest chemists now alive, analytical or otherwise, as you will. Learned sirs, will you kindly make us a mustard seed? You may take a mustard seed, and pound it and analyze it, and you may thus ascertain all its ingredients. So far, so good. Is not your work well begun? Now make a single mustard seed. We will give you a week. It is a very small matter. You have all the elements of mustard in yonder mortar. Make us one living grain; we do not ask for a ton weight. One grain of mustard seed will suffice us. Great chemists, have you not made so small a thing? A month has gone by. Only one grain of mustard seed we asked of you, and where is it? Have you not made one in a month? What are you at? Shall we allow you seven years? Yes, with all the laboratories in the kingdom at your service, and all known substances for your material, and all the world's coalpits for your fuel, get to your work. The air is black with your smoke, and the streams run foul with your waste products; but where is the mustard seed?

This baffles the wise men: they cannot make a living seed. No; and nobody can make a gospel, or even a new gospel text. The thinkers of the age could not even concoct another life of Christ to match with the four Gospels that we have already. I go further: they could not create a new incident that would be compatible with the facts we already know. Plenty of novel writers nowadays can beat out imaginary histories upon their anvils; let them write a fifth Gospel – say, the gospel according to Peter, or Andrew. Let us have it! They will not even commence the task. Who will write a new psalm, or even a new promise? Clever chemists prove their wisdom by saying at once, "No, we cannot make a mustard seed"; and wise thinkers will equally confess that they cannot make another gospel. My learned brethren are trying very hard to make a new gospel for this current century; but you teachers had better go on with the old one. The advanced men cannot put life into their theory. This living Word is the finger of God. That simple grain of mustard seed must be made by God, or not at all; and he must put life into the gospel, or it will not have power in the heart. The gospel of Sunday school teachers, that gospel of "Believe and live," however men may despise it, has God-given life in it. You cannot make another that can replace it, for you cannot put life into your invention. Go on and use the one living truth with your children, for nothing else has God's life in it.

I want you to see what a little affair the sowing seemed, as we answer the question, *What was it to him?* It was *a very natural act;* he sowed a seed. It is a most natural thing that we should teach others what we believe ourselves. I cannot make out how some professing Christians can call themselves Christians, and yet never communicate the faith to others. That the young people of our churches should gather other young people around them, and tell them of Jesus, whom they love, is as natural as for a gardener to put seeds into his prepared ground.

To sow a mustard seed is *a very inexpensive act.* It takes only one grain of mustard: nobody can find me a coin small enough to express its value. I do not know how much mustard seed the man had, for certainly it is not a rare thing; but he only took one grain of it, and cast it into his garden. He emptied no funds by that expenditure; and this is one of the excellencies of Sunday school work, that it exhausts the church neither of men nor of money. However much of it is done, it does not lessen the resources of our Zion; it is done freely, quietly, without excitement, and without sacrifice of life; and yet what a fountain of blessing it is!

Still, it was *an act of faith.* It is always an act of faith to sow seed, because you have, for the time, to give it up, and receive nothing in return. The farmer takes his choice seed, and throws it into the soil of his field. He might have made many a loaf of bread with it, but he casts it away. Only his faith saves him from being judged a maniac: he expects it to return to him fiftyfold. If you had never seen a harvest, you would think that a man burying good wheat under the soil had gone mad; and if you had never seen conversions, it might seem an absurd thing to be constantly teaching boys and girls the story of the Man who was nailed to the tree. We preach and teach as a work of faith; and remember, it is only as an act of faith that it will answer its purpose. The rule of the harvest is: *According to your faith be it unto you* (Matthew 9:29). Believe, dear teacher, believe in the gospel. Believe in what you are doing when you tell it. Believe that great results from meager causes spring up. Go on sowing your mustard seed of salvation by faith, expecting and believing that fruit will come thereof.

It was an act that brought the sower no honor. The Savior has chronicled the fact that the man took a grain of mustard seed and sowed it; but thousands of men had gone on sowing mustard seed for half a lifetime without a word. Nobody has ever spoken in your honor, my friend, though you have taught the truth. Dear teacher, go on sowing, though nobody should observe your diligence or praise your faithfulness. Sow the seed of precious truth in the garden of the child's mind, for much more will come of it than you have dared to hope.

It seems to me that our Lord selected the mustard seed in this parable not because its results are the greatest possible from a seed – for an oak or a cedar are much greater growths than a mustard tree – but he selected it because it is the greatest result as compared with the size of the seed. Follow out the analogy. Come to yonder school and see! That earnest young man is teaching a boy, one of those wild creatures of the street; they swarm in every quarter. A dozen young Turks are before him, or say, young Arabs of the street; he is teaching them the gospel. Small matter, is it not? Yes, very; but what may come of it? Think of how joyfully much may grow out of this little seed! What is that young man teaching? Only one elementary truth. Do not sneer; it is truth, but it is the mere alphabet of it. He touches upon nothing deep in theology; he only says, *Christ Jesus came into the world to save sinners.*

Dear boy, believe in the Lord Jesus, and live. That is all he says. Can any good thing come out of Nazareth? The teacher himself is teaching the one truth in a very poor way; at least, *he* thinks so. Ask him, when he is done, what he thinks of his own teaching, and he replies, "I do not feel fit to teach." Yes, that young man's teaching is sighed over, and in his own judgment it is poor and weak; but there is life in the truth he imparts, and eternal results will follow – results of which I have now to speak in the second part of my message. May the good Spirit help me so to speak as to encourage my beloved friends who have given themselves up to the Christlike work of teaching the little ones!

Secondly, let us ask, What came of it?

First, *it grew.* That was what the sower hoped would come of it; he placed the seed in the ground, hoping that it would grow. It is not reasonable to suppose that he would have sown it if he had not hoped that it would spring up. Dear teacher, do you always sow in hope? Do you trust that the Word will live and grow? If you do not, I do not think your success is very probable. Expect the truth to take root and expand and grow up. Teach divine truth with earnestness, and expect that the life within it will unveil its wonders.

But though the sower expected growth, he could not himself have made it grow. After he had placed the seed in the ground, he could water it, he could pray God to make the sun shine on it, but he could not directly produce growth. Only he that made the seed could cause it to grow. Growth is a continuance of that almighty act by which life is at first given. The putting of life into the seed is God's work, and the bringing forth of the life from the seed is God's work too. This is a matter within your hope, but far beyond your power.

A very wonderful thing it is, that the seed should grow. If we did not see it every day, we should be more astonished at the growth of seed than at all the wonders of magicians. A growing seed is God's abiding miracle. You see a piece of ground near London covered with a market-garden, and after a few months you go by the place, and you see streets, and a public square, and a church, and a great population. You say to yourself, "It is remarkable that all these houses should have sprung up in a few months." Yet that is not at all as wonderful as for a plowed field to become covered four feet high with corn, and all without the use of wagons to bring the material, or tools to work it up into a harvest. Without the noise of a hammer, or the ringing of trowels; without the handiwork of man, the whole has been done. Wonder at the growth of grace. See how it increases, deepens, and strengthens!

Growth in grace is a marvel of divine love. That a man should repent through the gospel, that he should believe in Jesus, that he should be totally changed, that he should have a hope of heaven, that he should receive power to become a child of God – these are all marvelous things; and yet they are going on under our eyes, and we fail to admire them as we should. The growth of holiness in such fallen creatures as we are is the admiration of angels, the delight of all intelligent beings.

To the sower this growth was very pleasing. How pleasant it is to see the seed of grace grow in children! Do you not remember when you first sowed mustard and cress as a boy, how the very next morning you went and turned the ground up to see how much it had grown? How pleased you were when you saw the little yellow shoot, and afterwards a green leaf or two! So it is with the true teacher: he is anxious to see growth, and he makes eager inquiry for it. What he expected is taking place, and it is most delightful to him, whatever it may be to others. An unsympathetic person cries, "Oh, I do not think anything of that child's emotions. It is merely a passing impression; he will soon forget it." The teacher does not think so.

The cold critic says, "I don't think much of a child's weeping. Children's tears lie very near the surface." But the teacher is full of hope that he sees in these tears a real sorrow for sin, and an earnest seeking after the Lord. The questioner says, "It is nothing for a child to say that he gives his heart to Jesus. Youngsters soon think that they believe. They are so easily led." People talk thus because they do not love children and do not live with the desire to save them. If you sympathize with children, you are pleased with every hopeful token, and are on the watch for every mark of divine life within them.

If you are a florist, you will see more of the progress of your plants than if you are no gardener, and have no interest in such things. Think then, of what my text says: *It grew.* Oh, for a prayer just now, from all of you this morning. "Lord, make the gospel grow wherever it falls! Whether the preacher scatters it, or the teacher sows it; whether it falls among the aged people, or the young; Lord, make the gospel grow!" Pray hard for it, brethren! You cannot make it grow, but you can prevail with God to bless it to his honor and praise.

Next, having started growing, *it became a tree.* Luke says, *It waxed a great tree.* It was great in itself, but the greatness was seen mainly in comparison with the size of the seed. The growth was great. Here is the wonder: not that it became a tree, but that, being a mustard seed, it should become *a great tree.* Do you see the point of the parable? I have already brought it before you. Listen! It was only a word spoken – "Dear boy, look to Jesus." Only such a word, and a soul was saved, its sin was forgiven, its whole being was changed, and a new heir of heaven was born. Do you see the growth? A word produces salvation! A grain of mustard seed becomes a great tree! A little teaching brings eternal life.

That is not all. The teacher, with many prayers and tears, took her girl home, and pleaded with her for Christ, and the girl was led to yield her heart to the dominion of Christ Jesus – a holy, heavenly life came out of that pleading. See! She becomes a thoughtful girl, a loving wife, a gracious mother, a matriarch in Israel, such a one as Dorcas among the poor, or Hannah with her Samuel. What a great result from a little cause! The teacher's words were tearfully spoken; they could not have been printed, for they were far too broken and childlike; but they were, in God's hands, the means of fashioning a life most sweet, most pure, and most beautiful.

A boy was about as wild as any roamer of our streets. A teacher knelt by his side, with his arm around the lad's neck. He pleaded with God for the boy, and with the boy for God. That boy was converted, and as a youth in business he was an example to the workroom; as a father, he was a guide to his household; as a man of God, he was a light to all around; as a preacher of righteousness, he adorned the doctrine of God his Savior in all things. There is much more that I might easily picture, but you can work it out as well as I can. All that is to be desired may spring out of the simple talk of a humble Christian with a youth. A mustard seed becomes a great tree; a few words of holy counsel may produce a noble life.

But is that all? Beloved, our teaching may preserve souls from the deep darkness of the abode of the lost. A soul left to itself might hurry down from folly to sin, from sin to callousness, from callousness to a fixed resolve to perish; but by the means of loving teaching all this is changed. Rescued from the power of sin, like a lamb snatched from between the jaws of the lion, the youth is now no longer the victim of sin, but seeks holy and heavenly things. Hell has lost its prey; and see up yonder, heaven's wide gate has received a precious soul. "Sweeping through the gates of the New Jerusalem," many have come who were led there from the Sunday school. They who once were foul are now robed in white, washed in the blood of the Lamb. Listen to their songs of praise! You may keep on listening, for those songs will never come to an end. All this was brought about through a brief address of a trembling brother who stood up one Sunday afternoon to close the school and talk a little about the cross of Jesus. Or all this came because of a gentle sister who could never speak in public, but yet was enabled to warn a young girl who was growing giddy, and seemed likely to go sadly astray. Wonderful, that a soul's taking the road to heaven or to hell should be made, in the purpose of God, to hinge upon the humble endeavors of a weak but faithful teacher! You see how the mustard seed grew until it *waxed a great tree.*

This great tree became a shelter. The fowls of the air lodged in the branches of it. Mustard in the East does grow very large indeed. The most common kind of it may be found eight or ten feet high; but there is a kind that will grow almost like a forest tree, and there probably were some of these latter trees in the sheltered region where our Lord was speaking. A mustard that grew here and there in Palestine was of surprising dimensions. When the tree grew, the birds came to it. Here we have *unexpected influences.* Think of it. That man took a mustard seed which you could hardly see if I held it up. When he took the mustard seed, when he put it into his garden, had he any thought of bringing birds to that spot? Not he.

You do not know all you are doing when you are teaching a child the way of salvation by Jesus Christ. When you are trying to bring a soul to Christ, your action has ten thousand hooks to it, and these may seize on innumerable things. Holy teaching is the opening of a well, and no one knows all the effects that the waters will produce on that spot. There seems no link between sowing a grain of mustard seed and birds of the air, but the winged wanderers soon made a happy connection.

There may seem no connection between teaching that boy and the reclaiming of cannibals in New Guinea, but I can see a very possible connection. Tribes in Central Africa may have their destiny shaped by your instruction of a tiny child. When John Pounds bribed an urchin with a hot potato to come and learn to read the Bible, I am sure John Pounds had no idea of all the Ragged schools in London; but there is a clear line of cause and effect in the whole matter. A hot potato might be the coat of arms of the Ragged School Union. When Nasmyth went about from house to house visiting in the slums of London, I do not suppose that he saw in his act the founding of the London City Mission and all the country town missions. No man can tell the end of his beginnings, the growth of his sowings. Go on doing good in little ways, and you shall one day wonder at the great results. Do the next thing that lies before you. Do it well. Do it unto the Lord. Leave the results with his unbounded liberality of love, but hope to reap at least a hundredfold.

How many birds came and roosted under that one mustard tree I do not know. How many birds in a day, how many birds in the year, came and found a resting place, and picked the seeds they loved so well, I cannot tell. When one person is converted, how many may receive a blessing out of him none can tell. Now is the day for romances: our literature is drenched with tales religious or irreligious. What stories might be written concerning benefits bestowed, directly and indirectly, by a single godly man or woman! When you have written a thrilling story upon the subject, I can assure you that I can match it with something better still. One single individual can scatter benedictions across a continent, and belt the world with blessing.

But what is that I hear? I see this mustard tree – it is a very wonderful tree; but I not only see, I also hear! Music! Music! The birds! The birds! It is early morning, the sun is scarcely up – what torrents of song! Is that the way to produce music? Shall I sow mustard seed, and reap songs? I thought we must buy an organ, or purchase a violin, or by some wind or stringed instrument get music; but here is a new plan altogether. Nebuchadnezzar had his flute, harp, trombone, zither, dulcimer, and all kinds of music, but all that mingled sound could not rival the melody of birds. I shall sow mustard seed now, and get music in God's own way.

Friends, when you teach your children the gospel of the Lord Jesus, you are sowing the music of heaven. Every time you tell the tidings of pardon bought with blood, you are filling the choirs of glory with sweet voices, which, to the Eternal Name, shall day and night trill out songs of devout gratitude. Go on, then, if this is to be the result. If even heaven's high harmonies depend upon the simple teaching of a Ragged school, let us never cease from our holy service.

Having said so much, I now close with these three practical observations. *Are we not highly honored to be entrusted with such a marvelous thing as the gospel?* If it be a seed achieving so much within it, which will come to so much if it be properly used, blessed and happy are we to have such good news to proclaim! I thought this morning, when I awoke in the fog and rain, and felt my bones complaining, that I shall be glad when four more Sundays shall have gone, and I shall be free to take a little rest in a sunnier climate. Jaded in mind, and weary in spirit, I braced myself with this reflection – what blessed work I have to do! What a glorious gospel have I to preach! I ought to be a very happy man to have such glad tidings to bear to my fellows. I said to myself, "So I am." Well now, beloved teacher, next Sunday, when you leave your bed and say, "I have had a hard week's work, and I could half wish that I did not have to go to my class," answer yourself thus: "But I am a happy person to have to talk to children about Christ Jesus. If I had to teach them arithmetic or carpentering, I might get tired of it; but to talk about Jesus, whom I love, why, it is a joy forever."

Let us be encouraged to sow the good seed in evil times. If we do not see the gospel prospering elsewhere, let us not despair; if there were no more mustard seed in the world, and I had only one grain of it, I should be all the more anxious to sow it. You can produce any quantity if only one seed will grow. So now today there is not very much gospel around; the church has given it up; a great many preachers preach everything but the living truth. This is sad, but it is a strong reason why you and I should teach more gospel than ever. I have often thought to myself, Other men may teach socialism, deliver lectures, or collect a band of fiddlers so that they may gather a congregation; but I will preach the gospel. I will preach more gospel than ever, if I can; I will stick more to the one key point. The other brethren can attend to the odds and ends, but I will keep to Christ crucified. To the men of vast ability, who are looking to the events of the day, I would say, "Allow one poor fool to keep to preaching the gospel."

Beloved teachers, be fools for Christ, and keep to the gospel. Don't you be afraid: it has life in it, and it will grow; only you bring it out, and let it grow. I am sometimes afraid that we may prepare our sermons and speeches too much, so as to make ourselves shine. If so, we are like the man who tried to grow potatoes – he never grew any, and he wondered much; "for," said he, "I very carefully boiled them for hours." So, it is very possible to extract all the life out of the gospel, and put so much of yourself into it that Christ will not bless it.

And, lastly, *we are bound to do it.* If so much will come out of so little, we are bound to go in for it. Nowadays people want ten percent for their money. Hosts of fools are readily caught by any scheme, or speculation, or limited liability company that promises to give them immense dividends! I would like to make you wise by inviting you to an investment that is sure. Sow a mustard seed, and grow a tree. Talk of Christ, and save a soul. That soul saved will be a blessing for ages, and a joy to God throughout eternity. Was there ever such an investment as this? Let us go on with it. If on our simple word eternity is hung, let us speak with all our heart. Life, death, and hell, and worlds unknown hang on the lips of the earnest teacher of the gospel of Jesus; let us never cease speaking while we have breath in our body. The Lord bless you! Amen, and Amen.

Chapter 18

The Pleading of the Last Messenger

Having yet therefore one son, his wellbeloved, he sent him also last unto them, saying, They will reverence my son. But those husbandmen said among themselves, This is the heir; come, let us kill him, and the inheritance shall be ours. And they took him, and killed him, and cast him out of the vineyard. What shall therefore the lord of the vineyard do? he will come and destroy the husbandmen, and will give the vineyard unto others. (Mark 12:6-9)

Brethren, you know the story of God's dealing with Israel, and Israel's dealing with God. The Lord chose their fathers, Abraham, Isaac, and Jacob; he made them a race separated unto himself; he brought them out of Egypt from under the iron yoke; he led them through the Red Sea; he fed them for forty years in the wilderness; he led them around and tutored them, even as a man teaches his son. In due time he brought them into the land that flows with milk and honey; and he put them under a dispensation exceedingly gentle and full of tenderness, where as a nation they might enjoy unbroken prosperity, and *they shall sit every man under his vine and under his fig tree; and none shall make them afraid* (Micah 4:4). All that he required of them was that he should be their God, that they should put no idols in his place, but should obey his statutes.

Alas! from the first they copied the nations among whom they dwelt. They set up the gods of Egypt when they were in the wilderness, and in Canaan they went astray after the polluted deities of the nations. They worshipped defiled gods with obscene rites; they even passed their children through the fire to Molech, and did horrible things that angered the Most High. In his long-suffering he sent to them prophets one after another – prophets who received unworthy treatment at their hands whenever they rebuked their sins. The prophets were derided, persecuted, and even slain with the sword. God in great patience sent them more of his messengers, some of them grandly eloquent, like Isaiah and Ezekiel; others of them full of tears, like Jeremiah; or clothed with dignity, like Daniel. They warned the people, and did not cease pleading with them, whether they would hear them or whether they would shun them. Cruel treatment awaited many of the servants of the Lord; they were stoned, they were sawn in two.

Israel rejected the servants that came from the great Householder asking for the rent of his vineyard. They repudiated the claims of God, and cast off allegiance to him with contempt and disdain, until at last the nation was led into captivity, and in the end only lingered on the chosen soil as a mere remnant. Judah wept upon the dunghill; whereas formerly she was adorned with bridal ornaments, and sat upon the throne. The adversary ruled in the halls of David; for the days of Herod, the Idumean tyrant, had come. The Roman yoke was heavy upon the people: their sins had brought them low. God, in his infinite compassion, gave them one more opportunity. He had one Son, his well-beloved Son, and he sent him to his Israel. With lips that dropped mercy, and with eyes that overflowed with tenderness, he came. *If thou hadst known,* said he, *even thou, at least in this thy day* (Luke 19:42). He wept over the city that would not be saved. But his warning and his weeping were lost upon the blinded people. Those who had rejected the prophets also rejected the Lord; the fate of the servants was repeated in *the heir. Let us kill him,* said they (Mark 12:7); and they put him to death on the cross.

You know the story. It is full of infinite mercy on God's part, and of immeasurable guilt on the part of man. God seemed to outdo himself in his long-suffering, and man seemed to outdo himself in his malicious defiance of the Most High. Sin culminated in the murder of the

Son of God; it reached its utmost height of horror when the cry was heard, *Crucify him, crucify him.* Yes, they crucified the Lord of Glory.

What has this to do with us? I am not going to preach this morning merely to rehearse a piece of ancient history that has no bearing on today; I do not so regard the death of our Lord. My anxiety is to reach the consciences of living men, and, if possible, to win to the Blessed Heir of all things, who has risen from the dead, some of those who have had a share in his death. I would bring to the great Householder the fruits of the vineyard that he himself has planted, and I would move many hearts to yield to him at the remembrance of the wicked injuries that have been done to his servants and to his Son. May the Spirit of God silently move over this audience at this time, as I try to use this passage, not in its strictest application, but with such an application as I am sure the Spirit of God will approve! May he bless the Savior's word to present uses, that we may this day repent!

The fact is, that unless changed by divine grace, we have all refused to pay to our great God the service that is due to him. He has put us here and given us this life, like a vineyard, for us to cultivate; but many have cultivated that vineyard entirely for themselves – themselves or their families and friends, and not for their God, their Maker. "God is not in all their thoughts." Now, the Lord has sent to such many messengers. We have had no prophets in these days living among us, but we have the Word of God and the record of the testimonies of his inspired messengers, and these virtually speak to us. We have Moses and the prophets; they are speaking to us even now. Besides that, we have been surrounded by men of God, and embraced by holy women who have appealed to us on God's behalf. They have been urged to speak by the love of their hearts, and they have tried to bring us to repent of past rebellion and to yield ourselves at once to God.

Many are the voices around us and within us that persuade us to render unto the great Householder his due; but in many cases none of these have been successful. Last of all God has sent to each one of us his Son, that he in his own person may lovingly repeat with greater emphasis the requirements of the Lord of love. The incarnate wisdom now cries to us, *My son, give me thine heart* (Proverbs 23:26). Jesus warns us, *Except ye repent, ye shall all likewise perish* (Luke 13:3). He sets before us the way of reconciliation, and bids us to believe in him and live. With many a charming parable he would draw the far-off prodigal home to the bosom of forgiving love. The very coming of the Son of God in human form, as Emmanuel, "God with us," is love's great plea for reconciliation. Who can resist so powerful an argument? It is in the person of Jesus Christ that God makes his last and strongest appeal to the human conscience. By the Christ of God, he virtually says this morning, *Turn ye, turn ye from your evil ways; for why will ye die, O house of Israel?* And I would to God that the answer might be from many a heart: *Come, and let us return unto the Lord: for he hath torn, and he will heal us* (Hosea 6:1). Cause it to be so, O great Spirit!

Three things I shall speak of this morning, and the first will be *the amazing mission. Having yet therefore one son, his wellbeloved, he sent him also last unto them, saying, They will reverence my son.* Secondly, *the astounding crime. They took him, and killed him, and cast him out of the vineyard.* And, therefore, thirdly, *the appropriate punishment,* of which the text says, *What shall therefore the lord of the vineyard do?* What vengeance can be sufficient for so wretched a deed?

First, then, let us dwell for a few moments upon the amazing mission: *Having yet therefore one son, his wellbeloved, he sent him also.*

Please remember concerning the Son of God, who was sent to us to reconcile us to the Father, that *he came after many rejections of divine love.* As to Israel he followed the prophets, so to us he comes after many others. There are none among us, I should think, who have been left without admonitions and challenges from God. He began early with some of us, calling us, like Samuel, when as yet we were children. He repeated those calls to us all through the days of our youth. It was never cheap to some of us to sin; we never went astray but what there was a something within that plucked us by the sleeve, and warned us of our wrongdoing. We have been called to God by most earnest pleadings of faithful men and affectionate women. Discourses have been addressed to us which might have moved hearts of stone; but yet, though stirred for the moment, we remain obstinate enemies to God, dishonest to his claims, anxious about this world, and forgetful of the world to come.

After all these refusals, if the Lord had closed the casket of mercy, and had opened the vials of vengeance and had poured them out upon us, who could have blamed him? Instead of this, he still, in his long-suffering pity, speaks to us by his Son Jesus Christ, by whom he made the worlds, who stoops to be the Messenger of the covenant of grace. He gently reminds us of our offenses against the great Father, of our willfulness in not returning to him, and of the tremendous peril that we incur by remaining in opposition to the great God. The very existence of our Savior gives us warning of our sin, of our ruin, and of the only way of escape.

If it be so, that we have rejected God's claims so often, will not the time past suffice us to have played this dreadful game? Have we not had enough of trifling with our souls? O Lord, how long shall men act the part of fools and risk their immortal souls? Oh, will they not at length yield to wisdom? Jesus himself, by the preaching of the gospel, pleads with us; are we determined to persevere in our evil ways? Do we not feel some tender yieldings? Does not a *still small voice* urge us to arise and go to our Father? After many provocations, will we not at length yield to the God of grace?

Remember that Jesus Christ, when he comes to us today as the messenger of the Father, *comes for no personal objectives.* When the messengers were sent by the householder, it was to claim the householder's rent; when the heir came, it was for the same purpose. So it is in the human emblem; but in the divine this becomes less conspicuous. When Jesus pleads with us, although he urges us to render unto God our love and our obedience, yet God does not stand in need of these as the householder stood in need of his rents. What is it to the infinite Jehovah whether you serve him or not? If you rebel against God, will he be less glorious? If you will not obey the Lord, what difference can it make to his boundless happiness? Will his crown shine less brightly, or his heaven be less glorious because you choose to be a rebel against him? What if the thing being towed contends with the fire; will the fire be quenched by that? If a gnat should contend with yonder blast furnace, you know what the end will be.

It is for your own sake that God would have you yield to him; how can it be for his own? If he were hungry, he would not tell you, for the cattle on a thousand hills are his. He can crush whole worlds to dust with his word or with his nod; and do you think he has anything to gain from you? You alone will be the gainer or the loser; therefore, when Jesus prays for you to repent, believe in the fairness of his heart; believe that it can be nothing but the most tender regard for your well-being that makes him warn you. Hear how Jehovah puts it: *As I live, saith the Lord God, I have no pleasure in the death of the wicked; but that the wicked turn from his way and live.* A messenger after many rejections, a messenger who comes solely out of love for us, ought to have our respectful attention.

Let us see for a minute who this messenger is. *He is one greatly beloved of his Father,* and in himself *he is of surpassing excellence.* The Lord Jesus Christ is so inconceivably glorious that I tremble at any attempt to describe his glory. Assuredly, he is very God of very God, co-equal and co-eternal with the Father, and yet he stooped to take upon himself a human form. He was born an infant into our weakness, and he lived a carpenter to share our toil. When he quits the bench and the saw, it is to follow still more laborious ways as a teacher and healer of the people. He was the lowly and suffering teacher of the blessed will of the Father. He took upon himself the form of a servant, and yet *in him dwelleth all the fulness of the Deity bodily* (Colossians 2:9). He is the Prince of the kings of the earth, and yet he took a towel and washed his disciples' feet.

Such is he who pleads with you. So majestic and so compassionate, so great, and yet so good; will you refuse him? If I plead with you, I am but as you are, flesh of your flesh; but if Jesus speaks to you, I beg you by the glory of his deity, as well as by the tenderness of his manhood, do not refuse him. Because of his deity you must not dare to harden your hearts. He is God's well-beloved; and if you are wise, he will be yours. Do not turn your back upon him whom all the angels worship. Beware, lest you reject One whom God loves so well; for he will take it as an insult to himself: he that despises the anointed of God has blasphemed God himself. You put your finger into the very eye of God when you disrespect his Son. In grieving the Christ you irritate the very heart of God; therefore, do not do so. I beg you, then, by the love that God bears to his Son, to listen to this matchless messenger of mercy, who would gladly persuade you to repent.

I have already said that he is so glorious that I cannot describe him; I will therefore only say that *his graciousness is as conspicuous as his glory.* There was never such a one as he. None of us loves men as Christ loves them; and if the loves of all the tenderhearted in the world could be run together, they would make but a drop compared with the ocean of the compassion of Jesus. Of old his delights were with the sons of men; and though he might have been happy enough among the angels, yet he left their company so that he might take up this inferior race. Yes, he adopted our nature, and became bone of our bone and flesh of our flesh, for love of that chosen company whom he calls his bride. He hid not his face from shame and spitting, nor his body from the shedding of blood, nor his soul from deadly agony; but he loved the church, and gave himself for it. It is this lover of souls that becomes God's advocate with us, and pleads with us that we would cease from our rebellion.

Do not refuse him! If he were stern and unloving, I could imagine that all the obstinacy of your nature might be aroused; but his love, which is better than the love we might receive from any man, deserves another treatment. If you reject him, he answers you with tears; if you wound him, he bleeds out cleansing; if you kill him, he dies to redeem; if you bury him, he rises again to bring us resurrection. Jesus is love made manifest.

> Heart of stone, relent, relent;
> > Break, by Jesu's cross subdued!
> See his body, mangled, rent,
> > Cover'd with a gore of blood;
> Sinful soul, what hast thou done?
> > Crucified God's only Son!

Furthermore, *his manner is most winning.* When I have been pleading for men with God, and I have ceased my pleading, I have feared that something in my tone or in my manner would cause my pleading to fail. I am not, perhaps, so tender as I should be, nor is there sufficient emotion of pity in my tones. If I could do better, I would go to any school to learn. God has put me often into the school of suffering to instruct me in this respect, and yet I do confess my failings with deep regret. But when Jesus, my Lord, pleads with you, this charge cannot be laid against him. His pleading is perfect. When Jonah preaches, his tones are harsh, and his spirit menacing; but that can never be said of Jesus. When Jeremiah weeps, there is an undertone of bitter complaint within the sweet sorrow of his love; but it is never so with Jesus. *Never man spake like this man.* If ever his words thunder – as they often do – even in that thunder there is heard the voice of love. When he flashes with the lightning of judgment against scribes and Pharisees, yet soft drops of mercy follow every flame of fire. He is stern because he is tender: his utterances of terror are born of a love that dares not conceal the truth, even though it breaks its heart in the telling of it. God is love, and Christ is God's love incarnate among men.

Therefore, my friend, if you see anything about *me* of which you disapprove, rebuke me if you will; but be all the more attentive to my Lord, about whom there is nothing but what is wooing and melting. God has sent to you his own well-beloved Son; I implore you, do not refuse him. My heart trembles at the bare suspicion that even one of you should reject the pleadings of one so jealous for your eternal welfare.

Yet again, when God sends his Son to plead with men, remember he does not urge us to do anything that will be for our loss and detriment: *obedience to him is happiness for ourselves.* He does not urge us to follow a life of misery, nor to begin a course that will end in our destruction. Far from it. The ways in which he would have us run are ways of pleasantness, and all the paths in which he would lead us are paths of peace. Even repentance is charming sorrow, and far more sweet than the joy of sin.

They that repent and turn to God through Jesus Christ find such joy, such happiness, that earth becomes to them the entryway of heaven. The joy-bells ring within the Father's house when a soul returns to its home. The great Father leads the joy, and all the household rejoice with him. To persuade you to be holy is to induce you to be happy; to urge you to seek God is to urge you to seek your own best welfare; to urge you to lay down the weapons of rebellion and be reconciled to the Most High is to set before you the wisest, safest, and best course that you can follow. Therefore, hear him. The Lord God out of heaven cries to you: *This is my beloved Son: hear him* (Mark 9:7). Well may you hear him, when every word that he speaks aims for your salvation.

Remember, once more, that if you do not hear the well-beloved Son of God, you have refused your last hope. *He is God's ultimatum.* Nothing remains when Christ is refused. No one else can be sent; heaven itself contains no further messenger. If Christ be rejected, hope is rejected. Neither would you be converted though one rose from the dead; for Jesus has risen from the dead, and you have refused him. I would like every person here that is unconverted to recollect that there is no other gospel, and no more sacrifice for sin. I have heard talk of "a larger hope" than the gospel sets before us: it is a fable, with nothing in Scripture to warrant it.

Rejecting Christ, you have rejected all; you have shut against yourself the one door of hope. Christ, who knows better than all pretenders, declares that *he that believeth not shall be damned.* There remains nothing but damnation for those who believe not in Jesus. *There is none other name under heaven given among men, whereby we must be saved.* This is clear; for heaven's grandest effort has been made. What more can God do? O heavens and earth! I appeal to you, what more can Jehovah do? If he gives his Son to die, and that great sacrifice is rejected, what remains? Infinite wisdom has done its best, and infinite love has surpassed itself. A fearful looking for judgment is all that despisers may expect.

Thus this amazing mission is set forth before you, and I pray you, as you love yourselves, do not refuse him that speaks; for if they escaped not who refused him that spoke on earth, how shall they escape who despise him that speaks from heaven?

I beg your attention while I look, in the second place, to the astounding crime. It was nothing less than an astounding crime, that when this householder sent his well-beloved son, the husbandmen said one to another, *This is the heir; come, let us kill him, and the inheritance shall be ours. And they took him, and killed him, and cast him out of the vineyard.* "No," says one, "we never killed the Son of God." I will not charge you with having done so *literally;* that would be to make myself chargeable with exaggeration. But a man may do virtually what he cannot do actually. If a murder be committed and I approve of it, if my own principles lead up to it, if I feel no indignation against it, but express myself very coolly about it, if there is reason to believe that if I had been there, I would have done the same, then I may be in the sight of God a partaker in the crime. There are many among us who are guilty of the body and blood of Christ. The hymn we just now sang does not bring a groundless charge.

Yes, thy sins have done the deed,
  Driven the nails that fix'd him there,
Crown'd with thorns his sacred head,
  Plunged into his side the spear,
Made his soul a sacrifice,
  While for sinful man he dies!

Now, I say this, that all those who persistently deny the deity of Christ, virtually kill him; for the Son of God is not alive if his deity be not in existence. It is essential to the idea of Christ, the heir of all things, that he be God, and to deny his deity is to stab at his heart.

All those who deny his atonement also slay him; for the blood of sacrifice is the life of the Christ of God. The very essence of his Christhood, the soul of his character as Jesus, lies in his having been appointed to be the atoning sacrifice for sin. No cross, no Christ; no atonement, no cross. Deny the great pardon for sin, and to the full extent of your power you have annihilated the Christ. As far as you can do it, you have destroyed the Savior.

"Well, we have not done that," cry some of you. "We have been no opposers of the deity or sacrifice of Jesus." But let me remind you that if you do not judge him to be worthy of your most careful thoughts, if you are indifferent to his claims and refuse to obey his gospel, you have virtually put him away. To you it is the same as if there were no Christ.

Is it nothing to you, all ye that pass by?
  Is it nothing to you that Jesus should die?

You have virtually answered, "It is nothing." You have set Christ down as nothing compared with the business of daily life, and thus you have virtually slain him. You have put him out of existence as far as you are concerned; in the little world of your mind there is no living Savior. He is dead and buried to you, and the claims of God that he pleads, you will not think upon. You have been occupied all the week with trivial amusements, or unimportant discussions, but you have not stooped to think of him whose advent into the world is so great a wonder, that if you never thought of anything else, you might be justified in a life of devout meditation. He who deserves all your thoughts gets none of them. You have nothing to do with Christ, his cross, his people, or his cause, and therefore – I say it with no harshness, but with much grief – you are killers of Christ, and are guilty of his blood. I charge you with killing your Savior. I press the accusation home, and trust that it will strike you with horror.

I have still closer work with some of you, who are most assuredly guilty. You were once members of the church; you came to the Communion table, where they gather who remember his precious body and blood; you used to glory in his name; but you have gone back, you have denied the faith, and you have ceased to be followers of the Lamb. Now, these are no words of mine, but inspired words: You have [crucified] to [yourselves] the Son of God afresh, and put him to an open shame (Hebrews 6:6). You are beyond all question among those who have cast the heir out of the vineyard and slain him, deliberately turning your backs upon his sacred cause. The Lord have mercy on you! You have had no mercy on Christ, or on yourselves.

I must press this home upon a great many more who have heard of Christ, and believe him to be God, and assent to all the truth about him, but who yet have never yielded themselves to his authority. O sirs, what have you done? You have preferred the world to Christ: you have chosen Barabbas and condemned the Savior. You have said to the claims of Jesus, "Wait." For whom has your Lord had to wait? What! For a harlot? For a bribe of gold? For your giddy pleasure? When a great question is postponed to let another take precedence over it, we do not object if that other is of preeminent importance; but can you say that anything has a greater claim on you than the Son of God? Is there anything that has a greater right to your thoughts, to your consideration, to your love, than the great salvation that Jesus Christ has worked out?

If you have pushed the Lord Jesus Christ out of the first place, he will occupy no other, and therefore you have virtually un-Christed him, and you are guilty of his blood. You must either be justified by him or you must be condemned by him. There is no third course to take: you must either believe in him or disbelieve him. Now, to refuse to believe in him is to make him a liar, and to make him a liar is virtually to slay the Lord of truth. His blood must be on you by faith to cleanse you, or else it will lie on you to condemn you, as it did the Jews of old.

What was the reason why these husbandmen, these dressers of the vineyard, dared thus to treat the heir? The reason is one that presses upon those present here who have rejected Christ. They did it, first, because *they had enjoyed a long immunity from punishment.* They had not been at once punished for their defiance of their lord. They had rejected his messengers without provoking him to war; they had gone on to stone and slay others of his servants, and the householder had not come upon them to overthrow them. The first time they mocked at the messenger they were somewhat afraid; they feared lest soon the sword of the prince whom they had defied would threaten their gates. But since there was no invasion, they grew bold.

The next messenger they killed, and washed their hands, in presumption, saying, "Nothing will come of it." They grew at last to be very hardened. I know not what they said, but I imagine that certain of them propagated the theory that their lord took no notice of what they did, or that he was too loving to punish them severely. "See!" said they. "He only sends fresh messengers if we kill the old ones; and even if we kill his son, he will bear it. Let us not imagine that he will take vengeance. He is love, and even if we would murder his son, he will lay up in store for us a larger hope." "At any rate," they seemed to say, "we will run all risks. We will test his graciousness. We will kill his son, and so challenge him to do his worst."

Ungrateful men abuse God's long-suffering today as they did of old. They say, "Well, I have refused the gospel for a long time; I have put aside many appeals; but I am not dead, nor struck with blindness, nor struck down with a stroke. I can go on at least a little longer in safety. I may refuse Christ yet again, for God is merciful." "Certain teachers," say you, "tell us that God is so good, that if we even kill his Son, he will take no account of it. We will kill his Son, and so we will reject the atonement, and trample on the precious blood, and yet we do not doubt that all will turn out to be right in the long run, and the evil of our crime will prove to be only temporary." You do not put your thoughts into those words, but you are saying as much by your actions. You dare not *say* it, and yet it lurks in your hearts, and works itself out in your deeds. You are going to run the dreadful risk of trifling with the Son of God. To you this seems a little thing, but horror takes hold of me at the thought of it.

O sirs, I will be no partner in your crime. I will not cease to warn you that it must be of all risks the most tremendous. Gracious as he is – and God has proved his grace by sending his Son – yet God is not unmanly nor unjust. If you refuse the mercy that he so freely offers you, he will deal with you in his justice. He is the judge of all the earth, and he must do right. Remember how he puts it: *My sword shall be bathed in heaven* (Isaiah 34:5). *If I whet my glittering sword, and mine hand take hold on judgment; I will render vengeance to mine enemies* (Deuteronomy 32:41). For as truly as he is love, so truly is he holiness. He is wondrous in his power to forgive; but he is also terrible out of his holy places. *If [the sinner] turn not, he will whet his sword; he hath bent his bow, and made it ready* (Psalm 7:12). Beware, *ye that forget God, lest [he] tear you in pieces, and there be none to deliver* (Psalm 50:22).

The great reason, however, why these husbandmen determined to kill the heir was this: they said, *The inheritance shall be ours.* This is what the heart of man vainly desires. It says, "Let us be rid of this troublesome talk of religion, and then we can live for ourselves, and study our own pleasure without remorse of conscience. Are we not our own? Who shall be lord over us? If we are rid of this Jesus, we shall not have this claim being always made upon us, that we are God's creatures, and that we ought to live to him. We do not intend to serve God. We will pay no rent to this householder. We will be our own proprietors. God shall have nothing from us. Who is the Lord, that we should obey his voice? If we can get rid of this Christ business we can live as we choose, and do as we please, and no one will call us to account. If we can persuade ourselves that religion is not true, we shall then care nothing for restraints and warnings, but we shall take our full swing and enjoy ourselves without limitation. A short life and a merry one will suit us. We might enjoy ourselves if this matter of God and Christ and eternity could be disposed of."

Yes, young man, this is what your prototype thought when he said to his father, *Give me the portion of goods that falleth to me* (Luke 15:12). Then he gathered all together, and went into a far country, and *wasted his substance with riotous living* (Luke 15:13). This is what you yearn for. But your folly is exceedingly great. I grieve as I look into your young face and read the idle dream of your heart. You little know what a tyrant he serves who lives as he pleases. May God grant that I may never live as my sinful lusts would make me live! I would rather be a machine and be compelled to do always what is right, than have free will, and with that free will give myself up to do that which is wrong. But there is no need to be made into a machine; the grace of God can make you as free in holiness as in sin. Grace can make you more free in the service of God than in the service of yourself.

Self lies at the bottom of all rejection of Christ – *Let us kill him, and the inheritance shall be ours.* Ah, my friend! It will not be yours; and if it were yours for a little while, and you could do just as you pleased with it, yet remember that the inheritance that is so gained will soon pass away, and you yourself will soon have to stand before the judgment seat of Christ to give an account of the deeds done in the body, whether they be good, or whether they be bad. And what will *you* do who have slain your Savior? What will you do in that day, who have lived and died unsaved?

I must close with that third topic, which is so dreadful to me: the appropriate punishment. I do not suppose that the thought of this subject will be half so dreadful to anybody here who is unconverted as it is to me. I tremble as I meditate upon the wrath to come. How glad I would be if I did not have to preach on such a theme! But I must preach on it, or be a traitor to God, and an enemy to you. If you perish, your blood will be required at my hands if I do not warn you of the punishment of sin. This is how the Savior put it: *When the lord therefore of the vineyard cometh, what will he do unto those husbandmen?* (Matthew 21:40). He leaves our conscience to award the penalty. He leaves our imagination to prescribe a doom sufficient for a crime so wretched, so daring, so cruel. They have killed the only son of their lord; what will he do unto those husbandmen?

Here I must interject a terrible passage, which it burdens me to deliver. At this present moment I am afraid that this parable is being written out again in the history of the church of God. God has put into his vineyard, or allowed to come into his vineyard, a number of religious teachers who are not rendering to him the honor due. Those religious teachers to whom I refer are not teaching the gospel as it is delivered in Holy Scripture, but they are adapting it to the age, and to the scientific knowledge of the period. They are described in the book of the prophet Jeremiah: *Thus saith the Lord of hosts, Hearken not unto the words of the prophets that prophesy unto you: they make you vain: they speak a vision of their own heart, and not out of the mouth of the Lord. They say still unto them that despise me, The Lord hath said, Ye shall have peace; and they say unto every one that walketh after the imagination of his own heart, No evil shall come upon you* (Jeremiah 23:16-17). The thoughts of their own minds are given instead of the revelation of God. Thus they set up another gospel, which is not another; but there be some that trouble you.

My fear is that the Lord will not much longer bear with these husbandmen. He will not long bear with these *prophets of the deceit of their own heart* (Jeremiah 23:26). He will bring an everlasting reproach upon them, and cut them off in his anger. He will destroy those wicked men, and he will give his vineyard unto other husbandmen who will deal more faithfully with the souls of men. I feel in my own soul that it must be so. I dare not live as a preacher of my own inventions. I dare not die as a preacher of my own thoughts, or of the thoughts of other men. I must tell my Master's message or be accursed. The spirit of the age is the spirit of proud self-sufficiency; be it ours, rather, to sit at Jesus' feet. My Lord will one day say to me, "I gave you a message; did you deliver it? I bade you to speak in my name; did you speak my words or your own? I gave you a revelation; did you deliver that revelation as best as you could? or did you invent a new thing out of your own brain?" I know how I shall answer.

I fear that a terrible doom awaits those who go after the fashionable falsehoods of the day. Be they clergymen or unorthodox ministers, an unutterably horrible damnation from the right hand of God awaits those who prostitute the office of the ministry for the delivery of human philosophies instead of teaching the gospel of the blessed God. Brethren, beware that none of us sin against the Holy Spirit by setting up our dreams in rivalry with his certainties. Pray for those who do so, lest God deal with them speedily in vengeance. The Lord have mercy upon all false prophets, and bring them humbly and tremblingly to his feet, lest they ensnare the people still more, to the overthrow of this nation, and the taking away of the candlestick out of its place.

I return to you whom I have already addressed. You have crucified the Son of God by refusing to believe in him. What shall the Lord do unto you when he comes? The sentence cannot be too severe, for the crime is beyond measure horrible. It must be the highest form of punishment known to the law. They slew the servants, and they slew the heir; no temporary punishment can suit the case. Those who plead for a light doom for such a crime must, in their own hearts, be rebels. Those who are evermore making light of hell are probably doing it in the hope of making it easy for themselves. He is the devil's advocate who would judge the punishment of the unrepentant to be a light one; God's true servants say, *Knowing therefore the terror of the Lord, we persuade men.* Our Lord leaves our own consciences to depict the overwhelming misery of those miserable men who carry their rebellion to its full length.

In the chapter that we read (Matthew 21), our Lord gives us a terrible word. Comparing himself to the stone that should be the foundation, but which the builders reject, he says, *On whomsoever it shall fall, it will grind him to powder* (Matthew 21:44). Sinner, if you reject the Savior, you will have to feel his full weight. Boundless in power, infinite in majesty, *the whole weight of him will fall on you.* Will you think that over? Since he breaks the nations in pieces with a rod of iron, judge his power; since from his presence heaven and earth flee away, judge his power. But whatever that power may be, you will have to feel the full force of it. This foundation stone falling upon you shall grind you to powder. I will not dwell further upon this tremendous thought, but I will repeat it in intentional and solemn form: the full weight of the incarnate God, in the day of his wrath, you will have to bear. It is put in another way in that expression – *The wrath of the Lamb* (Revelation 6:16). Is not that a marvelous combination: *the wrath of the Lamb*?

Love when it turns to jealousy is the fiercest of all passions; and when the love of Christ in infinite justice shall be turned into holy indignation against unrighteousness, then it will be something terrible to think of, and to bear it will be the second death. Are you prepared to bear the awful weight of a Savior's anger? No, you are not. Come, then, to Jesus. *Kiss the Son, lest he be angry, and ye perish from the way, when his wrath is kindled but a little.* O my friends, my dear friends, do not refuse the Lord Jesus, who now pleads with you. I am not worthy to be his ambassador; I am not fit for the office; but yet I would plead with you as a loving brother. Will you lose your souls? Will you reject Christ? O sirs, will you refuse the Son of God? Men and women, can you be so mad as to live and die without the Savior? Are you so far gone as this? Turn, I beg you, turn you this day. Lord, turn them, for your dear Son's sake! Amen.

Charles H. Spurgeon –
A Brief Biography

Charles Haddon Spurgeon was born on June 19, 1834, in Kelvedon, Essex, England. He was one of seventeen children in his family (nine of whom died in infancy). His father and grandfather were Nonconformist ministers in England. Due to economic difficulties, eighteen-month-old Charles was sent to live with his grandfather, who helped teach Charles the ways of God. Later in life, Charles remembered looking at the pictures in *Pilgrim's Progress* and in *Foxe's Book of Martyrs* as a young boy.

Charles did not have much of a formal education and never went to college. He read much throughout his life though, especially books by Puritan authors.

Even with godly parents and grandparents, young Charles resisted giving in to God. It was not until he was fifteen years old that he was born again. He was on his way to his usual church, but when a heavy snowstorm prevented him from getting there, he turned in at a little Primitive Methodist chapel. Though there were only about fifteen people in attendance, the preacher spoke from Isaiah 45:22: *Look unto me, and be ye saved, all the ends of the earth.* Charles Spurgeon's eyes were opened and the Lord converted his soul.

He began attending a Baptist church and teaching Sunday school. He soon preached his first sermon, and then when he was sixteen years old, he became the pastor of a small Baptist church in Cambridge. The church soon grew to over four hundred people, and Charles Spurgeon, at the age of nineteen, moved on to become the pastor of the New Park Street Church in London. The church grew from a few hundred attenders to a few thousand. They built an addition to the church, but still needed more room to accommodate the congregation. The Metropolitan Tabernacle was built in London in 1861, seating more than 5,000 people. Pastor Spurgeon preached the simple message of the cross, and thereby attracted many people who wanted to hear God's Word preached in the power of the Holy Spirit.

On January 9, 1856, Charles married Susannah Thompson. They had twin boys, Charles and Thomas. Charles and Susannah loved each other deeply, even amidst the difficulties and troubles that they faced in life, including health problems. They helped each other spiritually, and often together read the writings of Jonathan Edwards, Richard Baxter, and other Puritan writers.

Charles Spurgeon was a friend of all Christians, but he stood firmly on the Scriptures, and it didn't please all who heard him. Spurgeon believed in and preached on the sovereignty of God, heaven and hell, repentance, revival, holiness, salvation through Jesus Christ alone, and the infallibility and necessity of the Word of God. He spoke against worldliness and hypocrisy among Christians, and against Roman Catholicism, ritualism, and modernism.

One of the biggest controversies in his life was known as the "Down-Grade Controversy." Charles Spurgeon believed that some pastors of his time were "down-grading" the faith by compromising with the world or the new ideas of the age. He said that some pastors were denying the inspiration of the Bible, salvation by faith alone, and the truth of the Bible in other areas, such as creation. Many pastors who believed what Spurgeon condemned were not happy about this, and Spurgeon eventually resigned from the Baptist Union.

Despite some difficulties, Spurgeon became known as the "Prince of Preachers." He opposed slavery, started a pastors' college, opened an orphanage, led in helping feed and clothe the poor, had a book fund for pastors who could not afford books, and more.

Charles Spurgeon remains one of the most published preachers in history. His sermons were printed each week (even in the newspapers), and then the sermons for the year were re-issued as a book at the end of the year. The first six volumes, from 1855-1860, are known as *The Park Street Pulpit*, while the next fifty-seven volumes, from 1861-1917 (his sermons continued to be published long after his death), are known as *The Metropolitan Tabernacle Pulpit*. He also oversaw a monthly magazine-type publication called *The Sword and the Trowel*, and Spurgeon wrote many books, including *Lectures to My Students, All of Grace, Around the Wicket Gate, Advice for Seekers, John Ploughman's Talks, The Soul Winner, Words of Counsel for Christian Workers, Cheque Book of the Bank of Faith, Morning and Evening*, his autobiography, and more, including some commentaries, such as his twenty-year study on the Psalms – *The Treasury of David*.

Charles Spurgeon often preached ten times a week, preaching to an estimated ten million people during his lifetime. He usually preached from only one page of notes, and often from just an outline. He read about six books each week. During his lifetime, he had read *The Pilgrim's Progress* through more than one hundred times. When he died, his personal library consisted of more than 12,000 books. However, the Bible always remained the most important book to him.

Spurgeon was able to do what he did in the power of God's Holy Spirit because he followed his own advice – he met with God every morning before meeting with others, and he continued in communion with God throughout the day.

Charles Spurgeon suffered from gout, rheumatism, and some depression, among other health problems. He often went to Menton, France, to recuperate and rest. He preached his final sermon at the Metropolitan Tabernacle on June 7, 1891, and died in France on January 31, 1892, at the age of fifty-seven. He was buried in Norwood Cemetery in London.

Charles Haddon Spurgeon lived a life devoted to God. His sermons and writings continue to influence Christians all over the world.

Other Similar Titles

Life in Christ (Vol. 1 - 12),
by Charles H. Spurgeon

Men who were led by the hand or groped their way along the wall to reach Jesus were touched by his finger and went home without a guide, rejoicing that Jesus Christ had opened their eyes. Jesus is still able to perform such miracles. And, with the power of the Holy Spirit, his Word will be expounded and we'll watch for the signs to follow, expecting to see them at once. Why shouldn't those who read this be blessed with the light of heaven? This is my heart's inmost desire.

– Charles H. Spurgeon

Available where books are sold.

Jesus Came to Save Sinners, by Charles H. Spurgeon

This is a heart-level conversation with you, the reader. Every excuse, reason, and roadblock for not coming to Christ is examined and duly dealt with. If you think you may be too bad, or if perhaps you really are bad and you sin either openly or behind closed doors, you will discover that life in Christ is for you too. You can reject the message of salvation by faith, or you can choose to live a life of sin after professing faith in Christ, but you cannot change the truth as it is, either for yourself or for others. As such, it behooves you and your family to embrace truth, claim it for your own, and be genuinely set free for now and eternity. Come and embrace this free gift of God, and live a victorious life for Him.

Available where books are sold.

Words of Warning,
by Charles H. Spurgeon

This book, *Words of Warning*, is an analysis of people and the gospel of Christ. Under inspiration of the Holy Spirit, Charles H. Spurgeon sheds light on the many ways people may refuse to come to Christ, but he also shines a brilliant light on how we can be saved. Unsaved or wavering individuals will be convicted, and if they allow it, they will be led to Christ. Sincere Christians will be happy and blessed as they consider the great salvation with which they have been saved.

Available where books are sold.

According to Promise,
by Charles H. Spurgeon

The first part of this book is meant to be a sieve to separate the chaff from the wheat. Use it on your own soul. It may be the most profitable and beneficial work you have ever done. He who looked into his accounts and found that his business was losing money was saved from bankruptcy.

The second part of this book examines God's promises to His children. The promises of God not only exceed all precedent, but they also exceed all imitation. No one has been able to compete with God in the language of liberality. The promises of God are as much above all other promises as the heavens are above the earth.

Available where books are sold.

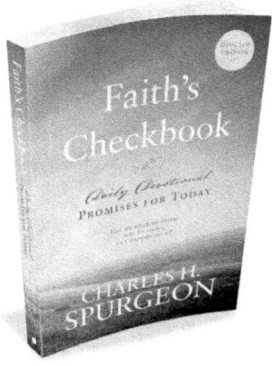

Faith's Checkbook, by Charles H. Spurgeon

Faith's Checkbook is a one-year devotional meant to encourage you to take God at His Word – to take hold of God's promises by faith. Each day you will be presented with a specific promise from the Bible, along with accompanying exhortation by Charles Spurgeon.

This is your "spiritual checkbook," if you will. God's bank account of provision is ample, and it cannot be overdrawn. Every situation you might face is equally met with a promise that, if accepted, will sufficiently see you through.

"God has given no promise that He will not redeem. He does not offer hope that He will not fulfill. To help my brethren believe this, I have prepared this little volume."
   – Charles H. Spurgeon

Available where books are sold.

Morning by Morning, by Charles H. Spurgeon

Charles H. Spurgeon's devotionals _Morning by Morning_ and _Evening by Evening_ have inspired, encouraged, and challenged Christians for generations. Spurgeon, with his masterful hand, carefully selected his text from throughout the Bible and covered a broad range of topics, in order to present a well-balanced and fruitful daily devotional for readers both young and old.

Now updated into more-modern English for today's readers, and again separated into two volumes as originally published, with morning devotionals in one volume and evening devotionals in the second. We chose a 11-point font for the sake of legibility, and formatted the devotionals so each fits on a single page.

Available where books are sold.

www.ingramcontent.com/pod-product-compliance
Lightning Source LLC
Chambersburg PA
CBHW071141130626
46553CB00004B/1474